Android 3.0 Application Development Cookbook

Over 70 working recipes covering every aspect of Android development

Kyle Merrifield Mew

PUBLISHING

BIRMINGHAM - MUMBAI

Android 3.0 Application Development Cookbook

First published: July 2011

Production Reference: 1150711

Published by Packt Publishing Ltd.
32 Lincoln Road
Olton
Birmingham, B27 6PA, UK.

ISBN 978-1-849512-94-7

www.packtpub.com

Cover Image by Javier Barría C. (jbarriac@yahoo.com)

Credits

Author
Kyle Merrifield Mew

Reviewers
Md. Mahmud Ahsan

Dr. Frank Grützmacher

Bob Kerns

Acquisition Editor
Tarun Singh

Development Editor
Alina Lewis

Technical Editor
Aaron Rosario

Copy Editor
Neha Shetty

Project Coordinator
Srimoyee Ghoshal

Proofreader
Aaron Nash

Indexer
Tejal Daruwale

Graphics
Nilesh Mohite

Production Coordinators
Kruthika Bangera

Adline Swetha Jesuthas

Cover Work
Kruthika Bangera

About the Author

Kyle Merrifield Mew lives in London and is currently a self employed writer and developer. Amongst other things he has also been a soldier, a cartoonist, a teacher, a charity fundraiser, and a web designer.

Kyle has been programming since the early eighties, has written for several technology websites, and also done three radio plays.

About the Reviewers

Md. Mahmud Ahsan has been developing web applications for over six years. He has developed some medium to large web applications and was also an architect on some web applications. He's a Zend Certified Engineer and an expert in Facebook, Linkedin, Twitter, Twilio API, and mashup application development. Beside his full time freelance work, he blogs at `http://thinkdiff.net` and writes articles on different technologies, especially Facebook application development. For the past year he's been developing iOS applications as a hobby and also developed some android applications. He lives in Bangladesh with his wife Jinat.

Currently he's working as a Freelancer, managing and developing social web applications and iOS applications.

He publishes his own iOS applications at `http://ithinkdiff.net`.

He was a technical reviewer for the titles *Zend Framework 1.8 Web Application Development* and *PHP jQuery Cookbook* by Packt.

I'm very grateful to my father who bought a computer for me in 2001, since then I have loved programming and working with various technologies.

Dr. Frank Grützmacher has spent some years in the research of distributed electronic design tools and worked for several German blue chip companies such as Deutsche Post and AEG. He was involved in android platform extensions for a mobile manufacturer. Therefore, on one hand he knows how to build large enterprise apps, and on the other hand he knows how to make android system apps.

He is currently working for the IT daughter of the largest German Telco company.

In the past he already reviewed Corba and Java related books for American and German publishers.

Bob Kerns has been writing software for 40 years, in fields as diverse as artificial intelligence, computer mathematics, computer networking, internationalization, device drivers, compilers, language design—and Android.

While studying at MIT, he worked on the pioneering Computer Algebra system Macsyma and helped maintain the MacLisp compiler and interpreter. He also created the first distance learning environment accessible over the Internet (then called Arpanet), teaching Lisp programming to all comers, young and old.

After ending his studies he continued to develop the Lisp language with NIL Lisp for VAX/VMS, before leaving MIT in 1981 to join the startup Symbolics, a vendor of Lisp workstations. During his tenure at Symbolics, he worked on virtually every part of the system. He extended the e-mail client to include early support for conversation management akin to what is provided in Gmail today. He enhanced the OS support for multiple languages, including support for Japanese. He managed development groups, and created and managed the group responsible for QA, release management, and software support.

After leaving Symbolics, he worked on expert systems and Lisp language development in Japan and the US, ported the **Common Lisp Interface Manager** (**CLIM**) to Macintosh, developed early tools for working with Unicode and international character sets. He worked with MCC and Digital Equipment Corporation on the Cyc knowledge engineering project.

He then worked for Expert System pioneer Inference on their ART*Enterprise expert system shell, and follow-on products, through a succession of spinoffs and acquisitions. In 1995, as the Web was just beginning to become popular, he pushed for and developed techniques for integrating ART*Enterprise into web services. This work then became the foundation for a series of further products combining AI and web technologies.

For the past decade Bob has worked with a wide array of technologies including AI, neuroscience, XML, knowledge representation, statistical inferencing, 3D computer graphics, Encryption, and software security, and of course web and mobile technologies.

He is currently working on AI technology for a major vendor to the financial sector.

Bob resides with his family in Marin County, California.

www.PacktPub.com

Support files, eBooks, discount offers and more

You might want to visit www.PacktPub.com for support files and downloads related to your book.

Did you know that Packt offers eBook versions of every book published, with PDF and ePub files available? You can upgrade to the eBook version at www.PacktPub.com and as a print book customer, you are entitled to a discount on the eBook copy. Get in touch with us at service@packtpub.com for more details.

At www.PacktPub.com, you can also read a collection of free technical articles, sign up for a range of free newsletters and receive exclusive discounts and offers on Packt books and eBooks.

http://PacktLib.PacktPub.com

Do you need instant solutions to your IT questions? PacktLib is Packt's online digital book library. Here, you can access, read and search across Packt's entire library of books.

Why Subscribe?

- ▶ Fully searchable across every book published by Packt
- ▶ Copy and paste, print and bookmark content
- ▶ On demand and accessible via web browser

Free access for Packt account holders

If you have an account with Packt at www.PacktPub.com, you can use this to access PacktLib today and view nine entirely free books. Simply use your login credentials for immediate access.

Table of Contents

Preface

This book covers every aspect of mobile app development, starting with major application components and screen layout and design, before moving on to how to manage sensors such as internal gyroscopes and near field communications. Towards the end, it delves into smartphone multimedia capabilities as well as graphics and animation, web access, and GPS.

Whether you are writing your first app or your hundredth, this is a book that you will come back to time and time again, with its many tips and tricks on the rich features of Android 3.

What this book covers

Chapter 1, Activities: Create and manage the fundamental components of any Android application.

Chapter 2, Layouts: Design and format screen layouts.

Chapter 3, Widgets: Include buttons, images and a wide variety of widgets in an application.

Chapter 4, Menus: Provide and manage pop-up menus for activities and applications.

Chapter 5, Data and Security : Store and share private or public data, set up databases, and control permissions.

Chapter 6, Detecting User Activity: Read sensors, detect gestures, and manage touch-screen events.

Chapter 7, Notifying the User: Use and customize dialog boxes pop-ups and the status bar.

Chapter 8, Graphics and Animation: Include and manipulate images and create animations.

Chapter 9, Multimedia: Add audio and video to an application and take control of the built-in camera.

Chapter 10, Telephony, Networks, and the Web: Incorporate phone and network functions in applications and connect them to the Internet.

Chapter 11, GPS, Locations, and Maps: Detect device location and include Google maps in applications.

Who this book is for

If you are new to Android application development and looking for a quick start, or if you are an experienced Android developer looking for a reference guide, then this book is for you. Ideally, you should know some Java and a little about mark-up languages but this is by no means necessary. This book will teach you how to write rich Android applications from scratch in no time.

Conventions

In this book, you will find a number of styles of text that distinguish between different kinds of information. Here are some examples of these styles, and an explanation of their meaning.

Code words in text are shown as follows: "We can include other contexts through the use of the `include` directive."

A block of code is set as follows:

```
<activity
   android:name=".DeclaringAnActivity"
   android:label="Welcome to the Android 3.0 Cookbook"
   android:screenOrientation="portrait">
   ...
</activity>
```

Any command-line input or output is written as follows:

```
keytool.exe -list -alias androiddebugkey -keystore "C:\Users\<user>\.
android\debug.keystore" -storepass android -keypass android
```

New terms and **important words** are shown in bold. Words that you see on the screen, in menus or dialog boxes for example, appear in the text like this: "clicking the **Next** button moves you to the next screen".

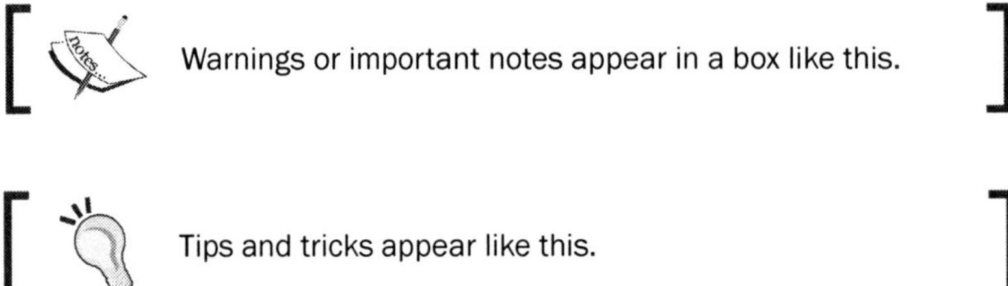

Warnings or important notes appear in a box like this.

Tips and tricks appear like this.

Reader feedback

Feedback from our readers is always welcome. Let us know what you think about this book—what you liked or may have disliked. Reader feedback is important for us to develop titles that you really get the most out of.

To send us general feedback, simply send an e-mail to `feedback@packtpub.com`, and mention the book title via the subject of your message.

If there is a book that you need and would like to see us publish, please send us a note in the **SUGGEST A TITLE** form on `www.packtpub.com` or e-mail `suggest@packtpub.com`.

If there is a topic that you have expertise in and you are interested in either writing or contributing to a book, see our author guide on `www.packtpub.com/authors`.

Customer support

Now that you are the proud owner of a Packt book, we have a number of things to help you to get the most from your purchase.

Errata

Although we have taken every care to ensure the accuracy of our content, mistakes do happen. If you find a mistake in one of our books—maybe a mistake in the text or the code—we would be grateful if you would report this to us. By doing so, you can save other readers from frustration and help us improve subsequent versions of this book. If you find any errata, please report them by visiting `http://www.packtpub.com/support`, selecting your book, clicking on the **errata submission form** link, and entering the details of your errata. Once your errata are verified, your submission will be accepted and the errata will be uploaded on our website, or added to any list of existing errata, under the Errata section of that title. Any existing errata can be viewed by selecting your title from `http://www.packtpub.com/support`.

Piracy

Piracy of copyright material on the Internet is an ongoing problem across all media. At Packt, we take the protection of our copyright and licenses very seriously. If you come across any illegal copies of our works, in any form, on the Internet, please provide us with the location address or website name immediately so that we can pursue a remedy.

Please contact us at `copyright@packtpub.com` with a link to the suspected pirated material.

We appreciate your help in protecting our authors, and our ability to bring you valuable content.

Questions

You can contact us at `questions@packtpub.com` if you are having a problem with any aspect of the book, and we will do our best to address it.

1
Activities

This chapter covers the following topics:

- ▶ Declaring an activity
- ▶ Starting a new activity with an Intent object
- ▶ Switching between activities
- ▶ Returning a result from an activity
- ▶ Storing an activity's state
- ▶ Storing persistent activity data
- ▶ Managing the activity lifecycle

Introduction

The Android SDK provides a powerful tool for programming mobile devices, and the best way to master such a tool is to get our hands dirty right from the very beginning.

You can work through this book step by step as a complete guide, and if you have ideas for your own applications, which I'm sure you do, then just look up the relevant chapter and recipe and dive right in.

The **Activity** class provides one of the fundamental building blocks of Android development, forming the primary interface between the user and an application.

Activities are the elements of an application that the user sees and interacts with and they are generally displayed within a rectangular portion (if not all) of the screen. For those with a background in Java, an activity can be thought of as being similar in function to the Swing JFrame.

This chapter explains how to **declare** and **launch** activities within an application, and how to manage several activities at once by sharing data between them, requesting results from them, and by calling one activity from within another.

This chapter also briefly explores the **Intent** object, which is often used in conjunction with activities (as well as other fundamental components) and is very handy for starting an activity from any point.

Before following the recipes in this book you will need to install the Android SDK, the Android AVD manager, and the Eclipse IDE, along with the ADT plugin. The ADT plugin, which stands for **Android Development Tools**, provides a seamless way to add Android-specific controls to the Eclipse IDE.

Instructions on how to do this can be found at `http://developer.android.com/sdk/installing.html`.

Declaring an activity

Activities and other application components, such as **services**, are declared in the **AndroidManifest** XML file. Declaring an activity is how we tell Android about how the activity can be requested, and what code to run when it is requested. For example, an application will usually indicate that at least one activity should be visible as a desktop icon and serve as the main entry point to the application.

Getting ready

As with most recipes, we will be using the **Eclipse IDE**. If you have not done so already, start up Eclipse and ensure that you have installed the **ADT Plugin**.

Android projects are built against a target platform or API level. Here we have used API level 8, which corresponds to the Android 2.2 platform (FroYo). It is quite possible to use any level for this task but if you intend to make use of the 'holographic' UI you will need to look at the recipe about optimizing for 3.0 in *Chapter 2, Layouts*.

How to do it...

The Eclipse Android **project wizard** is as good a place to start building an application as any and it will automatically generate a **manifest file** that includes a basic activity declaration:

1. Run the project wizard. From the Eclipse **File** menu select **New** and then **Android Project**.

2. Enter the details of your project as you can see in the next screenshot and click on **Finish**:

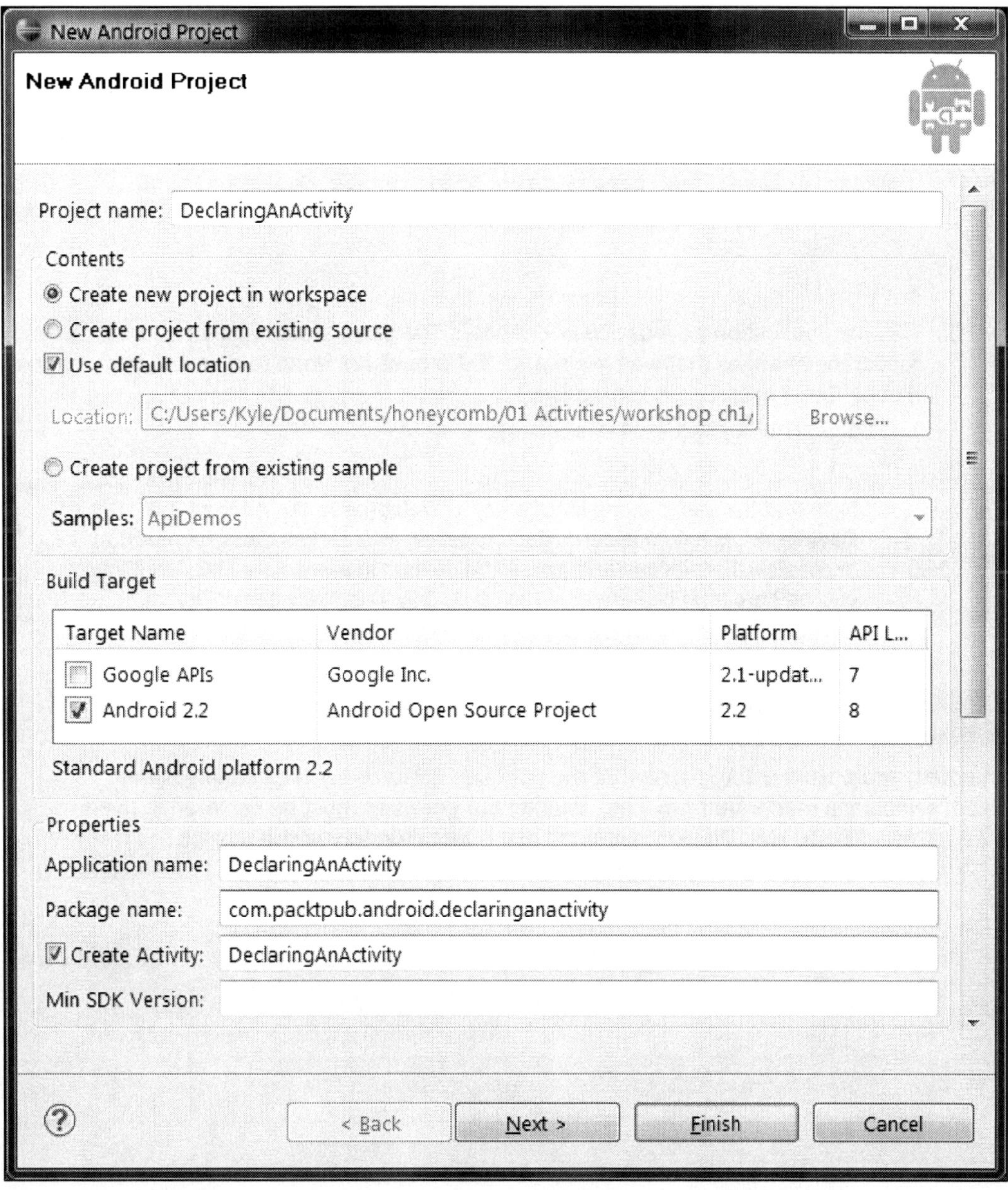

3. Open up the **manifest file** from the **Package Explorer,** and then click on the **AndroidManifest.xml** tab at the bottom to display the code that the IDE has produced.

4. Within the `<activity>` element, find the following attributes:

```
android:name=".DeclaringAnActivity"
android:label="@string/app_name"
```

5. Edit the code so that it matches the following snippet:

```
<activity
   android:name=".DeclaringAnActivity"
   android:label="Welcome to the Android 3.0 Cookbook"
   android:screenOrientation="portrait">

   . . .

</activity>
```

6. Run the application on a device or emulator. The title bar and screen orientation now reflect the changes that we have made. If you have not done this before, instructions can be found at `http://developer.android.com/guide/developing/building/building-eclipse.html`.

Note that the use of string literals, as in **"Welcome to the Android 3.0 Cookbook"**, is not considered good practice, as it makes translation next to impossible. String constants should be defined in a separate XML file; a literal is used here (and elsewhere in the book) only to simplify examples.

How it works...

An activity represents a single task that the user can perform, such as editing some text or selecting a media file from a list. Each of our activities must be declared in the `AndroidManifest` XML file, which resides in the root directory of the project.

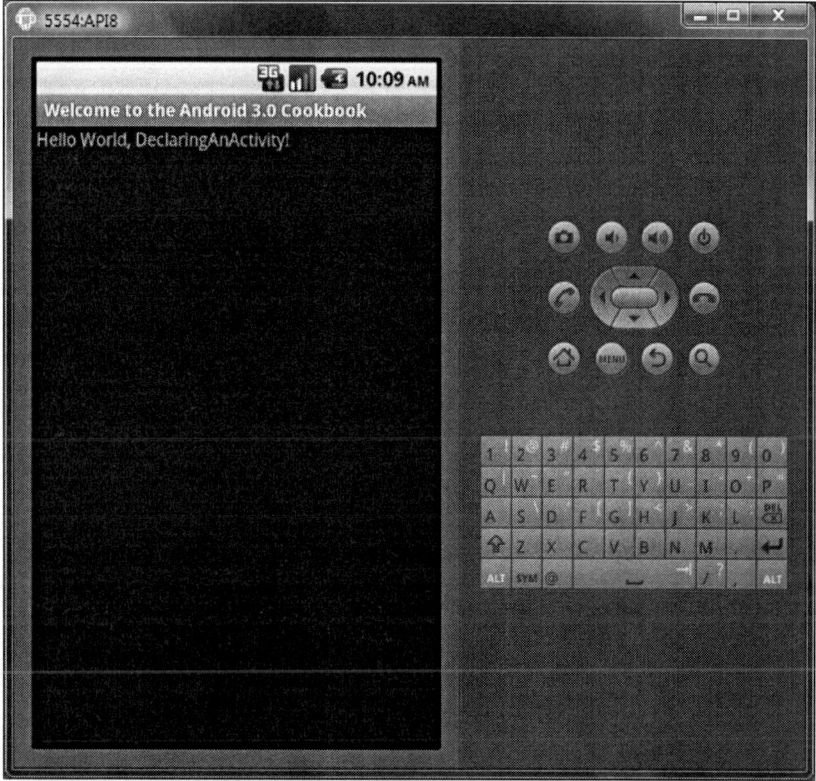

The project wizard provides us with two basic attributes:

- The *name* **DeclaringAnActivity** refers to the Java subclass that will contain our activity's methods and fields.

- The *label* **app_name** acts as a title for our application. It is displayed on the title bar of the device at runtime and also as the text under the application icon.

We also added an attribute of our own, `screenOrientation`, which does exactly what you might expect it to.

The manifest is used to control an activity's start-up state and to apply features such as themes, or as just demonstrated, screen orientation. As we will see later though, most attributes can be set and changed dynamically through Java code as well.

Starting a new activity with an intent object

The Android application model can be seen as a service-oriented one, with **activities** as *components* and **intents** as the *messages* sent between them. Here, an intent is used to start an activity that displays the user's call log, but intents can be used to do many things and we will encounter them throughout this book.

Getting ready

To keep things simple, we are going to use an **intent** object to start one of Android's built-in activities, rather than create a new one. This only requires a very basic application, so start a new Android project with Eclipse and call it `ActivityStarter` or something like that.

How to do it...

We are going to edit the Java subclass responsible for the main activity: the one declared in the manifest file. This class extends the activity class, and by overriding its `onCreate()` method we can introduce code that will be executed when the application is first launched:

1. Using the **Package Explorer**, open the Java file inside the `src` folder of the project. It will have the same name as the activity, entered when the project was created:

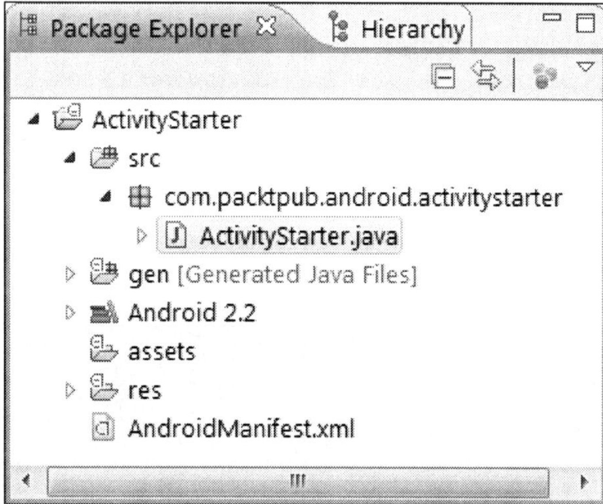

2. Add a new method to the class, similar to this one:

```java
void startActivity() {
   Intent myIntent = new Intent();
   myIntent.setAction(Intent.ACTION_CALL_BUTTON);
   startActivity(myIntent);
}
```

3. Now, call this method from the `onCreate()` method so that it executes when the application is launched:

```java
@Override
public void onCreate(Bundle state) {
   super.onCreate(state);
   setContentView(R.layout.main);

   startActivity();
}
```

4. Save and run the project. The application now displays the user's call log.

5. If this generates an error message, it may be that the correct libraries have not been imported. To use intents we have to import the relevant library, which can be done with `import android.content.Intent`; however it's easy to get Eclipse to import any missing libraries simply by pressing *Shift + Ctrl + O*.

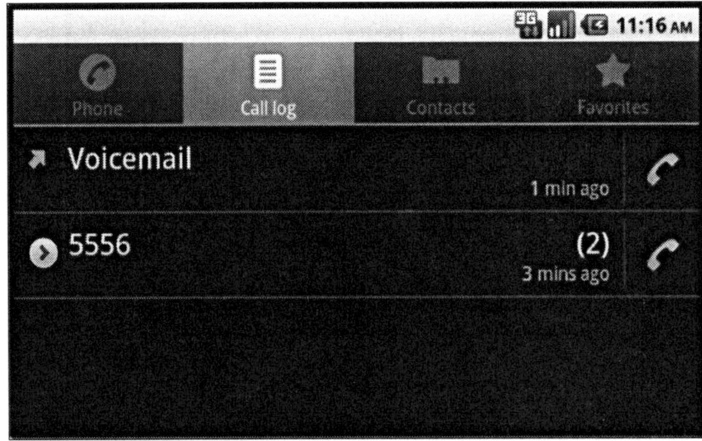

6. Press the *back* button on the device (or emulator) to see that the call log activity was actually called from our original main activity.

How it works...

Intents operate as asynchronous messages sent between application components and they are used to activate **services** and **broadcast receivers** as well as activities. Intents are passive data structures that provide an infrastructure for our activities and other components.

The `onCreate()` method is called as soon as the activity starts and so calling our `startActivity()` method from within it means that we are immediately taken to the call log activity. More often than not we would use a button or menu item to perform such an action, and we haven't done so in order to simplify the demonstration and make it easier to incorporate in your own application.

Again, note that this project was built against Android 2.2 (API level 8) but this choice was arbitrary as the libraries used have been available since Android 1.5 and you should, ideally, build against the target device that you are testing on.

There's more...

The previous example required only an **action** to be set but most intent objects make use of a `setData()` method as well as the `setAction()` method used.

Setting data and action

Replace the `setAction()` statement in the example with these two lines:

```
myIntent.setAction(Intent.ACTION_VIEW);
myIntent.setData(android.provider.MediaStore.Images.Media.INTERNAL_
CONTENT_URI);
```

This will open the device's image gallery when run and utilize both **data** and **action** parts of the intent.

Exploring other functions with auto-complete

Eclipse's **auto-complete** function allows us to explore Android's other baked-in activities. Simply start entering the code here and then scroll through the lists presented:

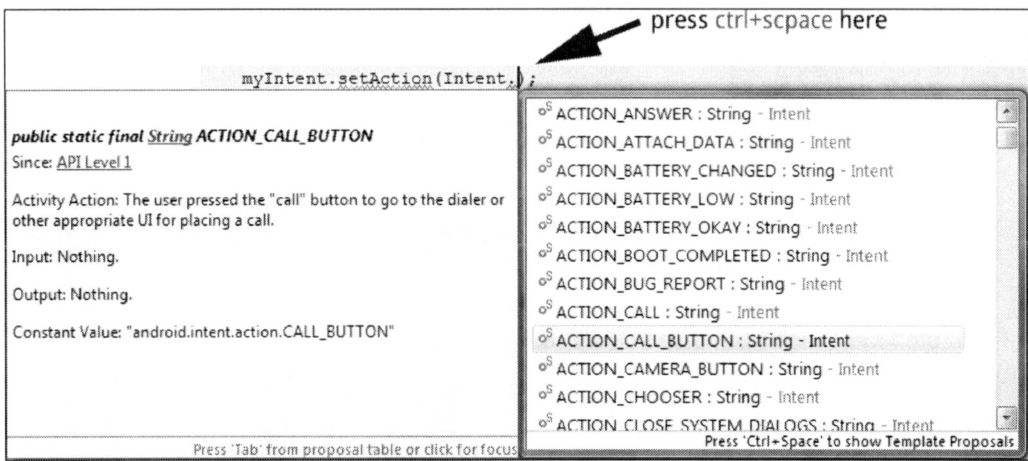

If the drop-down list fails to appear, press *Ctrl + Space* but note that when components share methods you may well see actions that correspond to other classes such as services or broadcasts, although the inline documentation is quite thorough and will mention when specific data or extra parameters are required.

See also

To start an activity from a menu selection, see the recipe *Handling menu selections* in *Chapter 4, Menus*.

Switching between activities

Often we will want to activate one **activity** from within another. Although this is not a difficult task, it will require more setting up than the previous two recipes as it will need two activities to be declared in the **Manifest**, a new **Class** to serve as our second activity, and a **button** along with a **click listener** to perform the switch.

Getting ready

This recipe can be started from scratch, so create a new Android project in Eclipse and call it `ActivitySwitcher`. Creating a project with the wizard automatically generates the first of our activities. This example can be built against any platform target and here we have used 2.2 (API level 8).

How to do it...

First we create a new **public class** that we will use to create the second activity:

1. Create a new **public class** in the same location as the original activity subclass using the tool bar's **New Java Class** icon or the package's context menu from the **Package Explorer**, selecting **New** and then **Class**.

2. Name the class `MySubActivity` or something similar and make sure to complete the **Superclass** field as seen in the following screenshot:

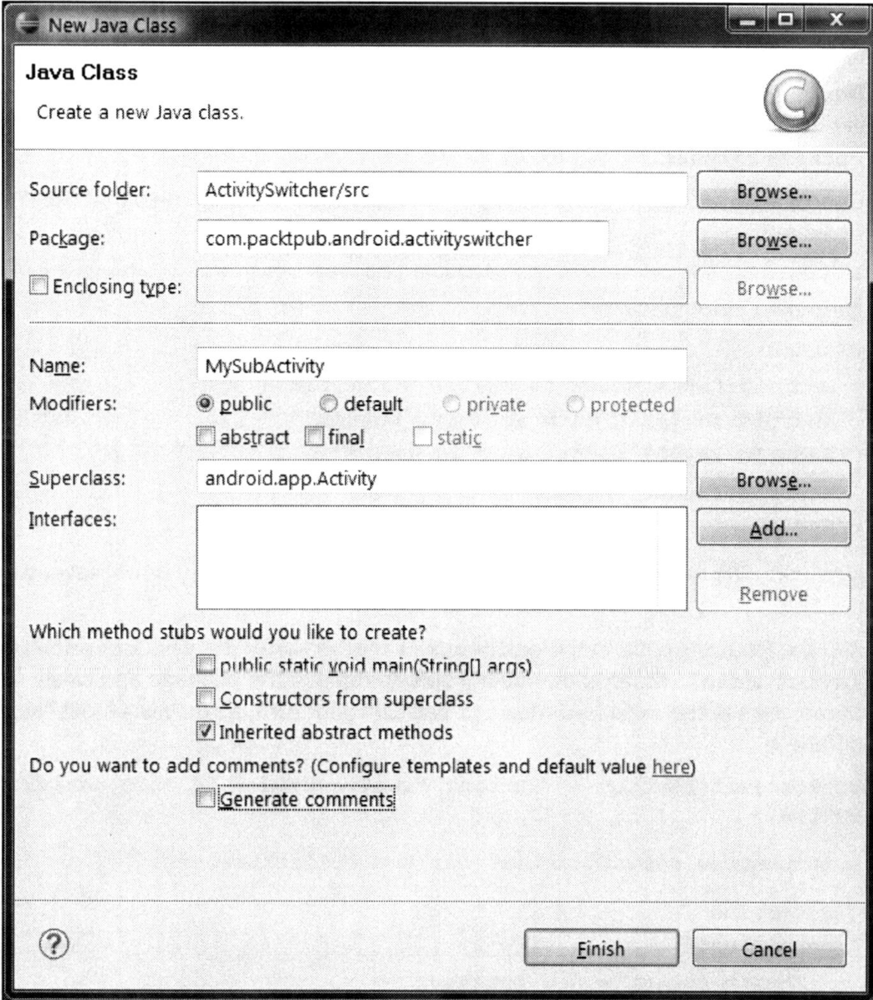

3. Next, we need to declare our new activity in the manifest file. Open the `AndroidManifest.xml` file from the **Package Explorer** and select the **Application** tab.

4. Under **Application Nodes**, click on the **Add...** button and then select **Activity**.

5. In the panel on the right-hand side, fill in the **Name** field as `.MySubActivity` and the **Label** field as `my sub activity`.

6. Open the **AndroidManifest.xml** tab and check whether these changes are reflected in the XML, which should look similar to the following snippet:

```
<activity
    android:name=".MySubActivity"
```

```
      android:label="my sub activity">
</activity>
```

7. Next, we must add a button that the user can click on to switch activities. This is
    set up through the `main.xml` file which resides in the `res/layout` folder in the
    Package Explorer.

8. Open the `main.xml` file and click on the **XML** tab at the bottom so that the code can
    be edited.

9. Add the following `<Button>` element just after the `<TextView>` element that was
    generated automatically:

```
<Button
   android:text="click to switch activities"
   android:id="@+id/main_activity_button"
   android:layout_width="wrap_content"
   android:layout_height="wrap_content">
</Button>
```

10. Now open the original Java activity class, `ActivitySwitcher` or whatever you
    called it.

11. Add the following code to the `onCreate()` method after the `setContentView(R.
    layout.main);` statement, making sure to replace the package and class
    parameters in the `setClassName()` call with your own, as they will most likely be
    different:

```
Button switchButton = (Button) findViewById(R.id.main_activity_
button);

switchButton.setOnClickListener(new OnClickListener() {

   @Override
   public void onClick(View v) {
      Intent intent = new Intent();
      String packageName =
         "com.packtpub.android.activityswitcher";
      String className =
         "com.packtpub.android.activityswitcher.MySubActivity";
      intent.setClassName(packageName, className);
      startActivity(intent);
   }

});
```

12. Run the application on a device or emulator. Clicking on the button will now start the
    sub activity.

How it works...

This new activity is not a very exciting application. Our activity does nothing but demonstrate how to switch from one activity to another, which of course will form a fundamental aspect of almost any application that we develop.

In most cases there would be a separate layout declaration alongside `main.xml` in the `res/layout` folder for each new activity. Also a button, or some other object, to return us to our original activity would be quite reasonable but these features have been omitted here simply to save us the extra typing, and of course, the user can always use the device's own *Back* button to achieve this.

We have seen how to create a new subclass for each new activity and how to declare these in the manifest. We have also seen how a UI element such as a button is declared in an XML file, `main.xml`, and then associated with a data member in Java with the `findViewById()` method.

Again we have made use of the intent object, not only to start the new activity but also to specify which activity class to run.

See also

To learn more about embedding widgets like the **Button**, see *Chapter 3, Widgets*.

Returning a result from an activity

Being able to start one activity from another is all well and good, but we will often need to know how the called activity has fared in its task or even which activity has been called. The `startActivityForResult()` method provides the most straightforward way to do this.

Getting ready

Returning a result from an activity is not that different from calling one the way we did in the previous recipe. Start up a new Android project in Eclipse and call it `GettingResults`.

How to do it...

In this recipe we will need to create a new activity class, provide it with an `onCreate()` method, then edit our default class and include our new activity in the manifest file:

1. Create a new class called `MyNewActivity` in the same package as the `GettingResults` class and give it the Superclass `android.app.Activity`.

2. Extend the class as an activity, provide it with an `onCreate()` method, and fill it out as given next.

3. Pressing *Ctrl + Space* once you have typed as far as `public void onCrea` will prompt Eclipse to complete most of this method for you:

```java
public class MyNewActivity extends Activity {

    @Override
    public void onCreate(Bundle state) {
    super.onCreate(state);

        setResult(42);
        finish();

    }

}
```

4. Press *Ctrl + Shift + O*. This will import the following libraries:

```java
import android.app.Activity;
import android.os.Bundle;
```

5. Open the `GettingResults` class and edit it to look like this:

```java
public class GettingResults extends Activity {

    @Override
    public void onCreate(Bundle state) {
        super.onCreate(state);
        setContentView(R.layout.main);

        Intent i = new Intent(this, MyNewActivity.class);
        startActivityForResult(i, 0);
    }

    @Override
    protected void onActivityResult(int requestCode,
        int resultCode, Intent data) {
        super.onActivityResult(requestCode, resultCode, data);
        Toast.makeText(this, Integer.toString(resultCode),
          Toast.LENGTH_LONG).show();
    }

}
```

6. Import any library the class needs with *Ctrl + Shift + O*.

7. Open the manifest file and include a new `<activity>` element underneath the one that is already there. Include the following attributes:

```
<activity
```

```
    android:name=".MyNewActivity"
    android:label="my new activity">
</activity>
```

8. Run the application on a device or an emulator. A small pop-up appears in the initial activity that has been passed from the called one:

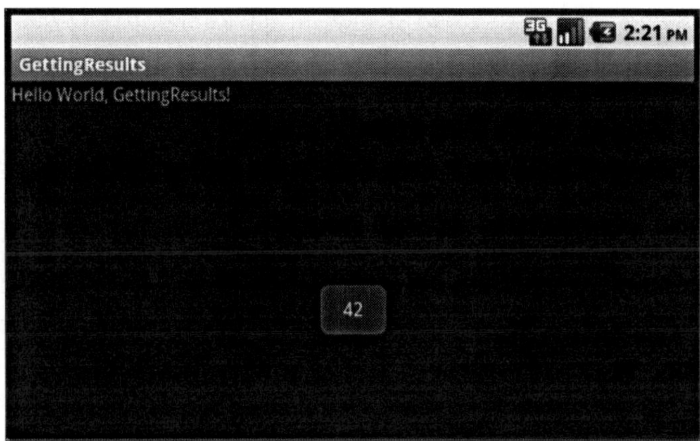

How it works...

Here, the called activity used `setResult()` to return a **result code** back to the calling activity. We used an arbitrary value in our example but a **result code** can be used to represent an outcome such as the index of a selected item.

The corresponding member in the calling activity is the `onActivityResults()` method. Besides the result code that we just sent from the called activity, the method receives a **request code**. This is simply the integer value that was passed with the `startActivityForResult()` call which takes the form:

```
startActivityForResult(Intent intent, int requestCode);
```

We used 0 as our **request code** because we knew where it came from—but this value can be used to identify where the request originated in less trivial applications with several activities.

> If `startActivityForResult()` is called with a negative request code it will act exactly as if it were a call to `startActivity()`—that is, it will not return a result.

Activity results are always handled by the calling activity's `onActivityResults()` method, which makes use of the **request code** as well as the **result code**.

We made use of the **Toast** object which is a neat little pop-up **view** that can be used to unobtrusively inform the user of some event or the other. It also functions as a handy little tool for on-the-fly debugging as it doesn't need setting up or *screen estate*.

There's more...

In the previous example, we only returned an integer with `setResult()` but there is an alternative format.

Returning an intent with the result code

To return an intent along with the result code back to the calling activity, use:

```
setResult(int resultCode, Intent data);
```

Applied to the previous demonstration, the code would then look something like this:

```
Intent i = new Intent();
setResult(42, i);
finish();
```

See also

To learn more about creating new activity classes refer to the previous recipe, *Switching between activities*.

For more information on Toasts see the recipe *Making a Toast* in *Chapter 7, Notifying the user*.

Storing an activity's state

A smart phone is a dynamic environment for software to exist in and an application can be interrupted for any number of reasons. Even turning the handset on its side will cause an activity to reload in orientation sensitive programs.

Android provides SQLite for storing and retrieving data but this would a little heavy handed for storing an instance value or two and fortunately the activity class has built-in methods that we can override and use to store primitive name or value pairs.

Getting ready

Our recipes get a little more involved from here on and so we will not be able to include all the code in the given examples. We will assume that the reader is familiar with the subjects covered in the past few recipes and will be able to create applications with the necessary elements without recourse to the exact text. If not, have a quick look through the preceding recipes. We will not introduce any new subjects without fully explaining them.

1. Create a new application project and call it `StateSaver`.

2. Include these elements within the `main.xml` layout file:

    ❑   An EditText

    ❑   A Button

    ❑   A TextView

3. Provide them with the following **android:id**s:

    ❑   @+id/edit_text

    ❑   @+id/button

    ❑   @+id/text_view

4. Change the text in the boxes to match the following screenshot:

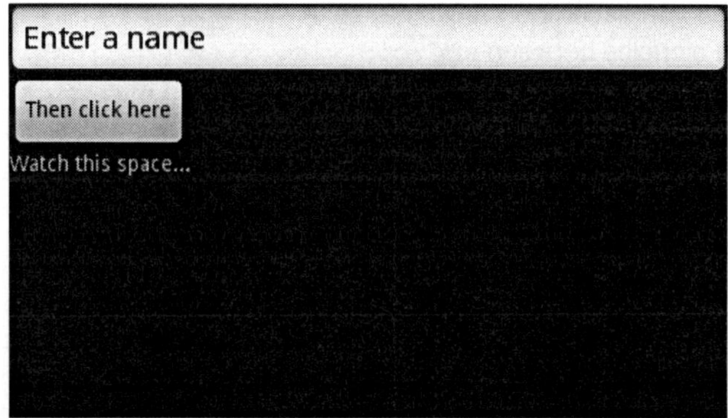

How to do it...

In this recipe we will create a simple application that 'remembers' a line of text that we enter when the activity is reloaded. To do this we override the activity's `onSaveInstanceState()` and `onRestoreInstanceState()` methods:

1. Declare the three UI elements that we just created as class-wide fields in the activity Java file, as follows:

```java
public class StateSaver extends Activity {
    private EditText mEditText;
    private Button mButton;
    private TextView mTextView;
```

2. We also need a `String` constant:

```java
    private static final String KEY = null;
```

3. Inside the `onCreate()` method and after the `setContentView()` statement associate these views with their **Resource ID**s:

```
mEditText = (EditText) findViewById(R.id.edit_text);
mButton = (Button) findViewById(R.id.button);
mTextView = (TextView) findViewById(R.id.text_view);
```

4. Create a click listener for our button (also inside `onCreate()`):

```
mButton.setOnClickListener(new OnClickListener() {

    @Override
    public void onClick(View v) {
       mTextView.setText(mEditText.getText().toString);
    }
});
```

5. Now is a good time to import any libraries. Pressing *Shift + Ctrl + O* will cause Eclipse to offer you a choice between `android.view.View.OnClickListener` and `android.content.DialogInterface.OnClickListener`. Make sure that you select `android.view.View`.

6. Beneath the `onCreate()` method, add the `onSaveInstanceState()` method:

```
@Override
public void onSaveInstanceState(Bundle state) {
    state.putString(KEY, mTextView.getText().toString());
    super.onSaveInstanceState(state);
}
```

7. Beneath this last method, include the `onRestoreInstanceState()` method:

```
@Override
public void onRestoreInstanceState(Bundle state) {
    super.onRestoreInstanceState(state);
    mTextView.setText(state.getString(KEY));
}
```

8. Run the project on a device or emulator. Enter some text into the **EditText** view and click on the button. Then restart the activity by exiting and restarting or by rotating the handset. When the activity begins afresh, the **TextView** restores to its remembered state.

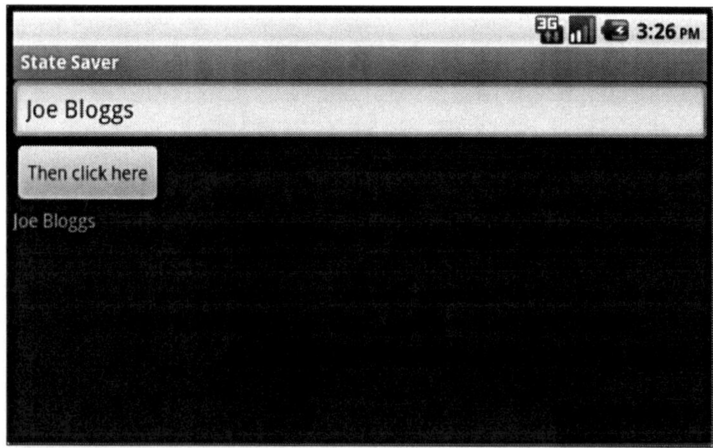

How it works...

The way these state saving methods work is really quite simple. When our application is dropped from memory, a **Bundle** of name/value pairs can be stored with the `onSaveInstanceState()` method. This **Bundle** is then handed back when the activity restarts to both the `onRestoreInstanceState()` and the `onCreate()` methods. This is an important point as the Bundle is made available to both procedures and gives us a choice over where and how to handle activity restarts. This is because `onRestoreInstanceState()` is not called until after `onStart()` meaning we can apply any initialization that we may need before restoring our values.

There's more...

The two methods introduced here are not the only way to ensure that a screen component's state is stored.

Using ID to include a view in the Bundle

Android will automatically include any view that has been supplied with an ID in the saved instance state Bundle when the activity is interrupted, regardless of whether we have included the two methods discussed here.

See also

Internal memory can also be used to store other private data and details on how to do this can be found in the recipe *Using internal storage for private data* in *Chapter 5, Data and Security*.

The recipe *Storing public data on external storage* in *Chapter 5, Data and Security* demonstrates how to use SD cards to store data available from outside an application.

Storing persistent activity data

Being able to store information about our activities on a temporary basis is very useful but more often than not we want our application to remember things across multiple sessions.

Obviously we can use an SQLite database, but this is a bit extreme if all we want to store the user's name or some preference or the other. Android provides a lightweight technique for doing this in the shape of the **SharedPreferences** interface.

Getting ready

It is possible to use **SharedPreferences** in any activity (as well as other application components). The example we use here makes use of a **TextView**, an **EditText**, and a **Button** to permanently store the user's name:

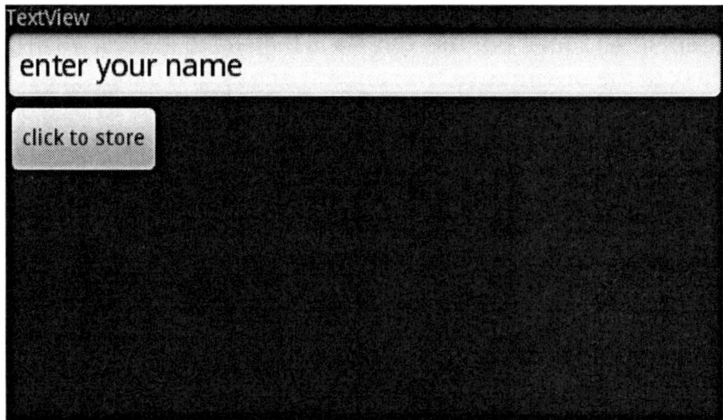

1. Create a new project with these elements and provide them with IDs in the layout. Also edit the text value of the EditText and the Button but leave the TextView as it is.

2. Connect these up in the Java code using `findViewById()`. In the code here we have named them `mTextView`, `mEditText` and `mButton`.

How to do it...

In this recipe the persistent data that we want to store is a string value used to represent the user's name. We will store this during the activity's `onPause()` method and restore the value in the `onCreate()` method (as they are called when we most likely need to restore and retrieve our preferences) but **SharedPreferences** can be applied anywhere:

1. Declare a class-wide String field, `mUserName` and a String constant KEY with value null.

2. Include the following lines in the `onCreate()` method after the `findViewById()` statements:

```java
SharedPreferences settings = getPreferences(MODE_PRIVATE);
mUserName = settings.getString(KEY, "new user");
mTextView.setText("Welcome " + mUserName);
```

3. Override the `onPause()` method and complete it as shown here:

```java
@Override
  protected void onPause() {
  super.onPause();

  SharedPreferences settings = getPreferences(MODE_PRIVATE);
  SharedPreferences.Editor editor = settings.edit();
  editor.putString(KEY, mUserName);
  settings.edit().putString(KEY, mUserName).commit();
}
```

4. Add a button and a listener to the `onCreate()` method so that we can actually enter a value to be stored, as follows:

```java
mButton.setOnClickListener(new OnClickListener() {
  @Override
  public void onClick(View v) {
    mUserName = mEditText.getText().toString();
    mTextView.setText("Welcome " + mUserName);
  }
});
```

5. Run the application on a device or an emulator. Once a new value has been entered it will persist across sessions. In fact we would have to clear it using the device's Applications Manager in Settings, or uninstall and reinstall the application to completely reset it.

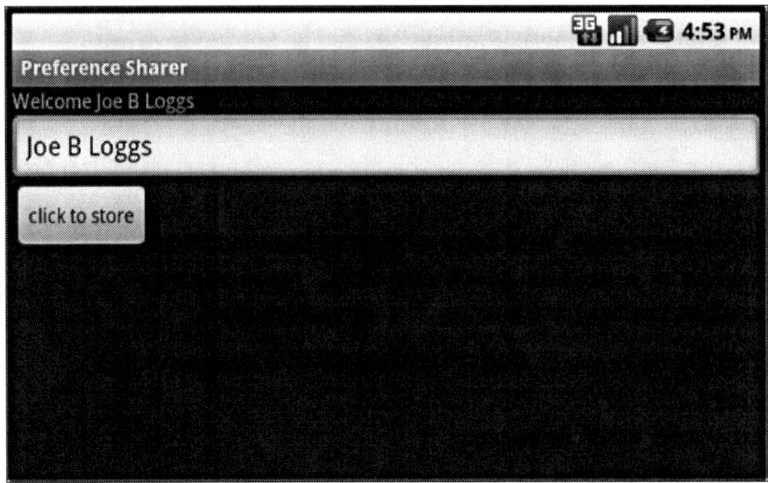

How it works...

We stored just one value here, the string KEY, but we could have stored any number of primitive name/value pairs. Each data type has equivalent getters and setters, for example `SharedPreferences.getBoolean()` or `SharedPreferences.setInt()`.

When we retrieve the value, in the `onCreate()` method we provided a string literal `"new user"`. This will be used in the absence of a stored value when the file has not yet been saved and is very useful for handling first-run events.

The saving of our preferences requires the services of the **SharedPreferences.Editor**. This is evoked with `edit()` and accepts `remove()` and `clear()` procedures as well as setters like the `putString()` one we used. Note that we must conclude any storing we do here with the `commit()` statement.

It is worth bearing in mind that the use of **SharedPreferences** is slow, and when more than half a dozen or so values are needed it is worth considering more serious techniques of retaining an application's data such as a database or accessing the device's internal memory directly.

There's more...

There is a slightly more sophisticated variant of the `getPreferences()` accessor, `getSharedPreferences()`, which can be used for storing multiple preference sets.

Using more than one preference file

Using `getSharedPreferences()` is no different from its counterpart but it allows for more than one preference file. It takes the following form:

```
getSharedPreferences(String name, int mode)
```

Here *name* is the file and the *mode* can be one of `MODE_PRIVATE`, `MODE_WORLD_READABLE` or `MODE_WORLD_WRITABLE` and describe the file's access levels.

See also

To store more complex data, see the recipe *Creating an SQLite database* in *Chapter 5, Data and Security*.

Managing the activity lifecycle

The Android OS is a dangerous place for an activity. The demand for resources on a battery-operated platform is managed quite ruthlessly by the system. Our activities can be dumped from memory when it's running low, without even a moment's notice, along with any data they contain.

It is therefore essential that we understand the activity lifecycle and where our activities are on the back stack.

Getting ready

Android supplies a series of callbacks that are executed at each stage of the **activity lifecycle** and can be overridden, enabling us to anticipate user actions and execute code when the **state** of an activity changes.

To prepare for this exercise, start up a new Android project in Eclipse.

How to do it...

We are going to record each lifecycle state with a persistent TextView whenever any of the activity's callbacks are executed:

1. In the `main.xml` file, define the default TextView with `android:id`—we used `android:id="@+id/text_view"`.

2. Open the main Java activity source file and declare a class-wide TextView to correspond with the one we just defined in XML:

   ```
   private TextView mTextView;
   ```

3. Next, complete the `onCreate()` method as follows:

   ```
   @Override
   public void onCreate(Bundle state) {
       super.onCreate(state);
       setContentView(R.layout.main);

       mTextView = (TextView) findViewById(R.id.text_view);
       mTextView.append("\n created");

   }
   ```

4. Now, override the `onPause()` callback like so:

   ```
   @Override
   public void onPause() {
       super.onPause();
       mTextView.append("\n pausing");
   }
   ```

5. Override the `onResume()` method in a similar fashion:

   ```
   @Override
   public void onResume() {
       super.onResume();
       mTextView.append("\n resuming");
   }
   ```

6. Repeat this for each of the remaining lifecycle callbacks, `onStart()`, `onRestart()`, `onStop()`, and `onDestroy()`.

7. Run the application and observe what happens when the activity is interrupted by pressing the *Back* and *Home* keys or when a call is sent to or from the phone.

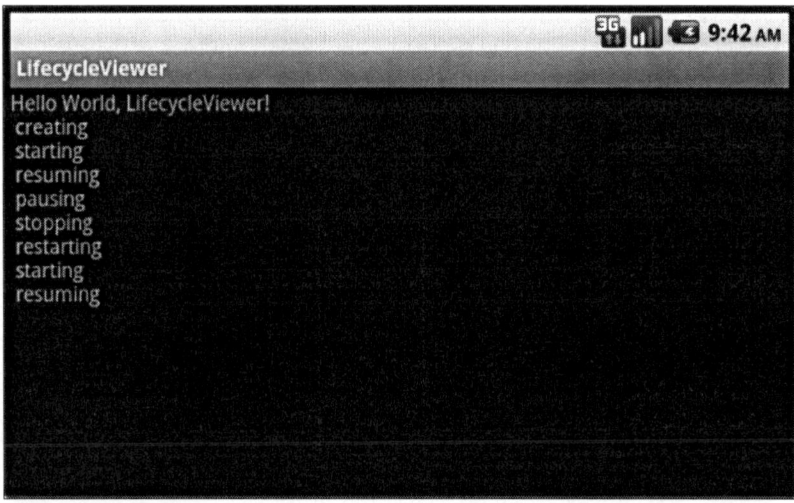

How it works...

Take a look at the next diagram. Our activity can exist in one of three states: **active**, **paused**, or **stopped**. There is also a fourth state, **destroyed**, but we can safely ignore it:

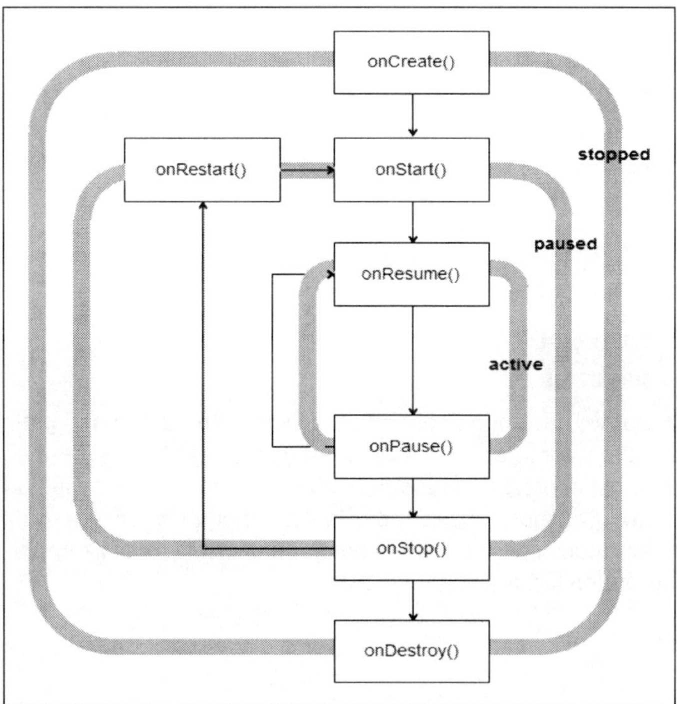

An activity is in the **active** state when its interface is available to the user. It persists from `onResume()` until `onPause()` which is brought about when another activity is pushed onto the stack. If this new activity does not entirely obscure ours, then ours will remain in the **paused** state until the new activity is finished or dismissed. It will then immediately call `onResume()` and continue.

When a newly started activity fills the screen or makes our activity otherwise invisible then our activity will enter the **stopped** state and resumption will always invoke a call to `onRestart()`.

When an activity is in either the **paused** or **stopped** state, the operating system can (and will) remove it from memory when memory is low or when other applications demand it.

In circumstances where resources are demanded suddenly, for example if the user receives a phone call, Android may kill our activity without even running the code in our `onDestroy()` method. Where possible we should use `onPause()` or `onStop()` to enable the user to navigate back to our activity seamlessly.

It is worth noting that we never actually see the results of the `onDestroy()` method, as by this point the activity has been removed. If you want to explore these methods further then it is well worth employing `Activity.isFinishing()` to see if the activity is really finishing before `onDestroy()` is executed, as seen in the following snippet:

```
@Override
  public void onPause() {
  super.onPause();

  mTextView.append("\n pausing");

  if (isFinishing()){
    mTextView.append(" ... finishing");
  }
}
```

There's more...

Despite the effort that we have had to put into preventing Android from shutting down our components prematurely, there are times when we want to deliberately exit an activity. Despite Android's robust approach to resource management it will not wipe our application if there is no demand or if memory is readily available. Although an activity that persists in this way is unlikely to have much of a negative impact, the user will most likely not see it that way and blame our application for draining their battery.

Shutting down an activity

To shut down an activity, directly call its `finish()` method, which in turn calls `onDestroy()`. To perform the same action from a child activity use the `finishFromChild(Activity child)` where `child` is the calling sub-activity.

It is often useful to know whether an activity is being shut down or merely paused, and the `isFinishing(boolean)` method returns a value indicating which of these two states the activity is in.

In this chapter we have seen the fundamental role that the **Activity** class plays in an Android application. Now that we can control the general structure of our projects, it's time to look more closely at the individual components such as layouts and fragments, components that make up the detail of our applications.

2
Layouts

In this chapter, we will cover the following topics:

- ▶ Declaring a layout
- ▶ Applying a relative layout
- ▶ Applying a table layout
- ▶ Using ListViews and ListAdapters
- ▶ Applying gravity and weight
- ▶ Controlling layout during run time
- ▶ Optimizing for tablets and multiple screens
- ▶ Dividing the screen into fragments
- ▶ Running 3.0 and higher applications on older platforms

Introduction

Android provides a useful variety of **Layout classes** for containing and organizing the individual elements of an activity such as buttons, checkboxes, and other **views**.

The Android User Interface is defined as a hierarchy of **Views** and **ViewGroups**. The `ViewGroup` is a container object that acts as the base class for Android's family of **Layout** classes, which are extended from it.

Layouts can be combined and nested to produce almost any configuration of visual screen components that we can imagine. This hierarchy of views can be, and mostly is, declared statically using XML files. The root node of these files must be a **ViewGroup**, that is, one of the provided **Layout** classes or a custom ViewGroup that we have created ourselves. Terminating nodes in the structure are all either **Views** or subclasses of the **View** object.

Android provides several built-in layout types designed for specific purposes, such as the `RelativeLayout` which allows views to be positioned with respect to other elements and the `TableLayout` for producing grids of views. We can also justify views with **Gravity** and provide proportional size with **Weight** control. Layouts and ViewGroups can be nested within each other to create complex configurations and Android provides over a dozen different **Layout** objects for managing widgets, lists, tables, galleries, and other display formats.

Starting with Android 3.0 it has been possible to produce multi-pane Activities with the `Fragment` class, which behaves in part like an Activity itself and part like a ViewGroup, and in addition these new features are made available to earlier platforms through the **Compatibility package**.

Declaring a layout

The Eclipse project wizard generates a **LinearLayout** automatically, in the form of the `res/layout/main.xml` file, and inflates it for us from the `onCreate()` callback with the `setContentView(R.layout.main)` statement. Here we will create two, slightly different layouts and switch between them with a button.

Getting ready

We will begin this task by editing our main layout file, so start a new Android project in Eclipse and open the `res/layout` folder.

How to do it...

1. Open and edit the `res/layout/main.xml` file so that it matches the following code:

```xml
<?xml version="1.0" encoding="utf-8"?>
<LinearLayout
    xmlns:android="http://schemas.android.com/apk/res/android"
    android:orientation="vertical"
    android:layout_width="match_parent"
    android:layout_height="match_parent">
    <TextView
        android:layout_width="wrap_content"
        android:layout_height="wrap_content"
        android:text="This layout is vertical." />
    <Button
        android:text="Click for a horizontal layout"
        android:id="@+id/horizontal_button"
        android:layout_width="wrap_content"
        android:layout_height="wrap_content" />
</LinearLayout>
```

2. Click on the **Graphical Layout** tab to check the appearance of this layout:

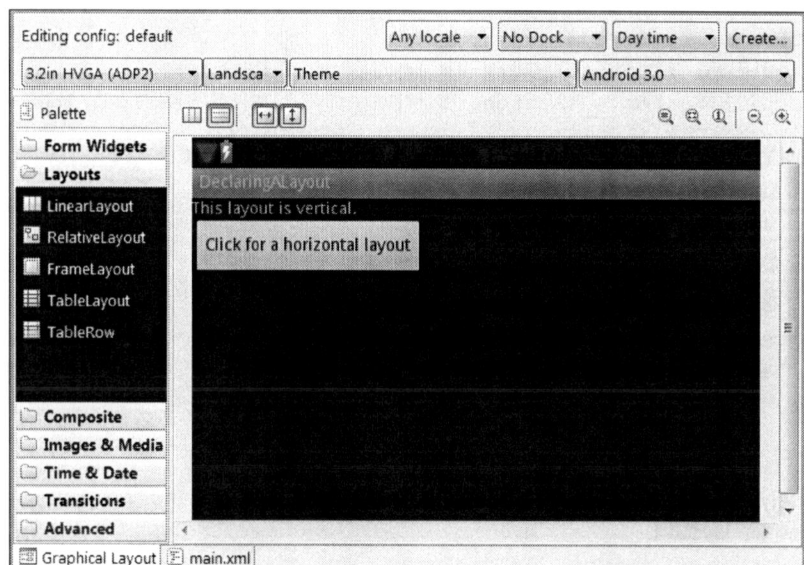

3. If your code contains the value `fill_parent` where our code has `match_parent`, you can safely ignore this as they mean exactly the same thing.

4. Inside the same folder make an exact copy of `main.xml` and call it `my_layout.xml`.

5. In this new layout file make changes only to the following four lines:

```
android:orientation="horizontal"
android:text="This layout is horizontal."
android:text="Click for a vertical layout"
android:id="@+id/vertical_button"
```

6. Preview the new layout by clicking on the **Graphical Layout** tab.

7. Now, open the main Java Activity file for editing and have the class implement the `OnClickListener` interface as follows:

```
public class DeclaringALayout
    extends Activity implements OnClickListener {
```

8. Directly beneath this declare two class wide buttons:

```
private Button mHorizontalButton;
private Button mVerticalButton;
```

9. Then directly under the `setContentView()` statement in `onCreate()`, associate the buttons with their XML counterparts:

```
mHorizontalButton =
    (Button) findViewById(R.id.horizontal_button);
mVerticalButton = (Button) findViewById(R.id.vertical_button);
```

10. Now, beneath the `onCreate()` method, implement the `onClick()` method of the `OnClickListener()` interface:

```
public void onClick(View v) {

    if (v == mHorizontalButton) {
       setContentView(R.layout.main);
    } else if (v == mVerticalButton) {
       setContentView(R.layout.my_layout);
    }

}
```

11. Finally, run this exercise on a handset or emulator and use the two buttons to switch between layouts.

How it works...

Clearly the key command here is the call to `setContentView()` which we have come across before, as Eclipse includes it in the `onCreate()` method, to automatically inflate the main layout, whenever we build a new project.

The setting of `orientation` to `horizontal` is not connected to screen orientation but controls whether each view in the layout is placed to the right-hand side of or beneath the preceding one, regardless of which way the handset is being held.

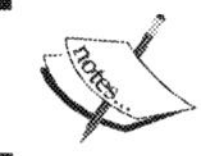

It is worth noting that vertical and horizontal orientation can also be set for a layout by clicking the icons to the top left of the **Graphical Layout** pane.

There's more...

As well as identifying a layout using a resource ID integer, as we did here, `setContentView()` can also take a View as an argument, for example:

```
findViewById(R.id.myView)
setContentView(myView);
```

For applications targeting Android 3.0 (API level 11) or higher, an alternative method of laying out view containers is available.

See also

▶ For an alternative way to separate screen elements see the recipe *Dividing the screen into Fragments* later in this chapter.

Applying a relative layout

The **RelativeLayout** subclass provides a container that allows us to position views, and even other layouts, based on each others' screen locations. Like the LinearLayout that we saw in the previous section, the RelativeLayout is also a ViewGroup; but it is particularly useful for reducing the number of other ViewGroups that we may have otherwise nested within it, which in turn saves vital memory.

Getting ready

We are going to set up a single `RelativeLayout` that contains widgets which are aligned both horizontally and vertically.

Start up a new Android project in Eclipse.

How to do it...

1. Open the `res/layout/main.xml` file with the **Graphical Layout** tab and delete the default TextView by selecting it and pressing *Delete*.

2. Open `main.xml` with the **main.xml** tab so that you can edit the code directly, delete the line `android:orientation="vertical"`, and change the opening and closing tag types from `LinearLayout` to `RelativeLayout`. The `main.xml` file should then look like this:

```xml
<?xml version="1.0" encoding="utf-8"?>

<RelativeLayout
    xmlns:android="http://schemas.android.com/apk/res/android"
    android:layout_width="match_parent"
    android:layout_height="match_parent"
    >

</RelativeLayout>
```

3. Again, if your code reads `fill_parent` where ours reads `match_parent`, there is no need to change this as these values are equivalent.

4. Next, return to the **Graphical Layout** and select **Form Widgets** from the **Palette** on the left of the layout pane.

5. Now drag a TextView from the **Palette** and drop it in the top-left corner of the layout. It should resemble the following screenshot just before you drop it:

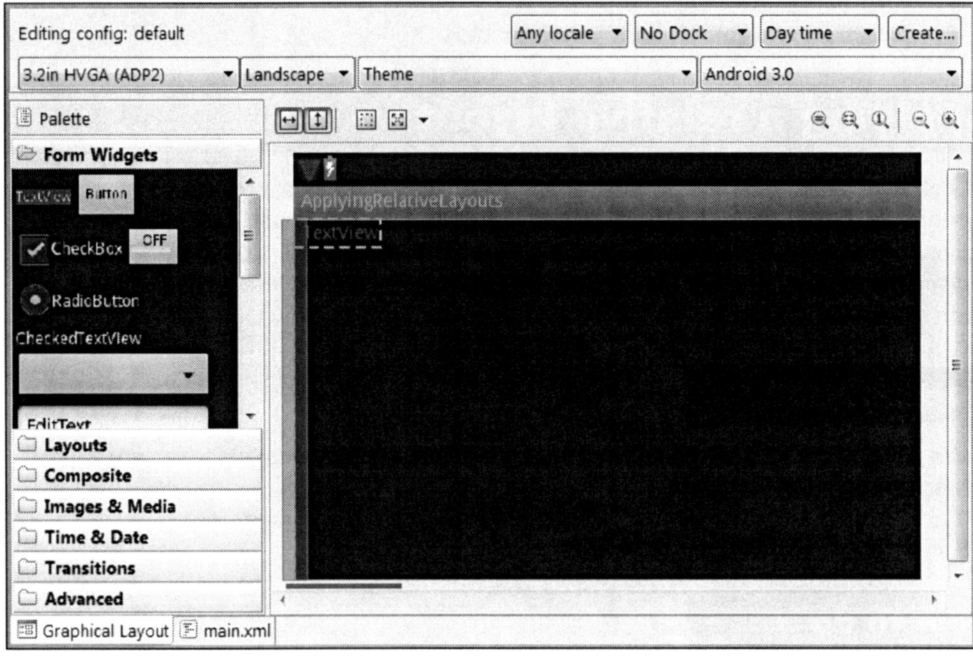

6. Next, drag a button and hold it for a moment above the TextView that we just created. A green grid should appear and when the button is held over any part of this grid, various properties will appear. Release the button when it is in the position seen here:

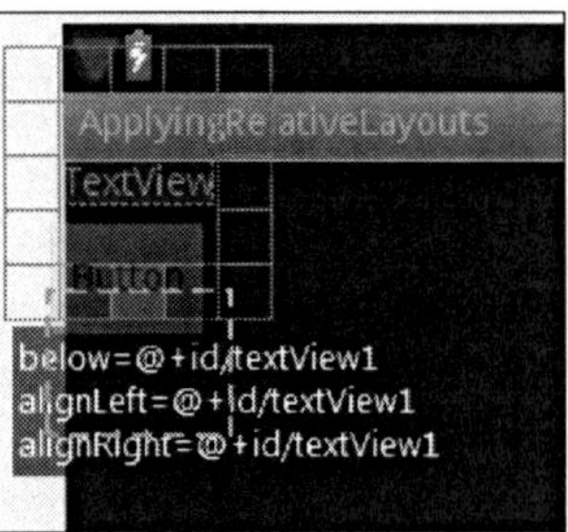

7. Continue dragging and dropping form widgets from the palette to the layout until you have reproduced the following pattern:

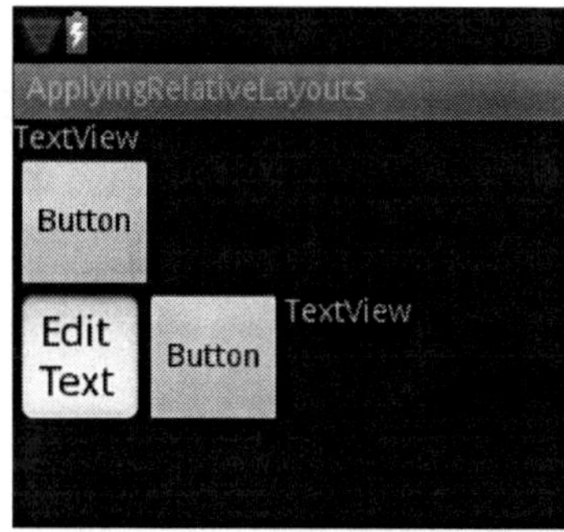

8. It is not necessary to run this code on a handset or emulator to follow how it works; instead, open the **main.xml** tab again and examine the code that the **XML Layout** has generated.

To make the XML layout code more readable, Press *Ctrl + Shift + F* to format it.

How it works...

This is a very straightforward exercise but it demonstrates a powerful aspect of relative layouts. If we only had the linear layout class available to us then creating rows within columns (or vice versa) would require a separate ViewGroup for each of these.

Examining the layout code shows that we can refer to sibling views, as in `layout_below`, `layout_toRightOf`, and `layout_alignLeft`, or to the parent ViewGroup, as we did with `layout_alignParentLeft`.

Note that a relative layout must have its `width` and `height` attributes set to `MATCH_PARENT` (or `FILL_PARENT`) for these parent aligning attributes to work, as using `WRAP_CONTENT` would create a circular reference.

There's more...

There are quite a few other relative properties available to views within a relative layout and the easiest way to explore these is by right-clicking a widget in the **Graphical Layout** and selecting **Properties**.

See also

For another example of a relative layout, see the recipe *Zooming in on a MapView* in *Chapter 11, GPS, Locations, and Maps*.

Applying a table layout

Very often we will want to lay out our information in columns and rows and when we do, Android provides us with the **TableLayout** and **TableRow** classes. TableLayout and TableRow are very similar to the HTML `<table>` and `<tr>` tags, although any Android view can be used as a cell, including another TableLayout. The system also includes several handy techniques for managing and organizing our tables.

Getting ready

Start up an Android project in Eclipse and navigate to the `main.xml` file in the `res/layout` folder.

How to do it...

1. Change the root node of the layout file from `LinearLayout` to `TableLayout`, and delete the default TextView and the `android:orientation="vertical"` attribute, leaving the code looking like this:

```xml
<?xml version="1.0" encoding="utf-8"?>

<TableLayout
    xmlns:android="http://schemas.android.com/apk/res/android"
    android:layout_width="match_parent"
    android:layout_height="match_parent">

</TableLayout>
```

2. Switch to the **Graphical Layout** tab and select **Layouts** from the **Palette** pane and drag a **TableRow** element from the **Palette** to the screen—it will appear as a shaded blue rectangle and also in the **Outline** pane.

3. Next, open the **Form Widgets** palette and drag three TextViews into the **TableRow**, following the orange guides, so that they lay side by side:

4. Now, provide each TextView with an `android:padding` of 6dip (**device independent pixels**). This is most easily done by right-clicking on the View and selecting **Properties | Padding** from the drop-down menu.

5. Copy the **TableRow** and paste two copies underneath the first, creating a 3 by 3 grid of TextViews. The **Outline** pane should look something like this:

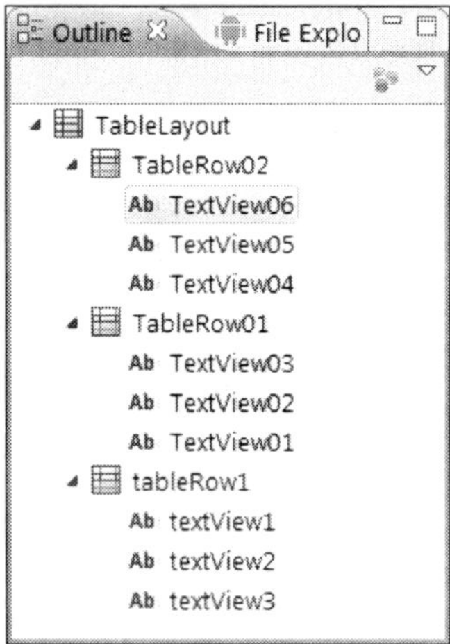

6. In the **Outline** view, right-click on **TableLayout** and select **Properties | StretchColumns...** from the drop-down menu. Now, enter a value of 1.

7. Select one of the central column's views to see the effect of the `android:stretchColumns` attribute and also take some time to examine the XML code:

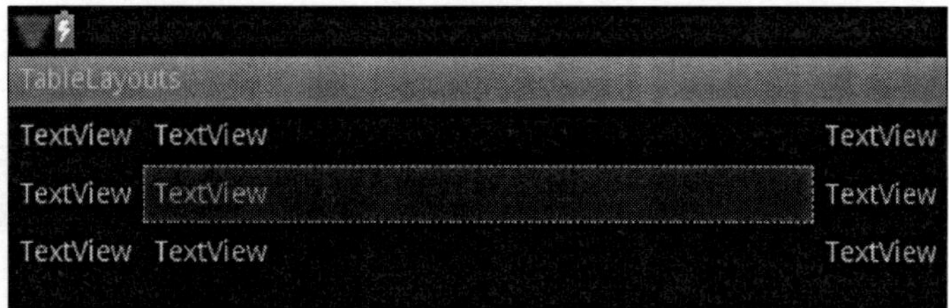

How it works...

Tables with as many columns and rows as we like can be built using the **TableLayout** and **TableRow** elements demonstrated here. Finer control over formatting can be achieved with the `stretchColumns` attribute, which causes its column to take up as much space as is available. We used the default column numbering, which begins with zero and so the second column is referred to here as 1, but there is a **TableRow** property `layoutColumn` which can be used to specifically index a column. For example:

```
<tableRow
    . . .
    android:layoutColumn="2" >
```

There's more...

Along with stretching a column to fill all available space, we can also command columns to take up no more space than they require, and even collapse completely.

Columns can shrink as well as stretch

The `shrinkColumns` attribute can be applied in exactly the same way that its `stretchColumns` partner is but has the opposite effect in that it will take up *no more room* than it requires.

Both these commands can be applied simultaneously to a single column to generate a *perfect* fit.

Hiding columns

It is often desirable to completely obscure an entire column, and the `collapseColumns` attribute can be used to do this, specifying the column index in the same way we did when stretching and shrinking columns.

It is possible to apply these controls to more than one column at a time by specifying more than one index, for example: `android:collapseColumns="0,2,4"` would cause the first, third, and fifth columns to collapse. Again, Android will conveniently ignore any illegal values.

To un-collapse a column from within Java call `setColumnsCollapsed(int column index, boolean false)`.

Using ListViews and ListAdapters

The layout classes covered so far are primarily graphical and their use is mainly design oriented, but there are layout classes that we can connect to various data structures such as the **ListView** and the **GridView**, both of which extend the base **AbsListView** class.

Getting ready

Here we will need to define a string array to populate our list as well as construct a **ListAdapter** to bind our data to our views. Start a new project with Eclipse and open the `res/values/strings.xml` file.

How to do it...

1. Select the **strings.xml** tab and include the following string array so that the whole file matches the one here:

```xml
<?xml version="1.0" encoding="utf-8"?>
<resources>

  <string
    name="hello">Hello World, ListViewsAndAdapters!</string>

  <string
    name="app_name">ListViewsAndAdapters</string>

  <string-array
    name="cities">
    <item>Bath</item>
    <item>Birmingham</item>
    <item>Bradford</item>
    <item>Brighton</item>
    <item>Bristol</item>
    <item>Cambridge</item>
    <item>Canterbury</item>
  </string-array>

</resources>
```

2. Create a new XML file inside the `res/layout` folder called `list_item.xml` and complete it as shown here:

```xml
<?xml version="1.0" encoding="utf-8"?>
<TextView
    xmlns:android="http://schemas.android.com/apk/res/android"
    android:layout_width="match_parent"
    android:layout_height="match_parent"
    android:textSize="28dip">
</TextView>
```

3. In the main activity file, change the Activity declaration so that it extends **ListActivity**:

```java
public class ListViewExample extends ListActivity {
```

Replace:

```java
setContentView(R.layout.main);
```

With:

```java
String[] c = getResources().getStringArray(R.array.cities);
setListAdapter(new ArrayAdapter<String>(this,
    R.layout.list_item, c));
```

4. Underneath this, create a `OnItemClickListener` with the following lines of code:

```java
ListView v = getListView();
v.setOnItemClickListener(new OnItemClickListener() {
    public void onItemClick(AdapterView<?> parent,
        View view, int position, long rowId) {
        String s = ((TextView) view).getText() + " "
            + position + " " + rowId;
        Toast.makeText(getApplicationContext(), s,
            Toast.LENGTH_LONG).show();
    }
});
```

5. Now run the project on an emulator or handset to see the populated list. Clicking an item displays its text, position, and row ID:

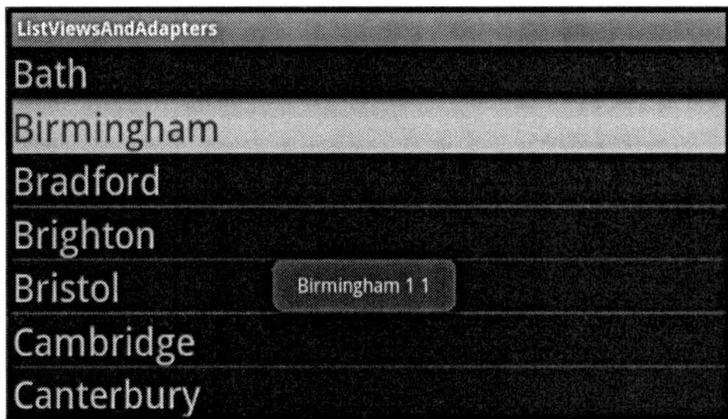

How it works...

The construction of the string array `cities` is fairly self explanatory, as should be the way it is referenced later with the `getStringArray()` call. The list is managed by an **ArrayAdapter**, which is a built-in class that connects our data to our `list_item` definition using the `setListAdapter()` call. We had, first, to reference our string resource in the usual way.

ListViews are more often than not activities in their own right and the **ListActivity** extension provides us access to the `setListAdapter()` method and also allow us to pass `this` as our context along with our view definition and the array, as required.

The use of a Toast pop-up in the click listener demonstrates not only that the list is working but also shows the values of the last two parameters in `onItemClick()`, which are positions of the View in the adapter and its row index, or ID. The first two parameters represent the **AdapterView** and the View within that were clicked on; here they are both anonymous.

There's more...

For applications targeting Android 3.0 (API level 11) or higher, it is possible for the user to make multiple selections on a list.

Setting up a multi-choice ListView

To change the choice mode of a ListView call `setChoiceMode(CHOICE_MODE_MULTIPLE_MODAL)` on your ListView and use a **MultiChoiceModeListener** to detect selected items with the listener's `onItemCheckedStateChanged()` callback.

See also

For another example of how to create a ListView, see the recipe *Dividing the screen into fragments* later in this chapter.

For more on Toasts and how to build custom pop-ups see the recipe *Making a Toast* in *Chapter 7, Notifying the User*.

Applying gravity and weight

Android provides some useful formatting tools when it comes to fine tuning our screen designs, including a way to specify relative size priorities for individual views and view groups. When one considers the wide variety of screen sizes and aspects that our application may end up running on, it is essential to be able to have a generalized control over the screen.

Getting ready

Start up a new Android project in Eclipse and from the `res/layout/main.xml` **Graphical Layout** tab, drag three **TextViews** onto the form, one beneath another. Also delete the default TextView.

How to do it...

1. From the **Graphical Layout** view change the layout width and height of the one at the bottom to `MATCH_PARENT` in both cases. This is easily achieved without having to edit the XML directly by right-clicking on the widget and selecting **Layout Height** and **Layout Width** from the pop-up menu.

2. Change the layout height of the middle TextView to `MATCH_PARENT` in the same way.

3. Finally, change the layout height of the top view to `MATCH_PARENT`. By now you will only be able to see one of the views, the topmost.

4. Open the **main.xml** tab and give each view a different background color. Here we have used three grays:

```
android:background="#333"

android:background="#666"

android:background="#999"
```

5. Now provide each view with a different layout weight, like so:

```
android:layout_weight="2"

android:layout_weight="3"

android:layout_weight="4"
```

6. View the resulting layout using the preview pane, which should now look something like:

7. With the top two text views, give each one either of the following attributes. Now we can see all our views. This can be done from the **Properties** menu:

```
android:layout_gravity="center"

android:layout_gravity="right"
```

8. View the results in the Layout tab to see how these commands are followed. Hopefully, the screen will now resemble the one shown here:

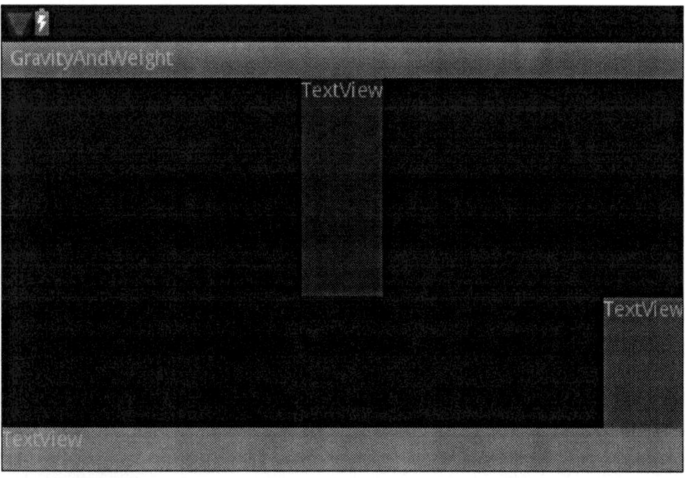

How it works...

The `layout_gravity` tag we used here is analogous to traditional text justification, and besides `center` and `right` we could also have used `left`, `top`, and `bottom`. It is also possible to differentiate between horizontal and vertical centering with the `center_horizontal` and `center_vertical` attributes.

The `layout_weight` attribute, even more than `gravity`, provides us control over screen elements without ever having to know exact dimensions. The system calculates the amount of screen estate allocated to each view based on the relative values of the **layout weights**. Only those views with a weight property are considered in this calculation so that, if we wish, we can omit views from the priority calculation by removing the weight attribute or setting it to zero.

There's more...

With the use of the pipe character (|)it is possible to apply more than one gravity attribute to a view or view group. For example, the following will both centre and raise its owner:

```
android:layout_gravity="top|center"
```

It should be noted that the `layout_gravity` and `gravity` tags are not the same thing. Where `layout_gravity` dictates where in its parent a view should lie, `gravity` simply controls the positioning of the contents of a view—for example the alignment of text in a button or text view.

See also

To learn how to adjust the gravity of pop-ups see the recipe *Making a Toast* in *Chapter 7, Notifying the User*.

Controlling layout during runtime

Specifying the UI with XML and keeping the layout separate from the application code makes for easily maintainable projects and allows us to specify different layouts based on locale, orientation, pixel density, docking status, and other configuration parameters.

Despite the tidiness of this approach there are occasions when we need to manipulate a layout or another view group at runtime from within a Java method. All XML code is interpreted by Java and we have access to ViewGroup parameters through various **LayoutParams** classes.

Getting ready

Here we will set up a simple layout with XML and use a **LinearLayout.LayoutParams** object to change the margins of a View during run time.

Start a new Android project and navigate to the `main.xml` file in the `res/layout` folder.

How to do it....

1. Open the **Graphical Layout** tab and edit the default TextView so that it looks like the one here:

```
<TextView
    android:text="This layout was defined in XML"
    android:id="@+id/text_view"
    android:layout_width="wrap_content"
    android:layout_height="wrap_content"
    android:textSize="18dip"
    android:padding="3dip" />
```

2. Beneath this, add a `Button` and change its ID and text properties like so:

```
<Button
android:id="@+id/button"
android:text="OK"
```

3. Also provide the containing LinearLayout with an ID:

```
<LinearLayout
    android:id="@+id/@+id/layout"
```

4. Open the main Java Activity code and declare a class wide TextView at the top:

```
TextView textView;
```

5. Set up the TextView and the Button, from within the `onCreate()` method:

```
textView = (TextView) findViewById(R.id.text_view);
Button button = (Button) findViewById(R.id.button);
```

6. Provide the button with the following click listener:

```
button.setOnClickListener(new OnClickListener() {

    @Override
    public void onClick(View v) {
        LinearLayout.LayoutParams params =
            (LinearLayout.LayoutParams) v.getLayoutParams();
        params.leftMargin = v.getRight()
            % (findViewById(R.id.layout).getWidth() - v.getWidth());
        textView.setText("This layout was changed dynamically");
    }

});
```

7. Compile and run the project on a handset or emulator. Clicking the button will change the specified layout parameters and move it across the screen:

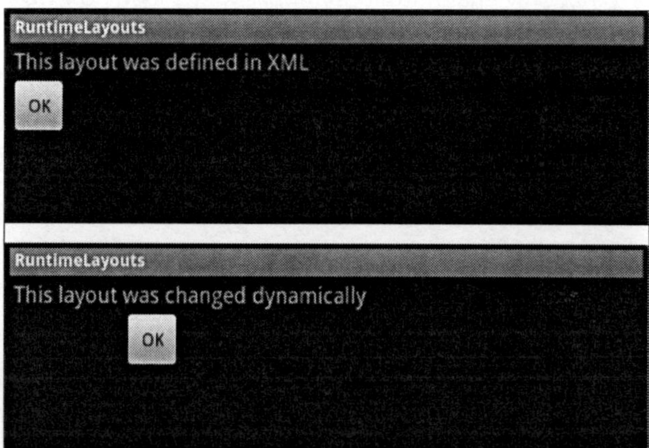

How it works...

Every view and view group has a set of layout parameters associated with it and in particular all views have parameters that inform their parent of their desired height and width. We express this in XML with the `WRAP_CONTENT` and `MATCH_PARENT` constants, which all views share, but every view class has its own appropriate set of parameters based on its purpose. For example, TextViews have parameters for controlling their text content.

Every View and ViewGroup has a `getLayoutParams()` method that we can use to access its layout width, layout height, and any class-specific parameters such as margin and padding. Here we used the LayoutParams of the view that was clicked on along with our original layout to move the button.

See also

To see how to change fragments rather than ViewGroups during runtime, see the recipe *Dividing the screen into fragments* later in this chapter.

Optimizing for tablets and multiple screens

Android can be (and is) installed on many devices and our applications can end up running on a wide variety of **screen resolutions** and range of **pixel densities**. Although the system generally scales applications to fit most situations rather well, there are nevertheless times when an application does not appear as we might wish. Differing pixel densities mean that screen elements can be larger or smaller than we might like depending on the handset they are running on.

Naturally we want our applications to run on as many devices as we can, but we do not want them installed on devices where the screen size makes them unusable. Fortunately, Android provides a way for us to not only ensure that our applications look how we want on any targeted screen configuration, but also make sure that they will not even be available to users with handsets that would not do our application justice.

In this recipe we will configure an application using the `<supports-screens>` element in the manifest and **resource qualified directories** to control how an application renders on screens of different sizes and/or densities.

Getting ready

Android only introduced compatibility for tablet sized screens in API level 9 (Platform 2.3.1). Start a new Android project in Eclipse with a **Build Target** of level 9 or higher—here we used 10. Next, open the `main.xml` file in the `res/layout` folder.

How to do it....

1. Edit the default TextView so that it has a height of `100dip`, text size of `26sp`, and a background color of `#333`:

    ```
    android:layout_height="100dip"
    android:textSize="26sp"
    android:background="#333"
    ```

2. Add another TextView beneath this one and give it both height and width of `MATCH_PARENT` (or `FILL_PARENT`) and a background color of `#666`.

3. Using the **AVD Manager**, set up an emulator with an API level to match the project (no lower than 9). Give it a **Resolution** of `640 x 1024` pixels and an **Abstracted LCD density** of `320` dpi:

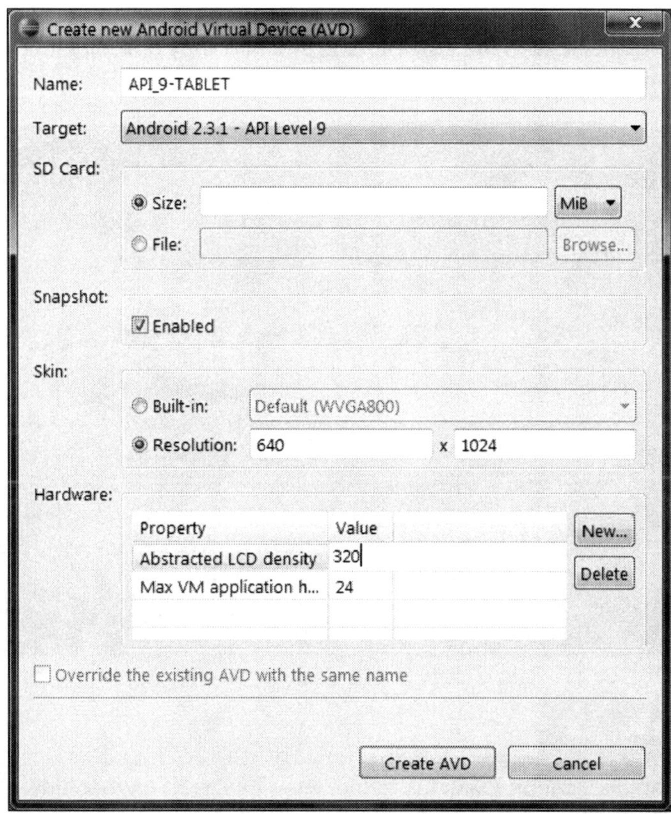

4. Set up a second emulator with a small screen of `240 x 320` pixels and a dpi of `160`.

5. Now, run the application on both emulators and observe the difference in the way they appear.

6. Make a copy of the `layout` folder that contains your `main.xml` file and paste it back into the `res` folder, calling it `layout-small.xml`.

7. Edit the `main.xml` file in the `layout-small` folder so that the top TextView has a height of `30dip` and a text size of `12sp`.

8. Open the manifest file and add the following `<supports-screens>` element to the `<manifest>` element:

```
<supports-screens
    android:resizeable="true"
    android:xlargeScreens="true"
    android:anyDensity="true" />
```

9. Test the project on both the emulators to see how they now maintain similar proportions across very different physical platforms:

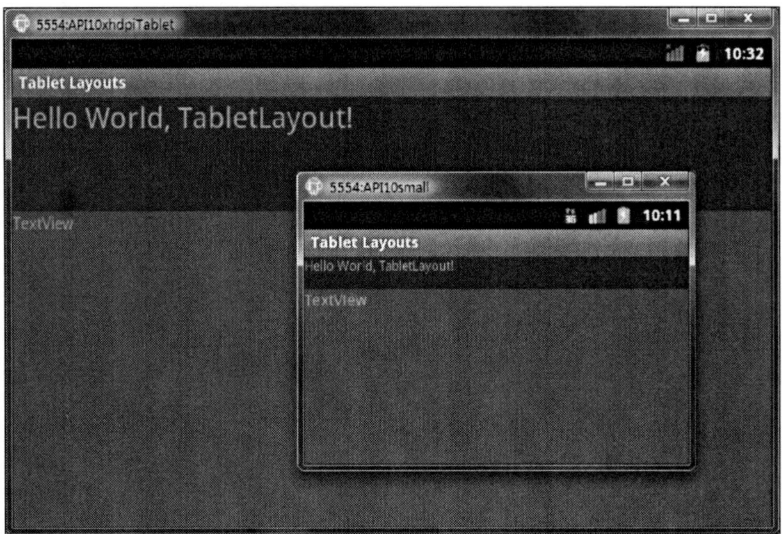

How it works...

For ensuring that an application looks the same when rendered on machines with different screen densities, Android provides the **density-independent pixel**, written as **dip**, **dp**, or **sp** for font sizes. The higher the screen density, the more the actual pixels will be displayed and this is why the text in the top view looked the same size when rendered on both emulators when we tested the project in step 5 previously.

This matching of size across screens is often desirable but when it is not, Android allows us to define resources that target screen sizes specifically by using **qualified directories**. In the previous example, we created a layout file in a folder called `layout-small` that will be automatically applied when the program is run on small screens, and we could have done the same with `layout-large` and `layout-xlarge` folders.

The exact same principle applies when we want to provide resources targeted at screens with different pixel densities, the qualifiers being **ldpi**, **mdpi**, **hdpi** and **xhdpi**, for example `layout-xhdpi` or `values-ldpi`. A good example of how this works can be seen by examining the contents of the qualified drawable folders that were generated with the project, where icon PNG files were provided with appropriate resolutions for the screens in question.

When resources are required to be a specific size on any screen and not scaled in any way we can use the **nodpi** qualifier as in `drawable-nodpi`.

Providing screen specific resources is only one way of controlling how an application manages multiple screens; we can also inform the system of which screens our application is designed to support with the `<supports-screens>` tag in the manifest. The four screen types being **smallScreens**, **normalScreens**, **largeScreens**, and **xlargeScreens** and setting their value as `true` indicates that the application is designed for such screens. Setting the value to `false` on the other hand can have two possible outcomes:

1. If the screen size is smaller than the target size, for example:

```
android:smallScreens="false"
android:normalScreens="true"
```

   Then, the application will be filtered out of the Android Market on devices with small screens.

2. If the screen size is larger than the target, as in the following:

```
android:normalScreens="true"
android:largeScreens="false"
```

   Then, the system will apply its own compatibility functions such as scaling to the larger screen.

There were two other attributes we applied to the `<supports-screens>` tag, **resizeable** and **anyDensity**. Setting `resizeable` is useful for ensuring that an Activity fills the screen. `anyDensity`, when true, will tell Android to assume that the application has been designed to work with all densities, and so not do any scaling.

See also

For other ways to manage tablet layouts see the next recipe, *Dividing the screen into fragments*.

Dividing the screen into fragments

So as to cater for the larger screens found on **tablet** devices, Android introduced the **android. app.fragment** package with version 3.0 (API level 11). **Fragments** simplify the process of designing and displaying **multi-pane** screens and are similar to layouts and view groups but provide some of the functionality of activities.

This recipe will demonstrate how to open a fragment from a list and how to control content.

Getting ready

Start a new Android project in Eclipse, making sure that the target build is API level 11 or higher by including the following tag to the `<manifest>` element of the manifest file:

```
<uses-sdk
  android:targetSdkVersion="11" />
```

How to do it....

1. The main layout for this example is a horizontal, LinearLayout containing a ListView and a fragment. The complete `main.xml` code looks like the lines below but substitute the package name in the class declaration with that of your own project:

```xml
<?xml version="1.0" encoding="utf-8"?>
<LinearLayout
   xmlns:android="http://schemas.android.com/apk/res/android"
   android:orientation="horizontal"
   android:layout_width="match_parent"
   android:layout_height="match_parent">

   <ListView
      android:id="@+id/list"
      android:layout_width="0px"
      android:layout_weight="1"
      android:layout_height="match_parent" />

   <fragment
      class="com.packtpub.android.fragmentexample.MyFragment"
      android:id="@+id/my_fragment"
      android:layout_width="0px"
      android:layout_weight="4"
      android:layout_height="match_parent" />

</LinearLayout>
```

2. Next, open the main Java activity code and alter the class declaration so that it implements an `OnItemClickListener`:

```java
public class FragmentExample
   extends Activity
      implements OnItemClickListener {
```

3. Beneath the `setContentView()` statement in the `onCreate()` callback, set up the ListView defined in the activity layout:

```java
@Override
public void onCreate(Bundle state) {
    super.onCreate(state);
    setContentView(R.layout.main);

    ListView list = (ListView) findViewById(R.id.list);
    ArrayAdapter<String> n =
        new ArrayAdapter<String>(getApplicationContext(),
          android.R.layout.simple_list_item_1,
          new String[] {
             "Ten", "Twenty", "Thirty", "Forty", "Fifty",
             "Sixty" });
    list.setAdapter(n);
    list.setOnItemClickListener(this);

}
```

4. Add a `onItemClick()` method to the activity and complete it as shown here:

```java
public void
    onItemClick(AdapterView<?> parent, View view, int pos,
       long id) {
    Fragment f = new MyFragment(pos + 1);

    FragmentTransaction t =
       getFragmentManager().beginTransaction();
    t.replace(R.id.my_fragment, f);
    t.setTransition(FragmentTransaction.TRANSIT_FRAGMENT_OPEN);
    t.addToBackStack(null);
    t.commit();
}
```

5. Create a new Java class, in a new file, call it `MyFragment`, and have it extend the `Fragment` class:

```java
public class MyFragment extends Fragment {
```

6. Give the new class a field and two constructors:

```java
private float mValue;

public MyFragment() {

}

public MyFragment(float v) {
    this.mValue = v;

}
```

7. Finally, give the class an `onCreateView()` method:

```java
@Override
public View onCreateView(LayoutInflater inflater,
    ViewGroup container, Bundle state) {
    Context context = getActivity().getApplicationContext();

    LinearLayout layout = new LinearLayout(context);

    TextView text = new TextView(context);
    text.setText("Size " + (mValue * 10));
    text.setTextSize(mValue * 10);

    layout.addView(text);

    return layout;
    }
}
```

8. Compile and run the project on a tablet or emulator. After pressing several list items, hit the *Back* key to see how the fragments have been stored:

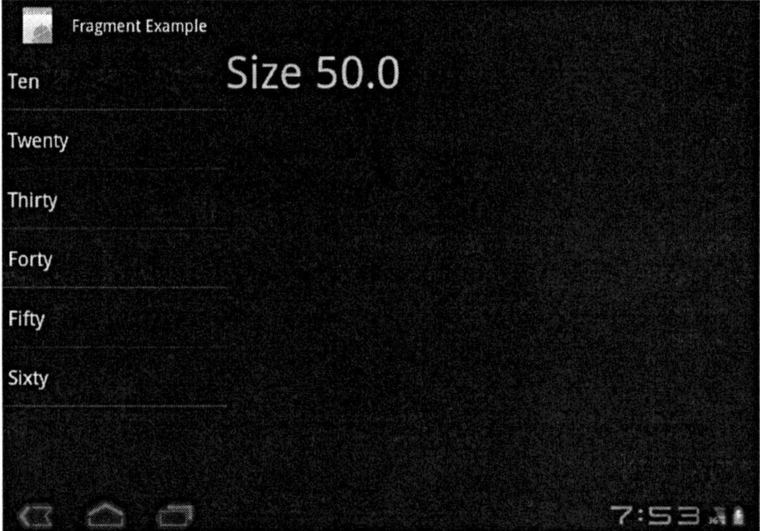

How it works...

The first thing we did here was to declare our fragment from within our activity's layout file. Most of this looks like any other view declaration with the exception of the class declaration, which simply points to the Java class that we created in steps 5, 6, and 7.

The **android.app.FragmentTransaction** object is how we perform operations on fragments, such as adding and removing them. A **FragmentTransaction** is obtained with `getFragmentManager().beginTransaction()` and can then be controlled directly through its own methods. Here we only had one fragment so we replaced each one using `replace(ViewGroup ID, Fragment)`, but had we wished, we could have created any number by using `FragmentTransaction.add(ViewGroup ID, Fragment)`. Fragment transactions also have `show(Fragment)`, `hide(Fragment)`, and `remove(Fragment)` methods, along with several others.

The way a fragment appears (or disappears) is controlled with the `FragmentTransaction.setTransition()` method. In this example we used the transaction `(int)` constant `TRANSIT_FRAGMENT_OPEN`, which simply opens our fragment. Along with the corresponding `TRANSIT_FRAGMENT_CLOSE` there is also `TRANSIT_FRAGMENT_FADE` and one or two others.

The `FragmentTransaction.addToBackStack()` method is how we ensure that each transaction is stored on the back stack so that previous transactions can be returned to with the *Back* key. The optional `(string)` parameter can be used as a name to identify a particular state.

The `FragmentTransaction.commit()` call is essential and is the final stage in each transition. The transition does not necessarily take place immediately but is scheduled to run on the main thread when it becomes available.

The `Fragment` class is very similar to the `Activity` class and contains many of the same methods such as `onCreate()`, `onPause()`, `onResume()`, and `onStop()`. Here, we only used the `onCreateView()` callback but we could have used these methods to store values as is often done with an Activity. For example:

```java
@Override
public void onCreate(Bundle state) {
  super.onCreate(state);

  if (null != state) {
    mValue = state.getFloat("mValue");
  }

}

@Override
public void onSaveInstanceState(Bundle state) {
  state.putFloat("mValue", mValue);

}
```

Fragments provide a useful bridge between Activities and ViewGroups. Each Fragment must exist with an Activity and, although it has its own lifecycle, when its parent enters the paused or stopped state, it will too.

See also

For more on including ListViews, see the recipe *Using ListViews and ListAdapters*, earlier in this chapter.

Fragments can be included on earlier versions of Android by using the compatibility package and this is demonstrated in the next recipe.

Running 3.0 and higher applications on older platforms

The advent of Android 3.0 introduced some significant new features, aimed in particular at tablet devices. However, there are a large number of Android tablets that run on earlier platforms and so Google produced a **compatibility package** so that most of these new features would run on older versions, going back as far as Android 1.6 (API level 4).

This chapter has introduced a lot of new concepts but we can conclude it with a nice and easy example showing how to install the compatibility library and how to include packages from it, so that we can take advantage of these wonderful new features on older platforms.

Getting ready

There is a strong chance that you have already downloaded and installed the Android **Compatibility Package** during a regular software update of your SDK. All the same, open the AVD manager, select **Installed packages**, and check that you have; it will look like this:

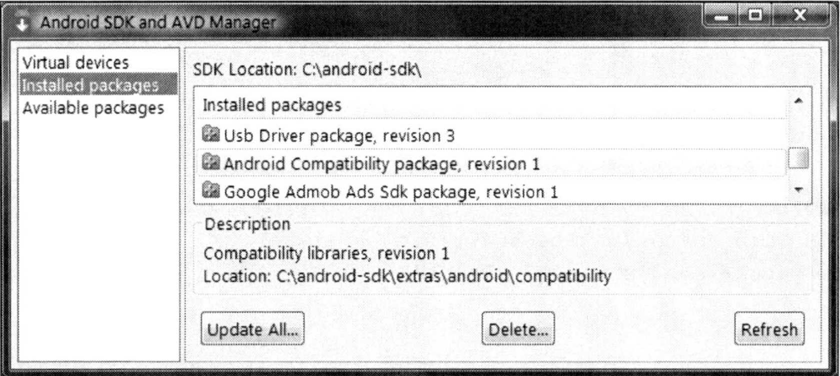

How to do it....

1. Having checked that the Compatibility package is installed, start up a new Android project in Eclipse with a Min SDK version of 4 and a Target SDK version of 10.

2. Open the project properties, which can be done with *Alt + Enter* on a PC, and select **Java Build Path** followed by the **Libraries** tab.

3. Click on the **Add External JARs...** button and browse to the `extras` folder in your `android-sdk` folder. Find the `android-support-v4.jar` file and click on **OK**.

4. There should now be a new folder in your project called **Referenced Libraries** containing the library:

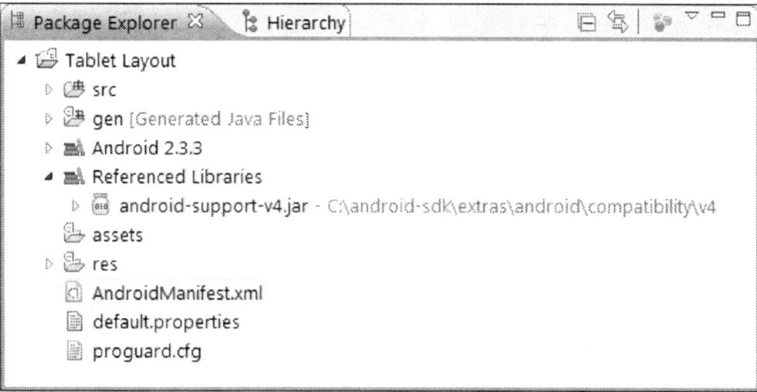

5. Change the declaration of your main Java Activity file from `extends Activity` to `extends FragmentActivity` and press *Shift + Ctrl + O* to include the line `import android.support.v4.app.FragmentActivity;` into your project.

How it works...

There is not much to explain when it comes to how this works. All we have done is import a new library so that we can use features introduced in 3.0 on earlier platforms. However, this is a remarkably useful function as it allows us to publish applications that will run on the widest possible range of devices.

The Android layout classes we have covered here allow us to set out our screens in a variety of useful ways. Of course it is the objects that we place inside these containers that provide their real functionality and it is these widgets that we will cover in the next chapter.

3
Widgets

In this chapter, we will cover the following topics:

- ► Inserting a widget into a layout
- ► Adding images to a widget
- ► Creating a widget at runtime
- ► Applying a style
- ► Turning a style into a theme
- ► Using a platform style or theme
- ► Creating a custom component

Introduction

Many of the individual on-screen components that we see in an Android application are provided by the **android:widget** package. It provides dozens of classes and interfaces for creating and using such objects. The system also allows us to extend the base **android.view. View** class to create custom widgets of our own.

The Android **Widget package** provides us with a wide variety of purpose-built components such as text views, date pickers, rating bars, and all kinds of other familiar UI elements. In addition, many widgets have associated **interfaces** such as the list adapters that we saw in the previous chapter.

It is worth making the distinction here, between **Widgets**, which are descended from the base View class, and **AppWidgets**, which are mini applications that can be embedded into an activity.

Many widgets can have images, sounds, and other media connected to them and these, along with most other properties, can be set and changed with static XML files or dynamically with Java code.

Our applications can be easily given a consistent look across different screens with the use of **styles**, which can, in turn, be encapsulated in a **theme** and applied to a wider scope of objects such as whole activities or even applications.

Another powerful feature of the Android UI is the ability to construct our own customized widgets, which can be done by extending the View class itself. These classes can again be reused and like built-in widgets, bound to data.

Inserting a widget into a layout

Android widgets are included into a layout just as the views and view groups that we have been previously using. Although each **widget** has its own unique characteristics, they all inherit from the View class.

Here we will insert a **CheckBox** widget but use a callback from the parent class to edit its properties.

Getting ready

Start up a new Android project in Eclipse and open the `main.xml` file in **Graphical Layout** mode.

How to do it...

1. Drag-and-drop a **CheckBox** from the **Form Widget** palette onto the default layout, as seen in the next screenshot:

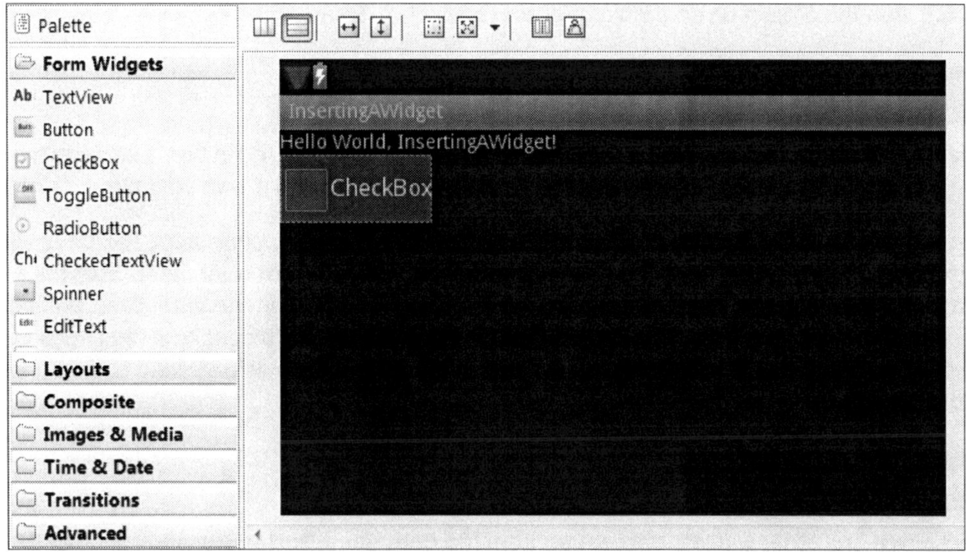

2. Open the **main.xml** tab and edit the new element so that it has the following properties:

```
<CheckBox
   android:text="A CheckBox"
   android:id="@+id/check_box"
   android:layout_width="wrap_content"
   android:layout_height="wrap_content" />
```

3. Include the following code inside the main Java activity's `onCreate()` method:

```
CheckBox checkBox = (CheckBox) findViewById(R.id.check_box);

checkBox.setOnClickListener(new OnClickListener() {

   public void onClick(View v) {

      if (((CheckBox) v).isChecked()) {
            ((CheckBox) v).setText("selected");
      } else {
            ((CheckBox) v).setText("not selected");
      }

   }

});
```

4. To import the necessary libraries, from Eclipse, press *Shift + Ctrl + O*. This will automatically add the following lines to the code:

```
import android.view.View.OnClickListener;
import android.widget.CheckBox;
```

5. Run the project on an emulator or handset.

How it works...

Widgets, like views, can be given a resource ID as part of their XML definition. Likewise, the `findViewById()` method can be used to associate a widget with a Java variable.

Most widgets lie at the bottom or close to the bottom of a hierarchy of classes. The **CheckBox**, for example, is descended from the **CompoundButton**, which in turn is inherited from the Button and View objects. The **OnClickListener** interface is defined in the View class, and so takes its argument as a View. This means that we have to cast the widget as a CheckBox so as to be able to use the methods not defined in the parent such as `setText()` and `isChecked()`.

There's more...

Checkboxes and other widgets descended from the **CompoundButton** class will change their states automatically when clicked, but it is possible to change this through code if we wish.

Changing a CheckBox's state with code

The **CheckBox** handles its own graphical state automatically, that is, it will toggle between the selected and unselected states without any extra code. If we need to change the state programmatically, we can use the **CompoundButton's** `setChecked()` method, which takes a Boolean argument to change the checkbox's state.

See also

To learn how to manage checkable menu items refer to the recipe *Building menu groups of checkable items* in *Chapter 4, Menus*.

Adding images to widgets

Along with being able to provide views (and many widgets) with a single background image, Android also allows us to add more than one image to certain views so that we can represent various states (such as pressed or focused) graphically. To create a widget with three states: pressed, focused, and normal, we will need three image files which can then be defined in XML as a single resource.

Getting ready

Select three different image files (JPG, PNG, BMP, or GIF) of the same size, but no wider than 200 pixels:

How to do it...

1. Start up a new Android project in Eclipse and locate the `res/drawable-mdpi` folder.

2. Drag the image files into the `drawable-mdpi` folder and name them as follows:

   - button_pressed.png
   - button_normal.png
   - button_focused.png

3. Create a new XML file in the same folder called `my_button.xml`.

4. Fill out the `my_button.xml` file as follows:

```xml
<?xml version="1.0" encoding="utf-8"?>
<selector
  xmlns:android="http://schemas.android.com/apk/res/android">
  <item
    android:drawable="@drawable/button_pressed"
    android:state_pressed="true" />
  <item
    android:drawable="@drawable/button_focused"
    android:state_focused="true" />
  <item
    android:drawable="@drawable/button_normal" />
</selector>
```

5. Add a new button to the `main.xml` layout file and ensure that it includes the attributes:

```xml
android:text=""
android:background="@drawable/my_button"
```

6. As it has been defined, our **drawable** can be accessed through the Button's context menu in the **Graphical Layout** by selecting **Properties | Background...**

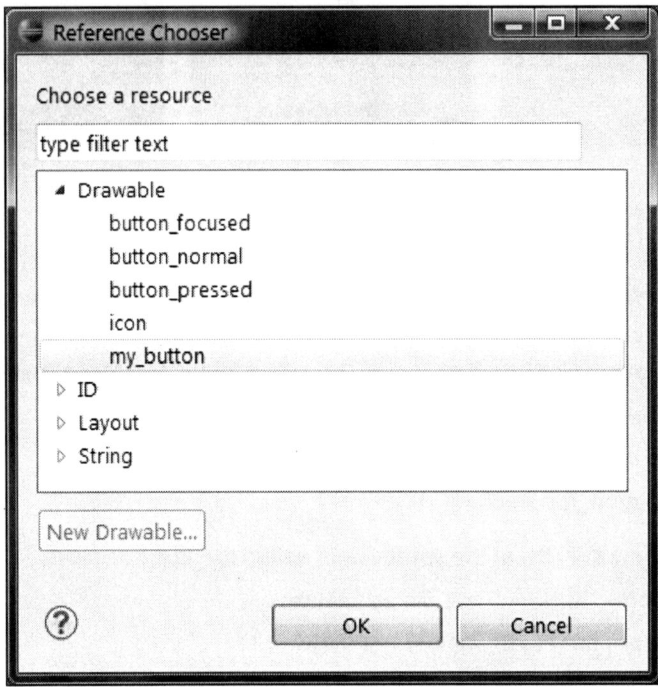

7. Run the project on an emulator or a handset and press the resultant button to view the various states.

8. You will see our button in its focused state and will need to use the *trackball* or *d-pad* keys.

How it works...

The essential process here is the `my_button.xml` file, which encapsulates our three images into a single drawable resource within the `<selector>` tag. The `state_pressed` and `state_focused` attributes are provided to allow us to define which image goes with which state.

Other widgets have states appropriate to their purpose and can be accessed in the same way.

It is important to realize that Android will check our `items` in the order we have written them and so the normal state must wait until the system has tested the other two possibilities, or we will only ever see the *normal* image.

With our three images combined in this way, we can refer to the `my_button` drawable in the same way we would with a single image or color value. We can also refer to this drawable from within Java at runtime in the same way we would with any other resource, adding the attribute `android:id="@+id/button"` to our button in the `main.xml` file.

Android stores these IDs as unique integer identifiers in the `R.java` file, the `@` symbol indicates that this is a resource, and the `+` sign tells the system that we are creating a new resource and therefore should be included. It is well worth taking a look at the `R.java` file but not worth editing it; at best, any edits will be written over, and at worst, they will crash our project.

Given such an ID, we can now associate both the button and the drawable using the resource file:

```
Button b = (Button) findViewById(R.id.button);
b.setBackgroundResource(R.drawable.my_button);
```

There's more...

We mentioned at the beginning of this recipe the need to make our three images the same size but this is not strictly necessary and Android provides means to control image size more deliberately.

Android will re-size images by default

If we had not made our images the same size, we would have seen a very similar output with images scaled and stretched to fit the size of the default image, which was `button_normal` here. This automatic scaling can be very handy, but bear in mind that Android applies a bi-cubic remapping, which requires a lot of processing.

The default behavior for Android is to perform this scaling just once when the image is first encountered, requiring a copy of our image and therefore using more memory.

Using designated folders for screen-specific resources

When Android encounters a `@drawable` reference, it expects to find the target in one of the `res/drawable` folders. These are designed for different screen densities: `ldpi` (low dots per inch), `mdpi` (medium), `hdpi` (high), and `xhdpi` (extra-high) and they allow us to create resources for specific target devices. When an application is running on a specific device, Android will load resources from the designated folder that most closely matches the actual screen density. If it finds this folder empty, it will try the next nearest match and so on until it finds the named resource. For tutorial purposes, a separate set of files for each possible density is not required and so placing our images in the `medium-dpi` folder is a simple but crude way to run the exercise on any device.

See also

For more on-screen specific resources and qualified directories, see the recipe *Optimizing for tablets and multiple screens* in *Chapter 2, Layouts* and also the documentation at `http://developer.android.com/guide/topics/resources/providing-resources.html#BestMatch`.

Creating a widget at runtime

We have already seen how it is possible to create a view or view group in XML and then to edit its properties from within Java code. It is in fact perfectly possible and quite easy to create any screen element from scratch at runtime. All of Android's built-in widgets are extensions of the View class and here we will use a **DatePicker**, create it, and then set some of its properties from within Java code.

Getting ready

As just mentioned, we will be doing very little in the way of XML in this recipe. Nevertheless, start a new Android project and navigate to the `res/layout/main.xml` file.

How to do it...

1. Remove any default views that the project wizard may have created, so that all we have is an empty `LinearLayout` filling the screen:

    ```xml
    <?xml version="1.0" encoding="utf-8"?>
    <LinearLayout
      xmlns:android="http://schemas.android.com/apk/res/android"
      android:layout_width="fill_parent"
      android:layout_height="fill_parent">
    </LinearLayout>
    ```

2. Give our layout object an ID so that we can refer to it from Java:

    ```xml
    android:id="@+id/layout"
    ```

3. Open the main Java activity class and include the following lines inside the `onCreate()` method after the `setContentView()` call:

    ```java
    LinearLayout = (LinearLayout) findViewById(R.id.layout);
    DatePicker picker = new DatePicker(this);
    layout.addView(picker);
    ```

4. Run the project on an emulator or handset to see the date picker widget.

5. Now, add the following line:

    ```java
    picker.updateDate(1969, 6, 21);
    ```

6. Directly after the date picker declaration, the entire method should now look like this:

```java
@Override
public void onCreate(Bundle state) {
    super.onCreate(state);
    setContentView(R.layout.main);

    LinearLayout layout =
        (LinearLayout) findViewById(R.id.layout);
    DatePicker picker = new DatePicker(this);
    picker.updateDate(1969, 6, 21);
    layout.addView(picker);
}
```

7. Run the project again to see the changes the new line has generated, as seen in the following screenshot:

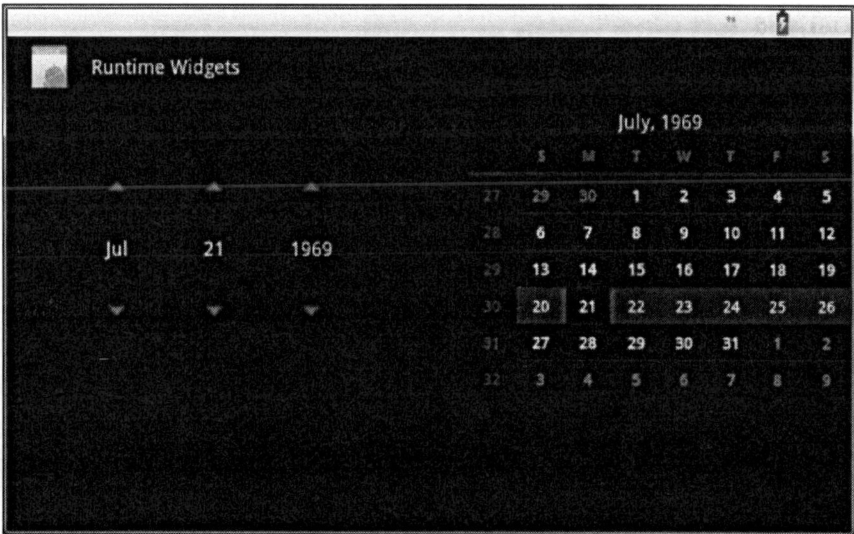

How it works...

Although all of our widget creation and manipulation was done from within the main activity, we still had to provide our layout object with an ID. This is in the same way we would with views and their subclasses, so that we can refer to it later.

Once we have declared our **LinearLayout** and **DatePicker** objects in code, it is a simple matter of using `findViewById()` to associate the layout with our variable and the `addView()` method, which is defined by the ViewGroup class to inflate our widget.

Every widget has its own set of appropriate methods specific to its purpose. For this example, we used the DatePicker's `updateDate(int year, int month, int day)` member.

> To view a list of available members for a widget in Eclipse, type the name of the object in a legal context and press *Ctrl + Space* after the period.

There's more...

We created our date picker by passing just the child object (`picker`) to the parent ViewGroup (`layout`) with the `addView()` method. This caused the widget to display itself with its default layout parameters, but the best way to master the SDK is to experiment with it and it is left as an exercise for the reader to apply other constructors and find ways to gain more control over this and other widget's appearances and behaviors.

Using addView() with width and height parameters

To directly specify a widget's width and height properties, use:

```
addView(View child, int width, int height)
```

> It is perfectly admissible to use the constants `MATCH_PARENT` and `WRAP_CONTENT` as the integer arguments here, although `WRAP_CONTENT` is the default setting and as such not generally used, although it *is* needed if you are going to use `MATCH_PARENT` for one dimension and `WRAP_CONTENT` for the other.

Applying a style

Android provides a system for separating our data from our design, in a manner similar to the way Cascading Stylesheets do in web design. Android **Styles** can be applied to single views or view groups and can inherit attributes from other styles.

Getting ready

Creating an Android **Style** requires a separate XML file to define it. Start up a new Android project in Eclipse and navigate to the `res/values` folder.

How to do it...

1. Using the `res/values` folder's context menu, create a new XML file and call it `my_style.xml`:

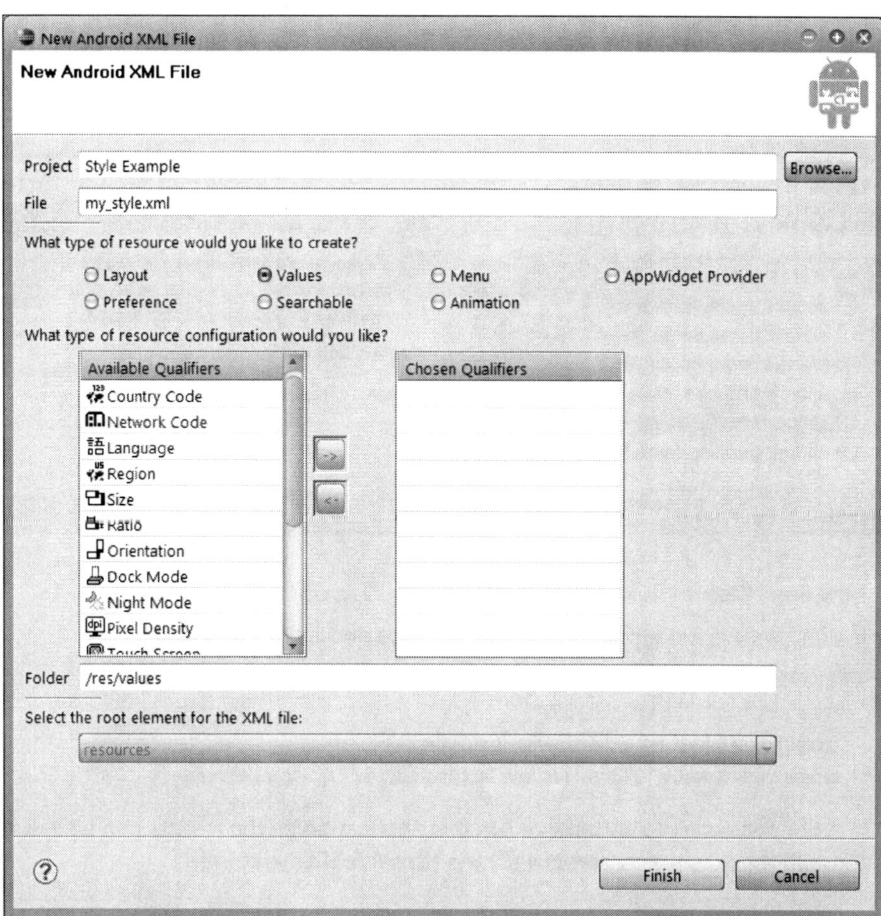

2. Open this file for editing. The wizard should have created a `<resources>` root node as follows:

```xml
<?xml version="1.0" encoding="utf-8"?>
<resources>
</resources>
```

3. Inside the `<resources>` node, nest the following `<style>` and `<item>` elements:

```xml
<style name="MyStyle">
    <item name="android:layout_width">wrap_content</item>
    <item name="android:layout_height">wrap_content</item>
```

```
        <item name="android:background">#60F</item>
        <item name="android:textColor">#AF0</item>
        <item name="android:textSize">20dip</item>
        <item name="android:padding">8dip</item>
    </style>
```

4. Alternatively, this can be done from the **Resources** tab, as seen in the next screenshot:

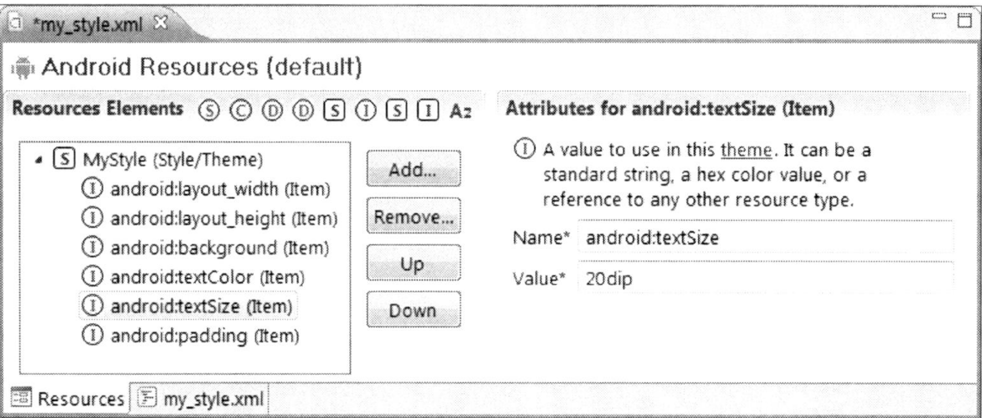

5. Now open the `main.xml` file inside the `res/layout` folder.

6. If a TextView is not already provided, add one and edit it to look like this:

```
<TextView
    style="@style/MyStyle"
    android:layout_width="match_parent"
    android:text="This is an example of a style" />
```

7. It is not necessary to compile or run this application as the results can be seen through the `main.xml` preview screen (**Graphical Layout** tab).

How it works...

We created an XML file in the `values` folder called `my_style.xml`. We could have called it anything we wanted, but it had to have the `.xml` extension. Likewise we *had* to nest our `<style>` inside the `<resources>` node for the system to know how to treat the file at compile time. The other compulsory element was the style name, `<style name="MyStyle">`, which we needed anyway to refer to it in the layout file.

Not only is the `main.xml` file far tidier than it might have been, we can now apply this style, or any other, wherever we want in our application, enabling us to easily create a consistent look and feel across different screen elements.

It is possible and often useful to be able to override a style's properties from the layout file and this was done here by defining the style's width as `wrap_content` and then deciding differently in the `main.xml` file and setting it to `match_parent`.

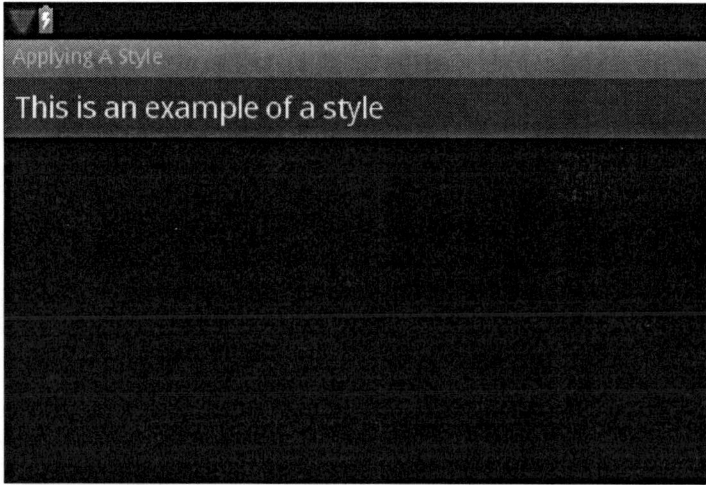

There's more...

It is not necessary that we create a new file for each defined style. We could have easily had as many styles as desired alongside each other inside the `<resources>` node and then referred to them, as we wished, later.

Not only can we define several styles together, but we can also create styles that inherit properties from other styles that we have made. For example, we could define a new style as follows:

```
<style name="MyStyle.skinny">
  <item name="android:padding">0dip</item>
</style>
```

This would take all the properties of `MyStyle` and override just the `padding` setting. In this way, complex hierarchies of styles can be constructed with very little effort.

Turning a style into a theme

A consistent visual design can be generated by applying a **style** to an entire activity or even to a whole application. This is done by including an `android:theme` attribute in the `manifest.xml` file, rather than in `main.xml` or another layout file. Styles applied in this way are referred to as **themes**, but are defined using the same `<resources>` and `<style>` tags and in the same location.

Once applied, an Android **theme** will change the properties of all views in its specified activity or application.

Getting ready

Themes are defined in the same resource folder as **styles**, so start a new Android project with Eclipse and navigate to the `res/values` folder in the **Package Explorer**.

How to do it...

1. In the `res/values` folder, create a new XML file as we did in the last recipe.

2. Call the file `my_theme.xml` and fill it out as follows:

```xml
<?xml version="1.0" encoding="utf-8"?>
<resources>

  <style name="MyTheme">
    <item name="android:textSize">20dip</item>
    <item name="android:textColor">#0F0</item>
    <item name="android:padding">8dip</item>
  </style>

</resources>
```

3. Open the `AndroidManifest.xml` file and edit the `<activity>` tag to include a **theme** element, like so:

```xml
<activity
    ...
    android:theme="@style/MyTheme">
```

4. Open the `main.xml` file in edit mode and replace the default TextView with two **TextViews** that have the following properties:

```xml
<TextView
    android:layout_width="wrap_content"
    android:layout_height="wrap_content"
    android:text="this text is green" />

<TextView
    android:layout_width="wrap_content"
    android:layout_height="wrap_content"
    android:text="and has padding" />
```

5. View the result in preview mode, as seen in the next screenshot:

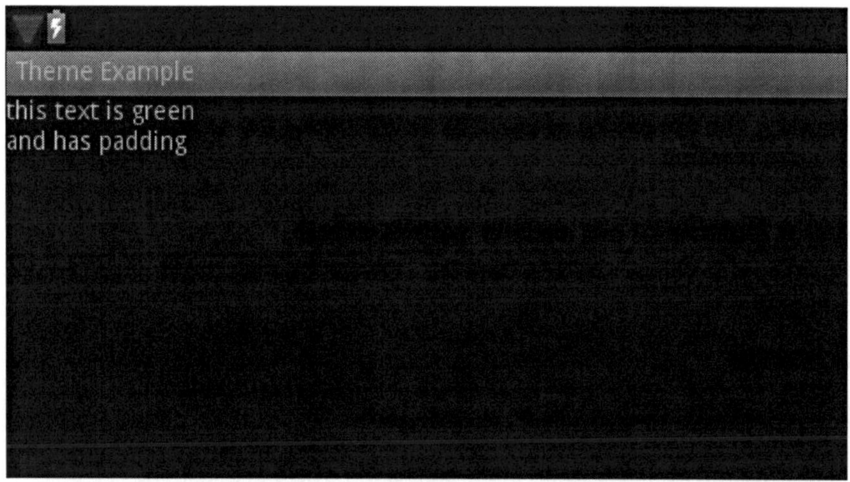

6. Unlike applying a **Style**, our **Theme** is not apparent until compiled, so compile and run the project on a handset or an emulator:

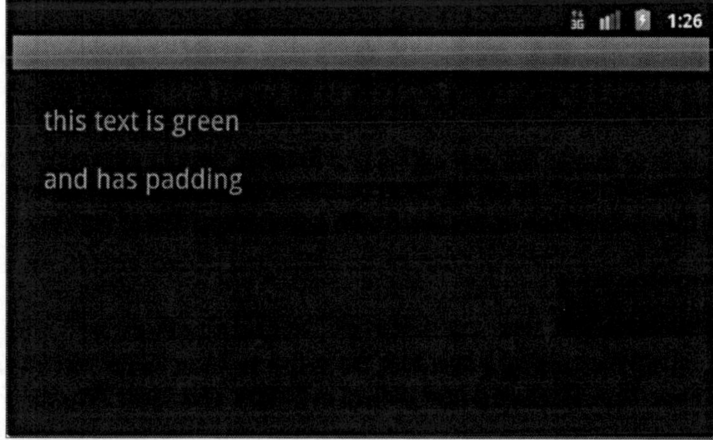

How it works...

Here we defined our **theme** with the `<style>` tag, just as we did in the previous recipe. The difference being that this time we introduced it into the **manifest file**, as part of the `<activity>` tag, with `android:theme="@style/MyTheme"`. This way, our theme was applied to all views in our activity.

Eclipse's **Graphical Layout** preview takes no notice of the manifest file, which means that it cannot be accessed from the **theme** drop-down and so we had to compile and run the project to properly appreciate the results.

There's more...

There are times when we would like to apply a theme to an entire application rather than just a specific activity, and this can be achieved by simply moving the `android:theme` attribute elsewhere in the manifest.

Applying a theme to an entire application

Moving the `android:theme` attribute from the `<activity>` tag to the `<application>` tag. For example:

```
<application
    . . .
    android:theme="@style/MyGlobalTheme">
```

This would cause `MyGlobalTheme` to apply across the whole application.

Where themes are referred to in both application and activity tags, the activity theme will override the application when attributes are shared and extend it when they are absent.

Using a platform style or theme

As well as being able to design our own **styles** and **themes**, we can also adapt and customize Android's built in themes such as dialog boxes and drop-down lists. Here we will take the provided **Dialog** theme and then customize it with some properties of our own.

Getting ready

In this exercise, we will be creating a new XML file in the `values` folder and editing both the `main` and `manifest` files. Start up a new project in Eclipse and open the `res/values` folder.

How to do it...

1. Inside the `res/values` folder, create a new XML file called `my_theme.xml`.
2. Complete `my_theme.xml` with the following code:

```
<?xml version="1.0" encoding="utf-8"?>
<resources>

    <style
        name="MyTheme"
        parent="@android:style/Theme.Dialog">
        <item name="android:typeface">monospace</item>
```

```
        <item name="android:background">#A00</item>
    </style>

</resources>
```

3. Inside the `res/layout` folder, replace the default **TextView** with the following in the `main.xml` file:

```
<TextView
    android:layout_width="wrap_content"
    android:layout_height="wrap_content"
    android:text="inherited from a dialog" />
```

4. In the Manifest file, ensure that the application tag has the following theme property:

```
<application
    ...
    android:theme="@style/MyTheme">
```

5. Run the project on a handset or emulator to view our customized dialog box:

How it works...

The theme here was created in the same way we did earlier, by nesting a `style` tag inside a `resources` tag and saving it in the `res/values` folder. The difference here was the use of the **parent** attribute which gave us the built-in dialog theme (`Theme.Dialog`) as the starting point.

There are many other such ready-made themes and styles which can be viewed from within the `main.xml` **Graphical Layout** tab (preview mode) by clicking on the **Theme** drop-down, although this does not display custom themes.

Once we have a theme as **parent**, we can edit it to suit our needs by defining item tags such as the `typeface` and `background` values set here.

By including `MyTheme` in the application tag in the manifest file, we ensured that our customized theme will be applied throughout the application and so there was no need to refer to it in the `main.xml` file, which was edited here simply to view the effect of the changes we made. As always, throughout this book, the reader is encouraged to experiment with these examples to gain a real feel for the SDK.

See also

For more on managing dialog boxes see the first three recipes in *Chapter 7, Notifying the user*.

Creating a custom component

Not only can we define widgets in XML, set their properties, and generally manipulate and edit them at runtime, but it is also possible to create widgets entirely from scratch by extending existing views (or subclasses) and overriding their methods.

Getting ready

We are going to create a custom widget solely from within Java, so start a new Android project in Eclipse and open up the main Java activity.

How to do it...

1. Inside our new activity, add a new inner class called `MyCustomView` that extends the **View** class. It is always a good idea to get into the habit of declaring instances as static where possible, because memory leaks on a battery-operated device have a far greater impact than they do on a PC:

```java
private static class MyCustomView extends View {
}
```

2. Give the new class a constructor:

```java
public MyCustomView(Context context) {
    super(context);
}
```

3. Now add and initialize a **Paint** field to this new class:

```
private static class MyCustomView extends View {
   final Paint paint = new Paint();
{
paint.setColor(Color.YELLOW);
      paint.setTextSize(18);
      paint.setAntiAlias(true);
      paint.setTextScaleX(2.0f);
}
```

4. In the `MyCustomView` constructor, change the following class setting:

```
this.setBackgroundColor(Color.GRAY);
```

5. Now, override the MyCustomView's `onDraw()` method, like so:

```
@Override
protected void onDraw(Canvas canvas) {
   super.onDraw(canvas);

   canvas.drawText("My Custom Widget", 2, 20, paint);
   canvas.drawCircle(160, 45, 25, paint);
   invalidate();
}
```

6. Replace the following `setContentView()` command:

```
setContentView(R.layout.main);
```

With the following:

```
setContentView(new MyCustomView(this));
```

7. Finally, compile the project and run the code on an emulator or handset to view the custom View:

How it works...

We built our custom widget by creating an anonymous inner class that extended the **View** object.

We imported three new `android.graphics` classes, namely, **Paint, Color,** and **Canvas**.

The **Paint** object is a useful class that allows us to define how text, bitmaps, and shapes are drawn to screen, allowing us to describe the colors and graphical appearance of our new class.

We also took advantage of the **Color** class, which provides common color constants such as `GRAY` and `RED` which we can use instead of hex color values. The Color class also has a `TRANSPARENT` value and methods for reading and converting colors, for example, an `RGBToHSV()` function. As with other classes, Eclipse's in-line documentation provides a comprehensive list of Color's constants and methods.

To make our changes visible, we had to override the new view's `onDraw()` method, which is called prior to a view being displayed. The **Canvas** object is how we control a view's appearance and contains all our drawing methods, such as the calls we made which are constructed thus far:

```
drawText(String text, float xOrigin, float yOrigin, Paint paint)
drawCircle(float centerX, float centerY, float radius,
    Paint paint)
```

We demonstrated how it is possible to set our new object's properties directly with `this.setBackgroundColor(Color.GRAY);`.

For simplicity's sake, we displayed our new widget by changing the `setContentView()` parameter but it is more common, and more useful, to refer to it in the same way as we would with any other view and this can be done with `setId(int id)`.

See also

To learn more about the `Paint` object, have a look at the *Using ShapeDrawable and Paint* recipe in *Chapter 8, Graphics and Animation*.

4
Menus

In this chapter, we will cover the following topics:

- ▶ Creating and inflating an options menu
- ▶ Designing Android compliant menu icons
- ▶ Building a context sensitive menu
- ▶ Handling menu selections
- ▶ Building menu groups of checkable items
- ▶ Applying shortcut keys and submenus

Introduction

Menus are an essential part of almost any operating system. On mobile systems where screen real estate is limited, they play an even more important role. Android provides similar mechanisms for menus as it does for other visual elements, making it possible to separate them from application code by the use of XML.

All Android handsets have a hard menu key for calling up secondary choices that do not need to be made available from a main screen, or perhaps need to be made available across an application.

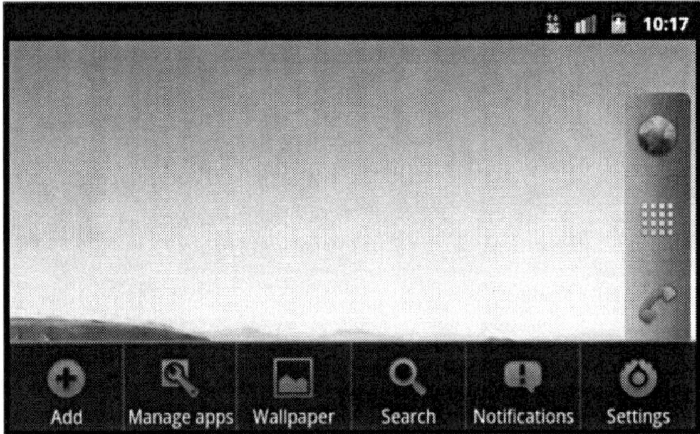

In concord with Android's philosophy of separating appearance from function, menus are generally created in the same way as other visual elements, that is, with the use of a definitive XML layout file.

There is lot that can be done to control menus dynamically and Android provides classes and interfaces for displaying context-sensitive menus, organizing menu items into groups, and including shortcuts.

Creating and inflating an options menu

To keep our application code separate from our menu layout information, Android uses a designated resource folder (`res/menu`) and an XML layout file to define the physical appearance of our menu; such as the **titles** and **icons** we see in Android pop-up menus. The **Activity** class contains a callback method, `onCreateOptionsMenu()`, that can be overridden to inflate a menu.

Getting ready

Android menus are defined in a specific, designated folder. Eclipse does not create this folder by default so start up a new project and add a new folder inside the `res` folder and call it `menu`.

How to do it...

1. Create a new XML file in our new `res/menu` folder and call it `my_menu.xml`. Complete the new file as follows:

```xml
<?xml version="1.0" encoding="utf-8"?>
<menu
    xmlns:android="http://schemas.android.com/apk/res/android">
    <item
        android:id="@+id/item_one"
        android:title="first item" />
    <item
        android:id="@+id/item_two"
        android:title="second item" />
</menu>
```

2. In the Java application file, include the following overridden callback:

```java
@Override
public boolean onCreateOptionsMenu(Menu menu) {
    MenuInflater inflater = getMenuInflater();
    inflater.inflate(R.menu.my_menu, menu);
    return true;
}
```

3. Run the application on a handset or emulator and press the hard *menu* key to view the menu:

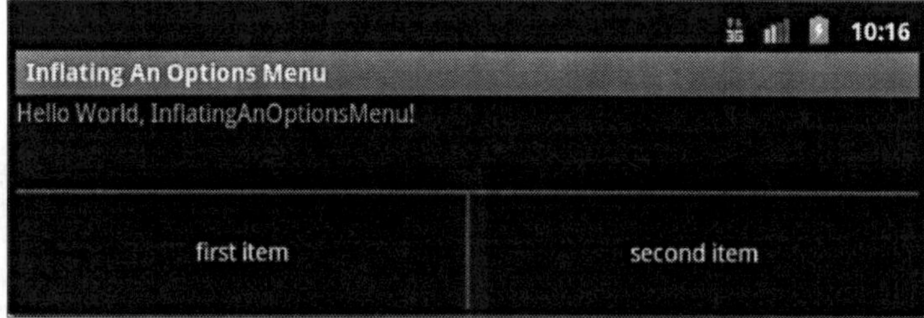

How it works...

Whenever we create an Android menu using XML we *must* place it in the folder we used here (`res/menu`). Likewise, the base node of our XML structure *must* be `<menu>`.

The purpose of the `id` element should be self explanatory and the `title` attribute is used to set the text that the user sees when the menu item is inflated.

There are nearly a dozen other menu attributes that we could use to control things such as menu order, or whether an item is enabled or not, and we will encounter most of these in this chapter. The reader is encouraged to explore these possibilities throughout.

The **MenuInflater** object is a straightforward way of turning an XML layout file into a Java object. We create a **MenuInflater** with `getMenuInflater()` which returns a MenuInflater from the current activity, of which it is a member. The `inflate()` call takes both the XML file and the equivalent Java object as its parameters.

There's more...

The type of menu we created here is referred to as an **options menu** and it comes in two flavors depending on how many items it contains. There is also a neater way to handle item titles when they are too long to be completely displayed.

Handling longer options menus

When an **options menu** has six or fewer items it appears as a block of items at the bottom of the screen. This is called the **icon menu** and is, as its name suggests, the only menu type capable of displaying icons. On tablets running API level 11 or greater the Action bar can also be used to access the menu.

> The **icon menu** is also the only menu type that cannot display radio buttons or check marks.

When an inflated options menu has more than six items, the sixth place on the icon menu is replaced by the system's own **More** item, which when pressed calls up the **extended menu** which displays all items from the sixth onwards, adding a scroll bar if necessary.

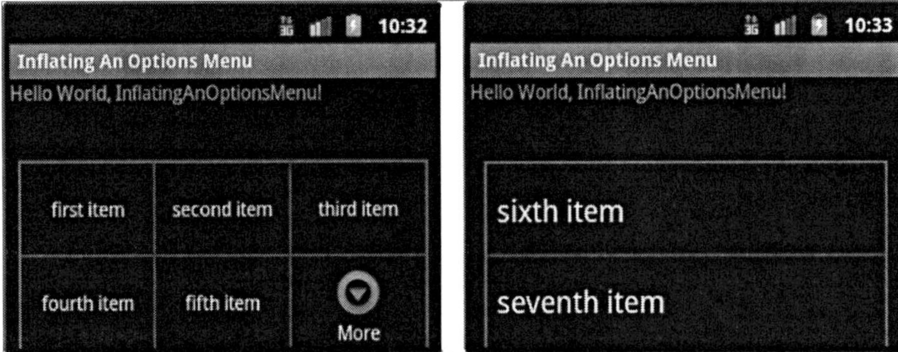

Providing condensed menu titles

If Android cannot fit an item's title text into the space provided (often as little as one third of the screen width) it will simply truncate it. To provide a more readable alternative, include the `android:titleCondensed="string"` attribute alongside `android:title` in the item definition.

Adding Option menu items to the Action Bar

For tablet devices targeting Android 3.0 or greater, option menu items can be added to the Action Bar.

Adjust the target build of the above project to API level 11 or above and replace the `res/menu/my_menu.xml` file with the following:

```xml
<?xml version="1.0" encoding="utf-8"?>
<menu
    xmlns:android="http://schemas.android.com/apk/res/android">
    <item
        android:id="@+id/item_one"
        android:title="first item"
        android:icon="@drawable/icon"
        android:showAsAction="ifRoom" />
    <item
        android:id="@+id/item_two"
        android:title="second item"
        android:icon="@drawable/icon"
        android:showAsAction="ifRoom|withText" />
    <item
        android:id="@+id/item_three"
        android:title="third item"
        android:icon="@drawable/icon"
        android:showAsAction="always" />
    <item
        android:id="@+id/item_four"
        android:title="fourth item"
        android:icon="@drawable/icon"
        android:showAsAction="never" />
</menu>
```

Note from the output that unless the `withText` flag is included, the menu item will display only as an icon:

Designing Android compliant menu icons

The menu **items** we defined in the previous recipe had only text **titles** to identify them to the user, however nearly all **Icon Menus** that we see on Android devices combine a text title with an icon. Although it is perfectly possible to use any graphic image as a menu icon, using images that do not conform to Android's own guidelines on icon design is strongly discouraged, and Android's own development team are particularly insistent that only the subscribed color palette and effects are used. This is so that these built-in menus which are universal across Android applications provide a continuous experience for the user.

Here we examine the colors and dimensions prescribed and also examine how to provide the subsequent images as system resources in such a way as to cater for a variety of screen densities.

Getting ready

The little application we put together in the last recipe makes a good starting point for this one. Most of the information here is to do with design of the icons, so you may want to have a graphics editor such as GIMP or PhotoShop open, or you may want to refer back here later for the exact dimensions and palettes.

How to do it...

1. Open the `res/menu/my_menu.xml` file and add the `android:icon` elements seen here to each item:

```xml
<?xml version="1.0" encoding="utf-8"?>
<menu
    xmlns:android="http://schemas.android.com/apk/res/android">
    <item
        android:id="@+id/item_one"
        android:icon="@drawable/my_menu_icon"
        android:title="first item" />
    <item
        android:id="@+id/item_two"
        android:icon="@drawable/my_menu_icon"
        android:title="second item" />
</menu>
```

2. With your graphics editor, create a new transparent PNG file, precisely 48 by 48 pixels in dimension.

3. Ensuring that there is at least a 6 pixel border all the way around, produce your icon as a simple two-dimensional flat shape. Something like this:

4. Fill the shape with a grayscale gradient that ranges from 47% to 64% (white) with the lighter end at the top.

5. Provide a black inner shadow with the following settings:

    ❏ 20% opaque

    ❏ 90° angle (top to bottom)

    ❏ 2 pixel width

    ❏ 2 pixel distance

6. Next, add an inner bevel with:

    ❏ Depth of 1%

    ❏ 90° altitude

    ❏ 70% opaque, white highlight

    ❏ 25% opaque, black shadow

7. Now give the graphic a white outer glow with:

    ❏ 55% opacity

    ❏ 3 pixel size

    ❏ 10% spread

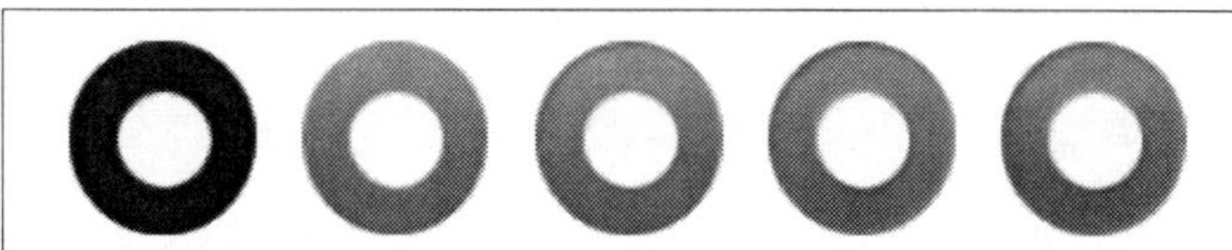

8. Make two copies of our graphic, one resized to 36 by 36 pixels and one 72 by 72 pixels.

9. Save the largest file in the `res/drawable-hdpi` as `my_menu_icon.png`.

10. Save the 48 by 48 pixel file with the same name in the `drawable-mdpi` folder and the smallest image in `drawable-ldpi`.

11. To see the full effect of these three files in action you will need to run the software on handsets with different screen resolutions or construct emulators to that purpose.

How it works...

As already mentioned, Android currently insists that menu icons conform to their guidelines and most of the terms used here should be familiar to anyone who has designed an icon before.

The designated **drawable** folders allow us to provide the best possible graphics for a wide variety of screen densities. Android will automatically select the most appropriate graphic for a handset or tablet so that we can refer to our icons generically with `@drawable/`.

It is only ever necessary to provide icons for the first five menu items as the Icon Menu is the only type to allow icons.

See also

For more on icons see the recipes *Optimizing for tablets and multiple screens* and *Dividing the screen into Fragments* in *Chapter 2, Layouts* and the recipes *Displaying an alert dialog, Making a toast, Notifying the user with the status bar,* and *Using the Notification.Builder class* in *Chapter 7, Notifying the User*.

Building a context sensitive menu

Very often we want our menus to present choices to the user in a context sensitive way, commonly achieved on PCs with a *right-click*. In Android a *long click* is used to produce such menus when they are available. All Android Views are capable of receiving this action and here we will create two different Views and connect them to a menu. Also we will examine one or two of the built-in features of the Android **ContextMenu**.

Getting ready

Just as in the previous two recipes, we will be defining a menu layout here in XML which we will then connect to our Views with Java using an activity callback. Start a new Android project in Eclipse and create a new folder `res/menu`.

How to do it...

1. Within the `res/menu` folder, create an Android XML file called `my_menu.xml`.

2. Complete `my_menu.xml` so that it contains two **items**, each with a **title** and an **id**, as we did before. You can of course copy much of this from the previous recipe if you wish:

```xml
<?xml version="1.0" encoding="utf-8"?>
<menu
    xmlns:android="http://schemas.android.com/apk/res/android">
```

```
<item
   android:id="@+id/item_one"
   android:title="first item" />
<item
   android:id="@+id/item_two"
   android:title="second item" />
</menu>
```

3. Open and edit the `main.xml` file in the `res/layout` folder, and also replace the default **TextView** and add an **EditText** to the vertically aligned **LinearLayout**, as seen in the following screenshot:

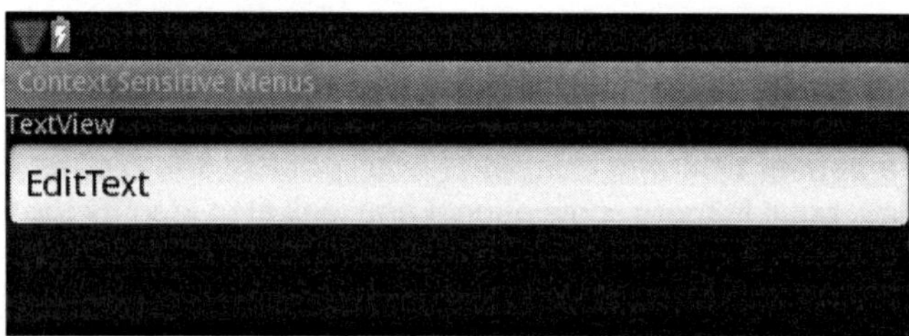

4. Provide each view with an appropriate ID, for example `android:id="@+id/text_view"` and `android:id="@+id/edit_text"`.

5. In our Java activity class, declare two private fields, `mTextView` and `mEditText`.

6. Retrieve the XML resources with `findViewById()` from within the `onCreate()` method:

```
mTextView = (TextView) findViewById(R.id.text_view);
mEditText = (EditText) findViewById(R.id.edit_text);
```

7. Still within `onCreate()` connect our views with our menu using:

```
registerForContextMenu(mTextView);
registerForContextMenu(mEditText);
```

8. Now override the `onCreateContextMenu()` activity method:

```
@Override
public void onCreateContextMenu(ContextMenu m,
   View v, ContextMenuInfo i) {
      super.onCreateContextMenu(m, v, i);
      m.setHeaderTitle("my title");
      MenuInflater inflater = getMenuInflater();
      inflater.inflate(R.menu.my_menu, m);
   }
```

9. Test the application on an emulator or handset, making sure to examine the context menu for both views.

How it works...

In terms of definition and inflation **Context Menus** are very similar to **Options Menus**. In fact the format of the XML and use of a **MenuInflater** are identical. It is the `registerForContextMenu()` call that makes the difference here and it is simply used to inform the system that a view has a context menu associated with it.

Our activity supplies us with the `onCreateContextMenu()` method, which performs the same function that the `onCreateOptionsMenu()` does for a standard menu, with the exception that we also need to pass the view that received the *long click* and a **ContextMenuInfo** object.

ContextMenuInfo is an interface belonging to **ContextMenu** and acts as an adapter passing any extra information about the menu inflation such as the item selected in a list view.

We gave our menu a **header title** with `ContextMenu.setHeaderTitle()`. Here we simply applied a string literal, but it is more conventional and logical to identify the view that was long-clicked in the title of its context menu. This value can be retrieved with `View.getID()`.

Note that if you remove the line `m.setHeaderTitle("my title");` and call up the menu from the **EditText**, then it will provide its own **header Edit text** which is overridden when we provide our own.

Android widgets such as **EditText** that contain editable text provide their own context menus with various cut and paste functions. This is why we call `onCreateContextMenu()` on its superclass, to handle menu items provided by the system.

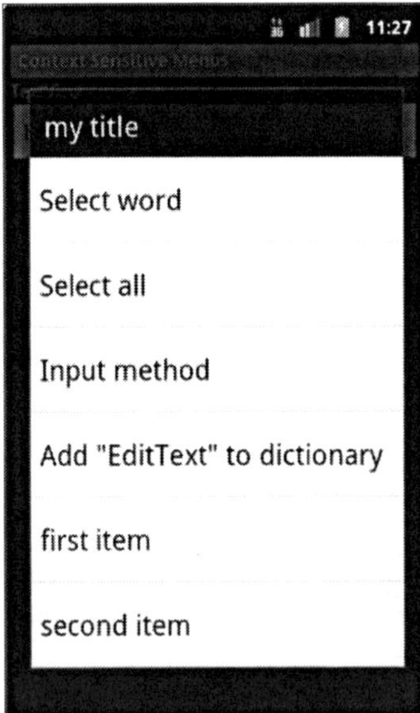

When we **register** our view with a context menu, we append our items to these readymade ones.

There's more...

It is not always possible to know in advance precisely what items may or may not be needed in a menu at runtime and so Android provides a way to add menu items from within our Java code.

Adding menu items dynamically

Menu items can be included either from within the `onCreateOptionsMenu()` method or the `onCreateContextMenu()` method, with Menu's `add()` member:

```java
@Override
public boolean onCreateOptionsMenu(Menu menu) {
  menu.add("a new item");
  . . .
```

We can also define menu item IDs as class fields, for example:

```java
public class MenuExample extends Activity {
  private static final int MENU1 = Menu.FIRST;
  . . .
```

This gives us greater control over our dynamically constructed items:

```java
menu.add(0, MENU1, 0, "another item");
```

The previous line, when included in one of our menu `onCreate` callbacks has the following structure:

```java
Menu.add(int groupId, int itemId, int order, CharSequence title).
```

See also

For more information about MenuInflater see the recipe *Creating and inflating an options menu* earlier in this chapter.

Handling menu selections

It is all very well to be able to design menus and have them inflate according to user actions but we also need some way to interpret and respond in return. Again the Activity class provides a hook for menu selections in the form of a callback, `onOptionsItemSelected()`.

Getting ready

In this recipe we will be using an XML menu definition identical to the previous one, so you may well wish to copy and paste this file to save time. Nevertheless start up a new Android project in Eclipse.

How to do it...

1. Define an XML menu called `my_menu.xml` in the `res/menu` folder, creating this folder if necessary, and provide it with two **items**, giving each at least an `id` and a `title`.

2. In the `res/layout` folder edit the `main.xml` file so that the layout contains a single **TextView** with an `android:id`, for example:

```xml
<TextView
    android:id="@+id/text_view"
    android:layout_width="match_parent"
    android:layout_height="wrap_content"
    android:textSize="20dip"
    android:text="Press menu" />
```

3. In our Java activity class create a **TextView** field and associate it with its XML resource equivalent.

4. Include code to inflate our menu by overriding the `onCreateOptionsMenu()` method as follows:

```java
@Override
public boolean onCreateOptionsMenu(Menu m) {
    MenuInflater inflater = getMenuInflater();
    inflater.inflate(R.menu.my_menu, m);
    return true;
}
```

5. Finally add the code to control the actual individual selections with the `onOptionsItemSelected()` method:

```java
@Override
public boolean onOptionsItemSelected(MenuItem item) {
    switch (item.getItemId()) {
    case R.id.item_one:
        mTextView.setText("You selected menu item one");
        return true;
    case R.id.item_two:
        mTextView.setText("You selected menu item two");
        return true;
    default:
```

```
        return super.onOptionsItemSelected(item);
    }
}
```

6. Run the project on a handset or emulator to test the menu selections:

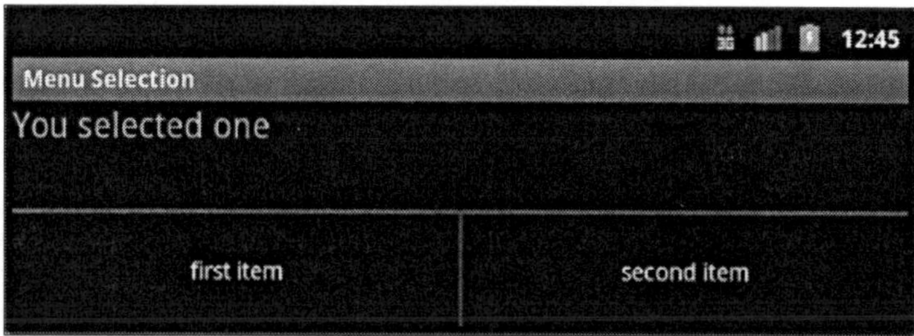

How it works...

The construction of an options menus was covered earlier in the chapter, as was its inflation. The activity member introduced here is `onOptionsItemSelected()` and the key identifier is `MenuItem.getItemId()`, which we used to differentiate between items.

We could of course use the passed **MenuItem** variable `item` to identify its source, and along with `getItemId()` we could have used `getTitle()` or `getOrder()` or several other public **MenuItem** methods.

We called `onCreateOptionsMenu()` on its superclass here more for completion than necessity and it is used to handle system menu items that may be called.

There's more...

As stated in its name the `onOptionsItemSelected()` is suitable only for Android's **Options Menu**. As one would expect, there is an equivalent method for **Context Menus**.

It is also possible to do more sophisticated things than change some text; for example we could start an activity from a menu item.

Selecting context menu items

To control the behavior of individual menu items for **Context Menus** use the `onContextItemSelected(MenuItem item)` activity callback.

Starting an activity from a menu

To start an activity from within the `onOptionsItemSelected()` or `onContextItemSelected()` methods, launch the activity with an Intent object using `startActivity()`.

Building menu groups of checkable items

Another common use for menus is to switch certain functions on or off and often this has to be done in a mutually exclusive manner such as when only one possible selection can be made from a list. For this purpose Android provides a framework for defining checkboxes and radio buttons using groups of menu items.

Getting ready

The Eclipse IDE provides another, more intuitive way to construct XML menu files in the form of a graphical pane that can be accessed with the **Layout** tab of any Android XML file. Start up a new project and inside the `res` folder, create a new folder called `menu`.

How to do it...

1. Create a new Android XML file inside `res/menu` and call it `my_menu.xml`.

2. View the new file through the **Layout** tab.

3. Using the controls provided (in particular the **Add...**, **Up**, and **Down** buttons) construct a menu as seen in the next screenshot. Give each item an `id` and a `title`. You will need to create the **Group** first:

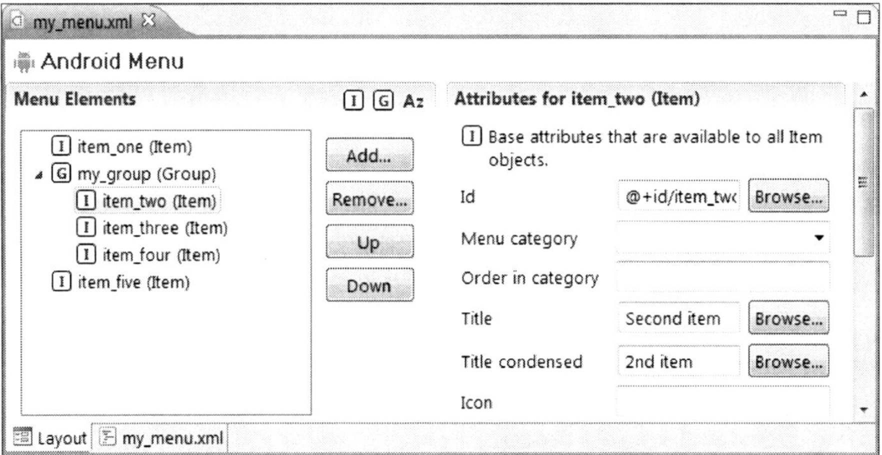

4. Give the menu group an `id` and set the **Checkable behavior** to `single`:

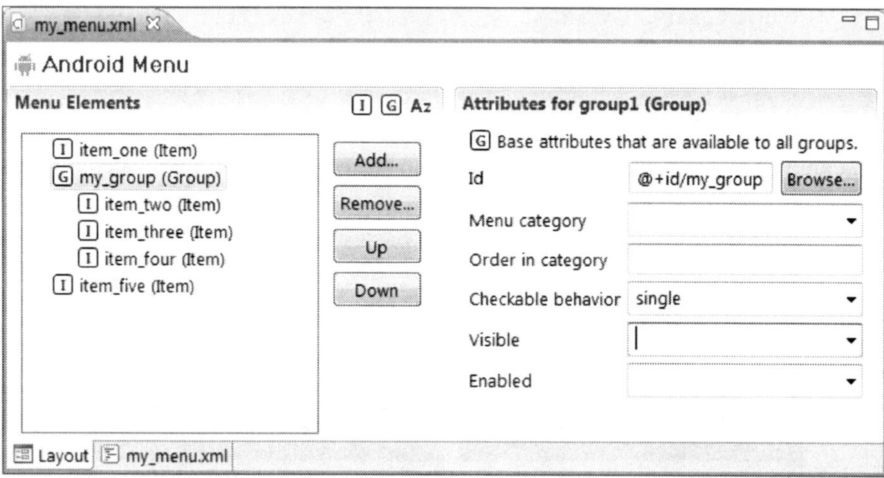

5. Edit the `main.xml` file in the `res/layout` folder so that the root layout contains a single **TextView**:

```xml
<TextView
    android:id="@+id/text_view"
    android:layout_width="match_parent"
    android:layout_height="wrap_content"
    android:textSize="20sp"
    android:padding="6dip"
    android:text="long click here" />
```

6. In the main Java activity file, connect the TextView in Java and **register** it for a Context Menu:

```java
private TextView mTextView;

@Override
public void onCreate(Bundle state) {
    super.onCreate(state);
    setContentView(R.layout.main);
    mTextView = (TextView) findViewById(R.id.text_view);

    registerForContextMenu(mTextView);
}
```

7. Override the `onCreateContextMenu()` hook as we have here:

```java
@Override
public void onCreateContextMenu(ContextMenu m,
    View v, ContextMenuInfo i) {
        super.onCreateContextMenu(m, v, i);
        m.setHeaderTitle("my title");
```

```
MenuInflater inflater = getMenuInflater();
inflater.inflate(R.menu.my_menu, m);
}
```

8. Now run the project on an emulator or a handset and call up our menu by long-clicking on the text view. The three items in the group should have radio buttons alongside them.

9. Using the **Layout** pane, edit our menu file so that the **Checkable behavior** of the group is `all` rather than `single`.

10. Run the program again to observe the difference this change makes. Our radio buttons are now checkboxes:

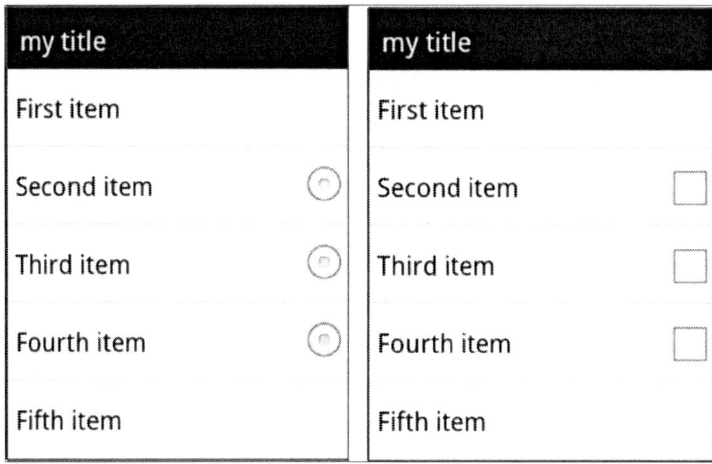

How it works...

Despite using Eclipse's visual XML editing capacities, the way we constructed our menu here was no different from previous recipes in this chapter and the same can be said for the way we **registered** a view with a menu and the way we **inflated** it. It is a good idea to take a look at the XML code directly to see how this exercise differs. The use of the `<group>` node should not be difficult to understand. The `android:checkableBehavior` element can take three values:

*   `single`—where only one item can be checked at a time, producing radio buttons
*   `all`—where any item can be checked, producing check boxes
*   `none`—making no items checkable

Individual items can be set as checkable with `android:checkable="true"` and their state can be controlled specifically with `android:checked="true"` or `"false"`.

There's more...

The state of checkable objects created in this way must be managed in code and Android provides the `isChecked()` and `setChecked()` methods for this purpose.

Changing checkable items dynamically

The state of an Android menu checkable item can be requested and changed from within our Java code. Generally speaking this would be done from one of the related callbacks such as the `onContextItemSelected()` method.

The `MenuItem.isChecked()` method returns a boolean reflecting the checked state of the item which can be changed by passing a boolean with `MenuItem.setChecked()`.

Applying shortcut keys and submenus

The **Menu, ContextMenu,** and **MenuItem** classes that we have covered in this chapter make up the key components of Android's menus. However there is still one class that we have not touched, the **SubMenu,** and no chapter on menus would be complete without a mention of shortcuts. As with other features, Android allows us to create and manipulate submenus and shortcuts using both XML and Java.

Getting ready

It is probably a good idea to use the project we created in the last recipe (*Building menu groups of checkable items*) but if you do not have it, start up an Android project and put together a quick menu XML file with three or four items in the `res/menu` folder. We will also need a TextView that is registered for a Context Menu.

How to do it...

1. Open the menu file inside `res/menu` and replace the first item with the code below:

```xml
<item
  android:id="@+id/sub_menu"
  android:title="sub menu">
  <menu>
    <item
      android:id="@+id/sub_one"
      android:title="submenu one" />
    <item
      android:id="@+id/sub_two"
      android:title="submenu two" />
  </menu>
</item>
```

2. In the same file, add one of the following elements to the second item and the other to the third:

```
android:numericShortcut="3"
```

3. In the Java activity file, implement an `onCreateContextMenu()` method to inflate our menu as follows:

```java
@Override
public void onCreateContextMenu(ContextMenu m,
    View v, ContextMenuInfo i) {
        super.onCreateContextMenu(m, v, i);
        MenuInflater inflater = getMenuInflater();
        inflater.inflate(R.menu.my_menu, m);
}
```

4. Next, provide the class-wide field:

```java
private static final int MENU1 = Menu.FIRST;
```

5. Then, add the following line before the **MenuInflater** declaration:

```java
m.addSubMenu(0, MENU1, 1, "my new submenu");
```

6. Finally, run and view the project on an emulator or a handset with a keyboard and call up the context menu followed by the submenu:

How it works...

SubMenus are created and accessed in almost exactly the same manner as other menu elements and can be placed in any of the provided menus, although they cannot be placed within each other, that is, a SubMenu cannot contain another SubMenu.

Shortcuts too are simple to include although they will only work on a handset or emulator with a keyboard. They can be assigned in Java as well with `setNumericShortcut(char)`.

SubMenus can be added dynamically as we did here and the `addSubMenu()` method allows us to specify the group, ID, position, and title.

See also

For more information about MenuInflater refer to the recipe *Creating and inflating an options menu* earlier in this chapter.

So far in this book we have covered the basic structure and physical appearance of an Android application. For software to be truly useful however, it needs to be able to manage information of some kind. In the next chapter, we will examine how to connect our applications to various kinds of data.

5

Data and Security

In this chapter, we will cover the following topics:

- ▶ Using internal storage for private data
- ▶ Storing public data on external storage
- ▶ Creating a SQLite database
- ▶ Sharing multimedia files across applications with Content Providers
- ▶ Defining and enforcing permissions
- ▶ Giving your users Android backup functionality

Introduction

The Android platform provides a variety of formats for us to store user data, from the basic name/value pairs and user preferences that we discussed in *Chapter 1, Activities*, to fully fledged SQLite 3 databases that can be used to store any data we want in an organized fashion.

A smart phone or tablet will come equipped with internal memory and this is often the ideal place to record and maintain our application data. Android provides classes and interfaces to handle data that will be familiar to anyone acquainted with Java.

Along with this generally small internal storage space, the system, more often than not, provides external memory in the form of at least one removable SD card which is also available to us as developers.

Perhaps the most powerful data tool available to the Android developer is the inclusion of **SQLite 3** and the system exposes all the methods we might need to administer such databases.

In addition to generating data, we can also control how (or even if) it is shared. Users of Android handsets can see the levels of data protection and choose whether to accept them at the point of installation. These permissions can be put in place by the developer and can be applied to individual program components such as activities as well as to entire applications.

The mobile nature of Android handsets exposes them to accidents and the elements more than many other electronic devices. This level of risk makes it more important than ever to protect our users' data, which we can do with Android using their **Backup Service Tool**.

Using internal storage for private data

As we saw in *Chapter 1, Activities*, Android provides a variety of methods for storing user preferences and settings but many applications require a more sophisticated filing system and a convenient way to do this is by using our handset's internal storage.

As one might expect the Java **OutputStream** object forms the basis for most of these types of operations.

Getting ready

Writing to internal storage is done through our Java activity class, so start up a new Android project in Eclipse and open the main activity pane.

How to do it...

1. Declare two string fields `FSPC` and `mString` to act as our filename and content:

```
final static String FSPC = "my_file.txt";
private final String mString = "a string";
```

2. Inside the `onCreate()` method add the following lines:

```
FileOutputStream outStream;

try {
   outStream = openFileOutput(FSPC, Context.MODE_PRIVATE);
   outStream.write(mString.getBytes());
   outStream.close();
} catch (FileNotFoundException e) {
   e.printStackTrace();
} catch (IOException e) {
   e.printStackTrace();
}
```

3. Run the project on a handset or emulator.

4. Once the program has run, open the **DDMS** (**Dalvik Debug Monitor Server**) perspective in Eclipse.

5. Use the **File Explorer** tab to open the folder `data/data` and find our application:

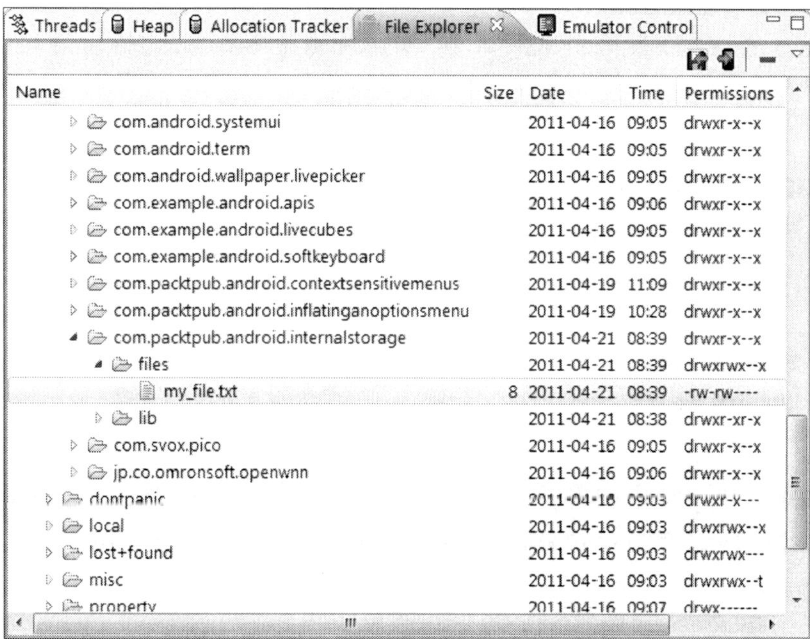

6. The file can be examined manually with the **Pull File...** command in the **File Explorer** drop-down menu.

How it works...

The key component here is the **FileOutputStream**, which is returned from the `openFileOutput()` call. While passing the file name we also provided a `content.Context` constant, `MODE_PRIVATE`. This was not strictly necessary as this is the default mode. It will overwrite our file each time the program is run. To append to an existing file we could have used `MODE_APPEND`.

> We can also make files created in this way available to other applications with the `MODE_WORLD_READABLE` and `MODE_WORLD_WRITABLE` constants.

Quite as we would expect, there is also a **FileInputStream** object with an equivalent `read()` function for inputting data. Again these operations need to be in a `try/catch` clause and closed properly to work correctly.

There's more...

Once we have more than one internal file, we will need to do more sophisticated things than simply read and write data, and often we will want to store static files of data internally. Android makes both these things possible.

Exploring internal memory

Temporary files can be disposed off with the `deleteFile(String filename)` method, which returns true if successful. We can also put together a list of all our files with `fileList()`, which returns a String array.

Storing static data

If we have data that we only need to read from, we can store it in the `res/raw` folder and access it with `R.raw.filename`, which returns a **FileInputStream**.

Storing public data on external storage

Nearly all Android devices come equipped with some form of external memory, very often in the form of an SD card. We can use such devices to store shared files that are available to the user from within our application.

The most straightforward way to write to an SD card is the Java **FileWriter** object but because of the removable nature of external storage, we need some way to check the status of our memory before we attempt to access it. Android provides the **android.os.Environment** class for us to accomplish this.

Getting ready

Most of this exercise is done using Java code but we will need a layout with a single **TextView** to observe our results, so start up a new Android project in Eclipse and edit the `main.xml` file so that it contains one **TextView**.

How to do it...

1. Provide the **TextView** we just created with an **ID** and associate it with a private field in Java with the `findViewById()` method.
2. Also create a private **FileWriter** called `mFileWriter`.

3. Inside the `onCreate()` callback add the following clause:

```
if (Environment.MEDIA_MOUNTED.equals(Environment.
getExternalStorageState())) {
    mTextView.setText(Environment.MEDIA_MOUNTED);
} else {
    mTextView.setText(Environment.MEDIA_REMOVED);
}
```

4. On your handset or an emulator, test this code with the SD card both mounted and ejected:

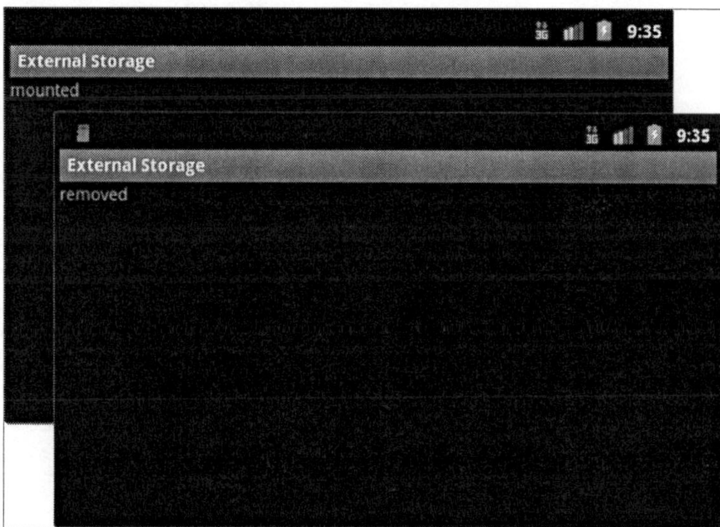

5. Now add this `try/catch` clause to the `if` part of the previous code to write our external file:

```
try {
    mFileWriter = new FileWriter("/sdcard/myfile.txt");
    mFileWriter.append("some text ");
    mFileWriter.flush();
    mFileWriter.close();
} catch (IOException e) {
    e.printStackTrace();
}
```

6. With the **File Explorer** window open in Eclipse, test the program again:

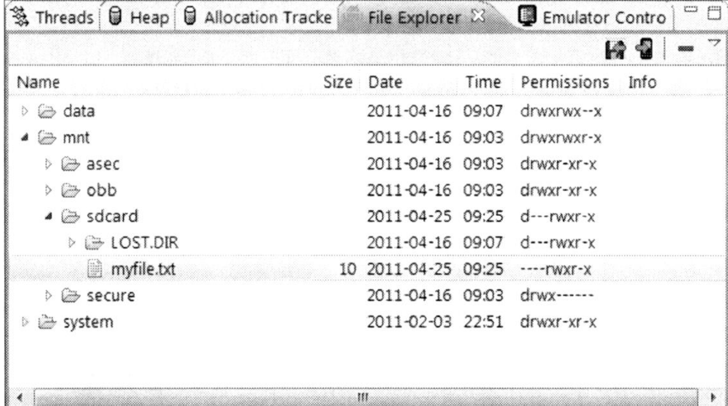

How it works...

The Environment constants `MEDIA_MOUNTED` and `MEDIA_REMOVED` are two of several useful string constants provided by the **Environment** class. Their actual values as we saw are *mounted* and *removed*. `getExternalStorageState()` returns other values such as `MEDIA_SHARED`, which allows us to check whether a card is also connected to a computer and `MEDIA_BAD_REMOVAL`, which can be used to discover if a card has been removed without being properly dismounted. The best way to become better acquainted with these values, as always, is for the reader to experiment further.

In cases where the media we are trying to access is read-only, `getExternalStorageState()` returns `MEDIA_MOUNTED_READ_ONLY`, which has a constant value of *mounted_ro*.

For a tiny file like the one we used here, the use of `FileWriter.flush()` might seem unnecessary but is generally advised for external files.

There's more...

Android makes use of several public directories for storing things such as ringtones or music. It is possible to take advantage of these and also to prevent our files from being automatically included in galleries or music collections by the system.

Public directories

Unless it has been stored in a public directory, any file created by our application will be deleted when that application is uninstalled. To prevent this, save any file to its appropriate public folder such as `Pictures`, `Alarms`, or `Movies`.

All the public folders can be found immediately in the root directory and will be created if they do not already exist.

Preventing files from being included in galleries

Android employs a **media scanner** that will automatically include sound, video, and image files in system collections. To avoid this, include an empty file called `.nomedia` in the same directory as the files you wish to exclude.

Creating a SQLite database

The methods outlined here provide some powerful techniques for storing and manipulating data, but providing a structured database this way would be a tiresome task. Fortunately Android incorporates **SQLite** (version 3 to be precise), a server-less, transactional database engine for this purpose. Instruction in **SQL** is beyond the scope of this book and it is assumed that the reader has some familiarity with self-contained databases, cursors, and queries.

In this recipe we will demonstrate how to set up a simple **SQLiteDatabase**, add a table and include some entries.

Getting ready

SQLite databases can be created and accessed through Java code, so to begin this task start up a new Android project with Eclipse and open the main Java activity file.

How to do it...

1. Inside the `onCreate()` method declare and assign an **SQLiteDatabase** as follows:

```
SQLiteDatabase db;
db = openOrCreateDatabase("my_database.db", SQLiteDatabase.CREATE_
IF_NECESSARY, null);
```

2. Underneath this, define a table for our database in the following manner:

```
final String CREATE_TABLE_CITIES = "CREATE TABLE tb_cities ("
    + "id INTEGER PRIMARY KEY AUTOINCREMENT,"
    + "city_name TEXT);";
```

3. Then execute this SQL statement:

```
db.execSQL(CREATE_TABLE_CITIES);
```

4. Now using a **ContentValues** object insert some entries:

```
ContentValues cv = new ContentValues();
cv.put("city_name", "Aberdeen");
db.insert("tb_cities", null, cv);
cv.put("city_name", "Dundee");
db.insert("tb_cities", null, cv);
```

5. And finally close the database:

```
db.close();
```

6. Run this code on an emulator or a handset connected to your computer and open Eclipse's **File Explorer** tab to locate our new database:

Name	Size	Date	Time	Permissions	Info
com.android.server.vpn		2011-04-16	09:05	drwxr-x--x	
com.android.settings		2011-04-16	09:06	drwxr-x--x	
com.android.soundrecorder		2011-04-16	09:05	drwxr-x--x	
com.android.spare_parts		2011-04-16	09:05	drwxr-x--x	
com.android.speechrecorder		2011-04-16	09:05	drwxr-x--x	
com.android.systemui		2011-04-16	09:05	drwxr-x--x	
com.android.term		2011-04-16	09:05	drwxr-x--x	
com.android.wallpaper.livepicker		2011-04-16	09:05	drwxr-x--x	
com.example.android.apis		2011-04-16	09:06	drwxr-x--x	
com.example.android.livecubes		2011-04-16	09:05	drwxr-x--x	
com.example.android.softkeyboard		2011-04-16	09:05	drwxr-x--x	
com.packtpub.android.contextsensitivemenus		2011-04-19	11:09	drwxr-x--x	
com.packtpub.android.databaseexample		2011-04-25	10:54	drwxr-x--x	
databases		2011-04-25	10:54	drwxrwx--x	
my_database.db	5120	2011-04-25	10:54	-rw-rw----	
lib		2011-04-25	10:52	drwxr-xr-x	
com.packtpub.android.externalstorage		2011-04-25	09:24	drwxr-x--x	
com.packtpub.android.inflatinganoptionsmenu		2011-04-19	10:28	drwxr-x--x	
com.svox.pico		2011-04-16	09:05	drwxr-x--x	
jp.co.omronsoft.openwnn		2011-04-16	09:06	drwxr-x--x	

How it works...

More often than not a database or at least its structure would be created beforehand, but we can use the **SQLiteDatabase** method `openOrCreateDatabase()` to produce one from scratch, as we did here. The `openOrCreateDatabase()` function takes a string *name*, an SQL *mode*, and a **CursorFactory** *object*, which is a public interface for handling **Cursor** objects.

The flag that we used in the SQL mode, `CREATE_IF_NECESSARY`, is just one of several we could have applied—the others being `OPEN_READWRITE`, `OPEN_READONLY`, and `NO_LOCALIZED_COLLATORS`.

We put together an SQL statement, `CREATE TABLE tb_cities (id INTEGER PRIMARY KEY AUTOINCREMENT, city_name TEXT)`, which we concatenated into a string constant, `CREATE_TABLECITIES`, for clarity. Any SQL statement can be constructed in this way and executed with `execSQL()`.

Inserting data is something we will need to do often with a working database and here we took advantage of the **ContentValues** class, which allows us to pass values to a **ContentResolver** that provides us access to the underlying *grammar* or *content model*.

Viewed as a database, what we have created would resemble the following screenshot:

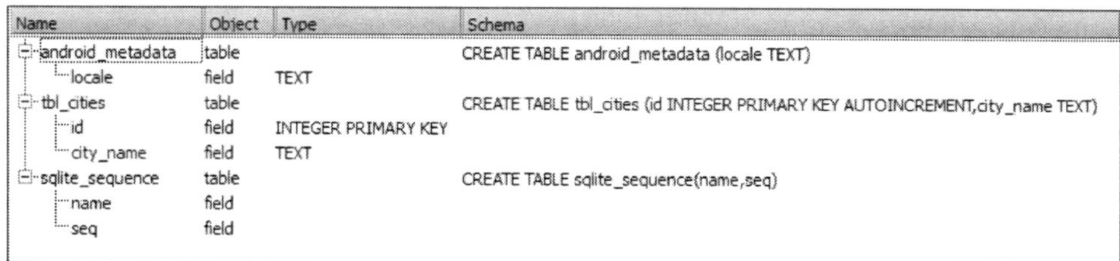

Name	Object	Type	Schema
android_metadata	table		CREATE TABLE android_metadata (locale TEXT)
locale	field	TEXT	
tbl_cities	table		CREATE TABLE tbl_cities (id INTEGER PRIMARY KEY AUTOINCREMENT, city_name TEXT)
id	field	INTEGER PRIMARY KEY	
city_name	field	TEXT	
sqlite_sequence	table		CREATE TABLE sqlite_sequence(name,seq)
name	field		
seq	field		

There's more...

On a battery-operated device it is even more important to keep the number of threads and processes to a minimum, and Android provides a technique for setting locks on critical sections of a database.

There will also be times when we want to version our database and this too is simple with Android.

Making a database thread safe

To apply locks around our database and therefore making it thread safe, use:

```
db.setLockingEnabled(true);
```

Versioning a database

An Android SQLite database can be versioned with:

```
db.setVersion(2);
```

Sharing multimedia files across applications with Content Providers

To enable the developer to share data from one application with another, Android provides the **android.content.ContentProvider** class. This vastly simplifies the management of common data types, such as audio, video, images, and contact details, and also provides several built-in providers under the **android.provider** package.

Getting ready

In this exercise we will use the **MediaStore** provider to examine the audio files on our device's SD card. Make sure that the handset or emulator being used for this recipe has some MP3 files loaded onto the SD card, then start up a new Android project in Eclipse.

How to do it...

1. Starting with the `main.xml` file in the `res/layout` folder, give the default TextView an `android:id` of `text_view` and set `android:text` to an empty string:

   ```
   android:id="@+id/text_view"
   android:text=""
   ```

2. In the main Java Activity code, inside the `onCreate()` method and after the `setContentView()` call, create and associate a TextView instance:

   ```
   TextView textView = (TextView) findViewById(R.id.text_view);
   ```

3. Beneath this add the following instances:

   ```
   String[] columns = new String[] {
      MediaStore.Audio.Media.TITLE,
      MediaStore.Audio.Media.DURATION };
   Uri myTunes = MediaStore.Audio.Media.EXTERNAL_CONTENT_URI;
   Cursor c = managedQuery(myTunes, columns, null, null,
      MediaStore.Audio.Media.DURATION);
   ```

4. Now, beneath this include the following:

   ```
   if (c.moveToFirst()) {

      String title;
      String duration;

      do {
         title = c.getString(
            c.getColumnIndex(MediaStore.Audio.Media.TITLE)
         );
   ```

```
    duration = c.getString(
      c.getColumnIndex(MediaStore.Audio.Media.DURATION)
    );

    textView.append(title + " " + duration + "\n");
  } while (c.moveToNext());
}
```

5. Compile and run the project on an emulator or handset to view MP3 files on the SD card sorted by duration:

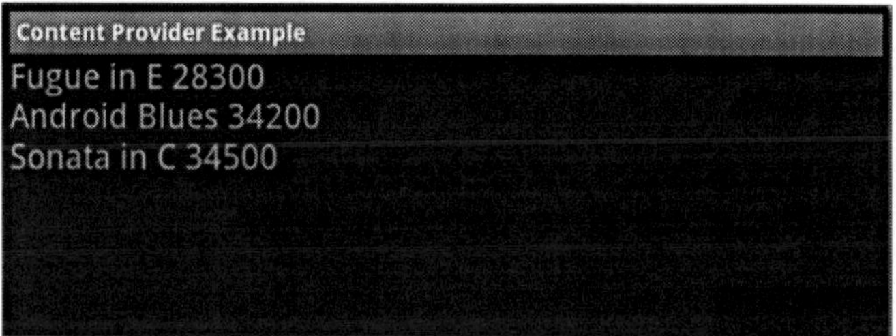

How it works...

The key class in this demonstration is the **Activity.managedQuery**, which allows us to query a **Provider**, in this case the **MediaStore** that provides access to common multimedia data types. Constructing a managedQuery returns a **Cursor** object based on the parameters we provided. The first is a URI, here pointing to the SD card. The second is a string array representing which columns we want to query. We used `MediaStore.Audio.Media` constants to select title and duration. The final parameter is the column that we wish our data to be sorted by. We ignored the third and fourth parameters in this example but we could have added selection criteria (in the form of an SQL `WHERE` clause, omitting the `WHERE` itself) and arguments respectively. Setting these as null, causes all columns to be selected.

We could have just as easily used a **ContentResolver.query** rather than a `managedQuery`. It would have taken the same arguments and returned the same Cursor, and if we had wanted to edit the data, this would have been the path to take. However, the `managedQuery` is very handy as it is handled directly by the activity and will unload itself automatically when the activity enters the paused or destroyed state.

This exercise only explored one of the built-in MediaStore providers to access audio files but there are also `MediaStore.Video`, `MediaStore.Files`, and `MediaStore.Images`.

Defining and enforcing permissions

As anyone who has downloaded and installed an Android application will
have seen, certain actions such as accessing the Internet or receiving SMS require explicit
permissions from the user at the point of installation. This is because the default security only
allows application processes to run isolated from each other unless specified.

Getting ready

We will be returning to the **Android Manifest** XML file in this recipe to set our **permissions**,
but we will need a screen with a **Button**, to trigger our action and some Java code to give our
application something to do.

Start a new Android project in Eclipse and edit the `main.xml` file in the `res/layout` folder
so that it contains a **Button** with an **ID**—`@+id/button` is fine.

How to do it...

1. Inside our main activity Java file, declare a **Button** widget and reference the XML in
   the usual way with `findViewById()`:

```
mButton = (Button) findViewById(R.id.button);
```

2. Create a click listener with an `onClick()` method and have it start the following new
   activity:

```
mButton.setOnClickListener(new OnClickListener() {
    @Override
    public void onClick(View v) {
        Uri uri = Uri.parse("http://www.packtpub.com");
        startActivity(new Intent(Intent.ACTION_VIEW, uri));
    }
});
```

3. Now open the `AndroidManifest.xml` file in the root folder of our project.

4. Include a `uses-permissions` tag with the following setting inside the root node
   (but no deeper) of the manifest:

```
    ...
</application>
<uses-permission
    android:name="android.permission.INTERNET" />
    ...
</manifest>
```

5. This can be typed directly using the **AndroidManifest.xml** tab or using buttons and drop-downs on the **Permissions** tab:

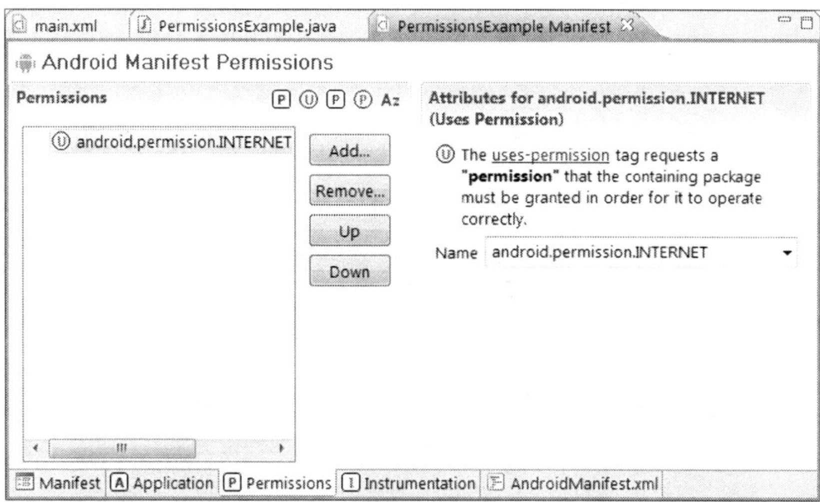

6. Run the code on an emulator or handset:

How it works...

Strictly speaking, setting permissions during the development stage will make no difference, but to view permissions on a handset or emulator select **Settings | Applications | Manage Applications** from the **Applications** menu, and then pick your application:

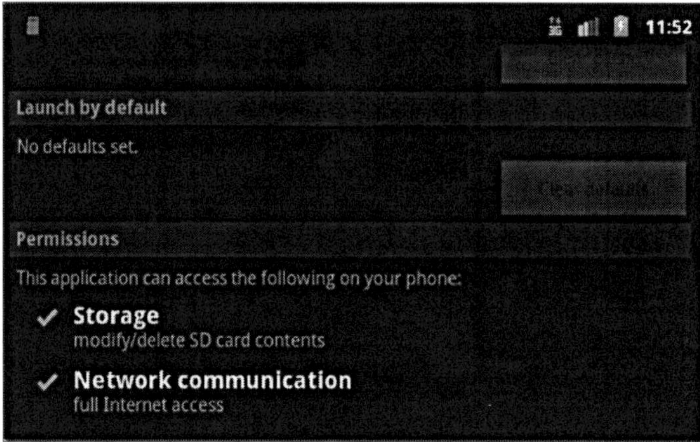

The **Manifest.permission** object comes with dozens of built-in constants such as `android.permission.INTERNET` and commonly used permissions include `READ_CONTACTS`, `READ_SMS`, and `SET_TIME_ZONE`.

Use Eclipse's **JavaDoc** facility to explore all the permission based constants in the **android.Manifest.permission** class.

There's more...

Despite the large number of built-in permissions available to us, it is often handy to be able to create a customized constraint for more specific control over individual components such as activities. Android allows us to define and enforce our own permissions and to control the protection level applied.

Defining and enforcing custom permissions

By placing a `<permission>` tag in the top level of our `<manifest>` we can set permissions for the entire application. To set permissions for single activities, place `<permission>` tags inside the respective activities. For example:

```
<activity>
<permission
  android:name
```

```
     ="com.packtpub.android.permissionsexample.MY_PERMISSION"
    android:label="@string/permission_label"
    android:description="@string/permission_description"
    android:protectionLevel="dangerous" />
. . .
```

Tags of this nature, when placed inside an `<activity>` node, can be checked from the `starytActivityForResult()` method. The label and description are both required and the description is often a whole sentence or two.

Custom permissions can also be given one of the several permission group headings: when an action may cost the user money, `COST_MONEY`, or make calls, `PHONE_CALLS`. The syntax of this `Manifest.permission_group` element is:

```
android:permissionGroup="android.permission-group.PHONE_CALLS"
```

Android gives us three usable **protection levels** to tell the system how to inform the user of the risk level of the permission. A setting of `normal` will generally not require confirmation from the user (although it will, as always, during installation). The `dangerous` setting will require user conformation and the `signature` setting will only accept request from applications that have the same signature—that is, applications that have been built to run as one package.

See also

For more on the `startActivityForResult()` method see the recipe *Returning a result from an Activity* in *Chapter 1, Activities*.

Providing backup functionality

One of the most useful security functions provided by Google for the Android platform is the cloud based **backup and restore service** for user data generated by our applications.

This functionality will come into play automatically when a user reinstalls or updates a backup-enabled application or when they get a new phone or restore factory settings for some reason.

Getting ready

As a developer you will require a **Backup Service Key**, which you receive when registering for backup service from Google. If you have not already done so you can register at `http://code.google.com/android/backup/signup.html`.

This demonstration can be applied to any application that requires backing up, so open any application you like, ideally one with some significant data such as shared preferences and/or internal files.

How to do it...

1. Open the `AndroidManifest.xml` file so that it is ready to edit.

2. Inside the `<application>` node include:

```
android:backupAgent="my_backup_agent"
```

3. Also inside `<application>` add the key and the `meta-data` code that you received when you registered for backup with Google:

```
<meta-data
   android:name="com.google.android.backup.api_key"
   android:value="your key goes here" />
```

4. Create a new class that extends **BackupAgentHelper** and override its `onCreate()` method as follows:

```
public class MyPrefsBackup extends BackupAgentHelper {

  void onCreate() {
    SharedPreferencesBackupHelper helper =
      new SharedPreferencesBackupHelper(
        this, "user_preferences"
      );
    addHelper("prefs", helper);
  }

}
```

5. If you have other internal files that you wish to include, then add another class and reference these files as laid out here:

```
public class MyFilesBackup extends BackupAgentHelper {
  void onCreate() {
    FileBackupHelper helper
      = new FileBackupHelper(
        this, "my_file", "another_file"
      );
    addHelper("all_my_files", helper);
  }

}
```

6. Our application is now backup-enabled.

How it works...

Despite there being little to show for our work, there is quite a lot going on here, not the least of which is the employment of **backup agent helpers** which reduces the amount of code by providing an interface for the underlying **backup agent** that we defined in the manifest. Without these helpers we would have to override the `onRestore()` and `onBackup()` methods in the **agent** itself.

In practice it would be preferable to have used constants rather than string literals which we did here simply to reduce the amount of typing. The string parameters `"prefs"` and `"all_my_files"` serve as a unique prefix to identify individual helpers.

To request a backup call the `dataChanged()` method on the **BackupAgent** or `onRestore()` to force a restore.

6

Detecting User Activity

In this chapter, we will cover the following topics:

- ▶ Reading a device's orientation
- ▶ Measuring motion with the accelerometer
- ▶ Listing available sensors
- ▶ Recognizing a touch event
- ▶ Detecting multi-touch elements
- ▶ Recognizing gestures
- ▶ Handling multi-touch gestures
- ▶ Controlling on screen keyboards

Introduction

If one aspect of modern smartphones makes them stand out from other digital devices, it is surely the large array of sensors that can be found on-board. Android handsets can detect speed, motion, gravitational pull, and even the Earth's magnetic field.

Combined with sensitive touch-screens capable of reading complex gestures, these new forms of input device make smartphones among the most versatile and fun devices a programmer can get his or her hands on.

Android provides us with many handy tools for detecting user activity of this nature along with an intuitive series of callbacks and listeners.

The ability of a phone to *know* which way it is being held, and so orient its on-screen content accordingly, is something users take for granted these days. As developers we need to be able to control this process and this chapter begins by exploring how to manage **configuration changes**. Not only can we intercept changes in **orientation** using these configuration tools, but also events such as the sliding in and out of a hard keyboard or the presence of a touch-screen.

Android devices generally contain several **sensors** and are able to take readings of various environmental conditions such as temperature and movement. Most of these instruments are accessed in the same way with the **android.hardware.SensorManager** class along with various listeners. We will see how to read and interpret the data that these devices produce and how to quiz a handset to discover which sensors are available to our applications.

Next, we will take a look at touch-screens and the **android.view.MotionEvent** class which plays a primary role in recognizing **touch events**. We will see how to distinguish between more than one digit in **multi-touch** settings.

Next we demonstrate how to detect **single pointer gestures** such as double taps, scrolls, and flings as well as **multi-touch gestures** like the pinch-zoom.

Finally we come to the **soft keyboard** and how to best manage the issue of the amount of screen space these items generally consume.

Reading a device's orientation

Perhaps one of the most useful features of the smartphone is the device's ability to detect its own **screen orientation** with regard to the user. Although much of this can be handled automatically when a user turns their device around, it is very useful at times to be able to take control of the process.

By informing the system through our manifest and overriding activity callbacks we can include code that will run when the device is rotated.

Getting ready

We are going to take over from the system's automatic handling of screen orientation with a callback method, but first we have to inform Android of this, which we do through our **manifest**. We will also need some way to observe results, so start up a new Android project in Eclipse and create a **TextView** with an **ID** in `main.xml`.

How to do it...

1. Open the `AndroidManifest.xml` file and inside the `<activity>` node add a `configChanges` element with the following value:

```
<activity
  android:name=".OrientationReader"
  android:configChanges="orientation"
  android:label="@string/app_name">
  ...
</activity>
```

2. Open the Java activity window and form an association between a private class member, `mTextView`, and the **TextView** that we created in XML:

    ```
    mTextView = (TextView) findViewById(R.id.text_box);
    ```

3. Override the `onConfigurationChanged()` method as follows:

    ```java
    @Override
    public void onConfigurationChanged(Configuration config) {
        super.onConfigurationChanged(config);

        if (config.orientation ==
          Configuration.ORIENTATION_LANDSCAPE) {
            mTextView.setText("landscape");

        } else if (config.orientation ==
          Configuration.ORIENTATION_PORTRAIT) {
            mTextView.setText("portrait");
        }

    }
    ```

4. Now compile and run the project on a handset or emulator. Rotate the phone or virtual device through 90 degrees to observe the `onConfigurationChanged()` method in action:

The screen can be rotated using a virtual device by pressing *Ctrl + F12* on the PC keyboard.

How it works...

By default, Android will restart an **Activity** when a device (or emulator) is rotated through 90 degrees. This is very useful for taking advantage of the system's designated resource folder `res/layout-land/` but reloading resources every time the device is turned can be expensive in some applications and Android provides the `configChanges` attribute value `"orientation"`, allowing us to control how an application behaves in these circumstances.

The `onConfigurationChanged()` method acts like many other hooks although it requires a **Configuration** object to operate. The **Configuration** object provides us with many useful fields such as `Configuration.orientation`, which we used here and which can also take the value `ORIENTATION_SQUARE`.

The next table contains a list of a few of the more useful **Configuration** fields and their associated constants:

Configuration.field	constants
.hardKeyboardHidden	*HARDKEYBOARDHIDDEN_NO, HARDKEYBOARDHIDDEN_YES.*
.keyboard	*KEYBOARD_NOKEYS, KEYBOARD_QWERTY, KEYBOARD_12KEY.*
.navigation	*NAVIGATION_NONAV, NAVIGATION_DPAD, NAVIGATION_TRACKBALL, NAVIGATION_WHEEL.*
.navigationHidden	*NAVIGATIONHIDDEN_NO, NAVIGATIONHIDDEN_YES.*
.touchscreen	*TOUCHSCREEN_NOTOUCH, TOUCHSCREEN_STYLUS, TOUCHSCREEN_FINGER.*

These configuration fields are extremely useful when you consider that we have little idea in advance about what hardware will be available for our applications in the wild.

Measuring motion with the accelerometer

There are a wide and growing variety of **sensors** that can be found on an Android handset, from accelerometers and gyroscopes to light and proximity sensors. Most of these devices can be accessed with the **android.hardware.SensorEvent** class, although naturally they each produce their own specific data sets.

Here we will use `Sensor.TYPE_ACCELEROMETER` to measure a handset's motion in three dimensions before going on to explore other sensor types.

Getting ready

Gathering information from sensors is quite straightforward as Android provides a handy interface, **android.hardware.SensorEventListener**, to facilitate this. Nevertheless there is a little more housekeeping required than previous tasks as we must take control of the registering of these listeners with the **SensorManager** class.

Start up a new Android project in Eclipse and create a TextView with an ID in `main.xml`.

How to do it...

1. Inside our main activity's Java class edit the declaration so that it implements **SensorEventListener**, like so:

```java
public class MotionDetector extends Activity implements
SensorEventListener {
```

2. Just below this, declare a class field of type **SensorManager**:

```java
private SensorManager mSensorManager;
```

3. At the end of the `onCreate()` method add the following **SensorManager** assignment:

```java
mSensorManager = (SensorManager) getSystemService(SENSOR_SERVICE);
```

4. We need to disable our sensors when we are not using them, so add an `onPause()` and an `onResume()` method, completed as seen here:

```java
@Override
protected void onResume() {
    super.onResume();

    mSensorManager.registerListener(
      this,
      mSensorManager.getDefaultSensor(
        Sensor.TYPE_ACCELEROMETER
      ),
        SensorManager.SENSOR_DELAY_UI);
}

@Override
protected void onPause() {
    super.onPause();

    mSensorManager.unregisterListener(this);
}
```

5. Eclipse will probably have informed you of an error by this point and will offer to **add the unimplemented methods**. Accept this suggestion and fill out the body of the `onSensorChanged()` method as follows:

```
public void onSensorChanged(SensorEvent e) {
  synchronized (this) {

      if (e.sensor.getType() == Sensor.TYPE_ACCELEROMETER) {
        mTextView.setText("x= " + e.values[0] +
            "\ny= " + e.values[1] +
            "\nz= " + e.values[2]);
      }

    }
}
```

6. The `onAccuracyChanged()` method is not used in this example but must be included anyway—you can leave it like this:

```
public void onAccuracyChanged(Sensor sensor, int accuracy) {
  // TODO Auto-generated method stub
}
```

7. Provided you have assigned the TextView with `findViewById()`, this program can be run on any emulator or handset with an accelerometer:

How it works...

Reading a sensor's values requires several components, including the **SensorEventListener** interface that implements two callbacks which we use to respond to changes in sensor values or accuracy. The `onAccuracyChanged()` callback is required less often but is nevertheless useful as demands on battery and environmental conditions can cause this setting to change. The possible constant `int` values for this can be:

```
SENSOR_STATUS_ACCURACY_HIGH,
SENSOR_STATUS_ACCURACY_MEDIUM
SENSOR_STATUS_ACCURACY_LOW
```

Many sensors, including the accelerometer, are a powerful drain on a device's battery so we need to disable them when not in use. We did so in the `onPause()` callback using SensorManager's `unregisterListener(SensorEventListener)` method. Registering the listener, on the other hand, was slightly more complex, requiring a `SensorEventListener`, an `int` **type**, which here was the default accelerometer, and a delay value. This delay (`int`) value controls how quickly the sensor operates and can have a dramatic affect on power usage. There are four settings:

- `SENSOR_DELAY_FASTEST`
- `SENSOR_DELAY_GAME`
- `SENSOR_DELAY_NORMAL`
- `SENSOR_DELAY_UI`

The actual reading of the accelerometer's values was done in the `onSensorChanged()` method. We managed the SensorEvent's `sensor.getType()` method to select the accelerometer and we can also use this to gain other information about a sensor such as `sensor.getPower()`, which returns the power the sensor uses in micro amps or `sensor.getMaximumRange()`, which returns a distance based on the sensor's own measurements.

The accelerometer, along with the magnetic field sensor and the gyroscope, returns three values based on a coordinate system. In our example here the three values describe the acceleration of the device along each of the three axes of this coordinate system measured in m/s^2. Relative to the handset the three directions are as shown in the next image:

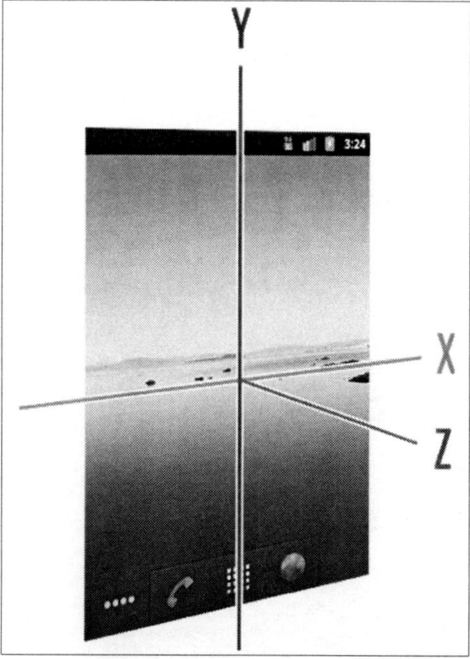

 Note that the force of Earth's gravity (approximately 9.8 m/s^2) will always register with the accelerometer. For example, if a phone is perfectly upright, as in the diagram, then the Y axis, `event.values[1]`, will read **-9.8**.

There's more...

The technique we used to register and access the accelerometer is very similar in operation and structure to the way we would access the other sensors.

Accessing any available sensor

We referred to our accelerometer with the Sensor constant `TYPE_ACCELEROMETER` in the two lines:

```
mSensorManager.registerListener(this,
mSensorManager.getDefaultSensor(Sensor.TYPE_ACCELEROMETER),
    SensorManager.SENSOR_DELAY_UI);
...
if (e.sensor.getType() == Sensor.TYPE_ACCELEROMETER)
```

We could have used any one of several constants provided by the **Sensor** object. Here is a comprehensive list of sensor types:

- `TYPE_ACCELEROMETER`
- `TYPE_ALL`
- `TYPE_GRAVITY`
- `TYPE_GYROSCOPE`
- `TYPE_LIGHT`
- `TYPE_LINEAR_ACCELERATION`
- `TYPE_MAGNETIC_FIELD`
- `TYPE_ORIENTATION`
- `TYPE_PRESSURE`
- `TYPE_PROXIMITY`
- `TYPE_ROTATION_VECTOR`
- `TYPE_TEMPERATURE`

These are largely self explanatory with the possible exception of `TYPE_ALL`. This special case is used to detect any sensor.

Listing available sensors

Android handsets come with a wide variety of sensors but which sensors are included is a matter for manufacturers to decide and differs from model to model. As developers we need some way to detect which sensors are available to us. In particular we may want to select between sensors that perform similar functions. For example it may be preferable to measure motion with a gyroscope if one is available but prepare a function that utilizes the accelerometer when one is not.

Getting ready

The project we put together in the last recipe is as good a place to start this exercise as any, as we will be doing little in the way of coding. You can of course apply this task to any of your own applications if you prefer.

How to do it...

1. Open up the Java activity file and declare the following private members:

```
private SensorManager mSensorManager;
private TextView mTextView;
private List mList;
```

2. You will have needed to define the TextView in XML and provide it with an `android:id`.

3. Inside the `onCreate()` method assign our **SensorManager** and TextView like this:

```
mSensorManager = (SensorManager) getSystemService(SENSOR_SERVICE);
mTextView = (TextView) findViewById(R.id.text_view);
```

4. Finally, add the following statement block just beneath this:

```
mList = mSensorManager.getSensorList(Sensor.TYPE_ALL);

for (int i = 1; i < mList.size(); i++) {
  mTextView.append("\n" + mList.get(i));
}
```

5. When run on a handset or emulator this routine will display a list of all available sensors for that device:

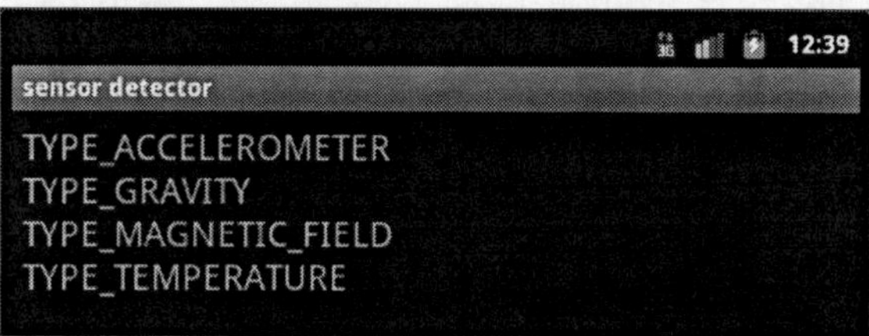

How it works...

This is a nice simple exercise and all we have done is demonstrate the usefulness of **SensorManager's** `getSensorList(int)` method. In practice we would probably only make inquiries regarding a particular sensor type and this is simply a matter of replacing the `Sensor.TYPE_ALL` constant with the appropriate type in the `mSensorManager.getSensorList()` call.

Being able to test for the presence of sensors enables us to develop for a wide variety of handsets without necessarily knowing in advance what hardware is available.

Recognizing a touch event

One of the most challenging aspects of smartphone programming is the often very small amount of screen estate available, with some handsets having screen sizes of less than 3". Programming such devices would prove very frustrating if it were not for the presence of **touch-screens** on most of them.

Here we will create a slider button that we can drag across the screen with a finger using the **view.View.OnTouchListener** and **view.MotionEvent** classes. This will demonstrate how to make any View respond to a touch event and read the position of any movement we make.

Getting ready

Although there is quite a lot of code in this example, to start with all we need is a new Android project and a Button to use as a slider. Start a new project and in the `res/layout/main.xml` file add the following Button:

```xml
<Button
    android:text="slide me"
    android:id="@+id/button"
    android:layout_width="wrap_content"
    android:layout_height="wrap_content"
    android:padding="6dip" />
```

How to do it...

1. Inside the `onCreate()` method in our Java file, add the following code:

    ```java
    final Button slider = (Button) findViewById(R.id.button);

    slider.setOnTouchListener(new OnTouchListener() {
        int sldrX;
        int wndwX;

    });
    ```

2. We need to implement the **OnTouchListener's** `onTouch()` method. To do this quickly, use Eclipse's help function by hovering over the marked code and selecting **Add unimplemented methods** from the quick fix window:

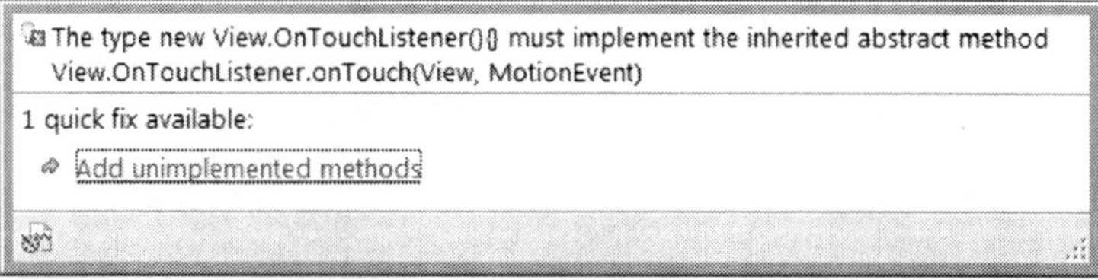

3. Fill out our new method as we have here. Although, as you can see, the `case MotionEvent.ACTION_UP` clause is not actually required for this demonstration:

```java
@Override
public boolean onTouch(View view, MotionEvent event) {
    int action = event.getAction();

    switch (action) {

    case MotionEvent.ACTION_DOWN:
        sldrX = (int) event.getX();
        wndwX = (int) event.getRawX();
        break;

    case MotionEvent.ACTION_MOVE:
        int l = (int) event.getRawX() - sldrX;
        int r = l + view.getWidth();
        view.layout(l, view.getTop(), r, view.getBottom());
        break;

    case MotionEvent.ACTION_UP:
        // actions to be completed
        // when the button is released
        break;
    }

    return false;
}
```

4. That's it. Run the project on a handset or an emulator with the touchscreen enabled. Our button will now respond to touch events and slide across the screen:

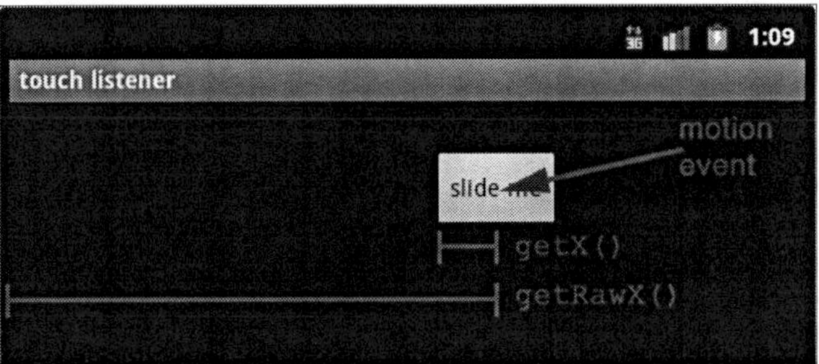

How it works...

The `OnTouchListener.onTouch()` method gives us access to the **View** that was touched as well as the **event** itself. This event is returned in the form of a **MotionEvent** instance and we used its public method's `getX()` and `getRawX()` to return the position of the event. The first method returns the position within the view (that is, how far from the button's left edge it was touched) and the second, *Raw*, version returns the position on the entire screen.

We could just as easily have used `getY()` and `getRawY()` to return the view's vertical position in a similar fashion.

> The units returned by these methods are in pixels and the origin is found in the top left corner of the screen or view being measured.

The **MotionEvent** class is able to do far more than tell us where our finger is on the screen, and methods such as `getEventTime(long)` and `getDownTime(long)` tell us when and for how long (in milliseconds) our event occurred.

The other useful feature of the MotionEvent class is the `getAction()` method which allowed us to capture the three parts of a screen swipe: `ACTION_DOWN`, `ACTION_MOVE`, and `ACTION_UP`. There is also a fourth `ACTION_CANCEL` value for when a touch event is interrupted or ends unexpectedly.

Other **View.view** methods that we used were `getWidth()` and `getTop()` for retrieving our view's location and `layout(int,int,int,int)` for positioning it.

> It is well worth noting that in releases prior to API 11 (Android 3.0) only a single view could receive a touch event at any one time. If, for reasons of backwards compatibility, you wish to disable the multi-view touch feature, provide the `android:splitMotionE vents="false"` attribute to the layout concerned.

There's more...

A lot of mobile applications, in particular maps and games, make use of the edges of the screen as a method of input. The **MotionEvent** class provides us with constants to record screen edge activity.

It is also possible to **detect pressure** on some handsets and in the absence of such a sensor, a **size detector** is usually available which can provide a crude but effective approximation of pressure by registering the spread of contact.

Edge detection

There are four flags, available to us as **MotionEvent** constants:

- `EDGE_TOP`
- `EDGE_BOTTOM`
- `EDGE_LEFT`
- `EDGE_RIGHT`

These can be used in the manner we applied above to detect when a touch event intersects the edges of the physical screen.

Pressure and size detection

To find the pressure of an event use `MotionEvent.getPressure()`, which will return a float between 0.0 for no pressure and 1.0 for maximum pressure.

If this method returns values greater than 1.0 then the device itself may need calibrating and the same may apply if this value never reaches close to 1.0.

The `MotionEvent.getSize()` method provides a measure of how spread out the point of contact is and also returns a float between 0.0 and 1.0

See also

For further examples of the onTouchListener see the recipes *Drawing with a Canvas* in *Chapter 8, Graphics and Animation* and *Capturing photos with the camera* in *Chapter 9, Multimedia*

Detecting multi-touch elements

Detecting touch on just a single point is useful enough, but far more information can be gathered from a **touchscreen** that can detect and distinguish the presence of more than one finger. Android can, in theory, detect up to 256 touch events at once, although one can see how this might be difficult to achieve in practice.

The programming of **multi-touch events** is necessarily more complex than tracing a single point but thankfully for us, it is achieved in a similar manner. Here we will see how to determine the number of touch events at a given moment and how to differentiate between them.

Getting ready

As mentioned earlier, detecting **multiple touch events** is similar to detecting single touch events. Start this task from where we left off in the previous recipe or apply the techniques laid out here to a project of your own.

How to do it...

1. We will be adding to our previous **OnTouchListener** so open the Java activity and scroll down to the `onTouch()` method.

2. Near the top of `onTouch()` add the following two declarations:

    ```java
    int index =
        (action & MotionEvent.ACTION_POINTER_INDEX_MASK)
           >> MotionEvent.ACTION_POINTER_INDEX_SHIFT;
    int id;
    ```

3. Replace the `switch` expression:

    ```java
    switch (action) {
    ```

    With:

    ```java
    switch (action & MotionEvent.ACTION_MASK) {
    ```

4. Now add two more `case` clauses to the `switch` statement as follows:

    ```java
    case MotionEvent.ACTION_POINTER_DOWN:
        id = event.getPointerId(index);
        Toast.makeText(getApplicationContext(),
          "finger " + id + " pressed", Toast.LENGTH_LONG);
        break;
    case MotionEvent.ACTION_POINTER_UP:
        id = event.getPointerId(index);
        Toast.makeText(getApplicationContext(),
          "finger " + id + " released", Toast.LENGTH_LONG);
        break;
    ```

5. To allow us to touch our view with more than one finger, we need to make it a bit wider. In `main.xml` change the width with the following:

    ```
    android:layout_width="match_parent"
    ```

6. Our project will now respond to more than a single touch event. Compile and run the code either on a handset or emulator with multi-touch capacity to try it out.

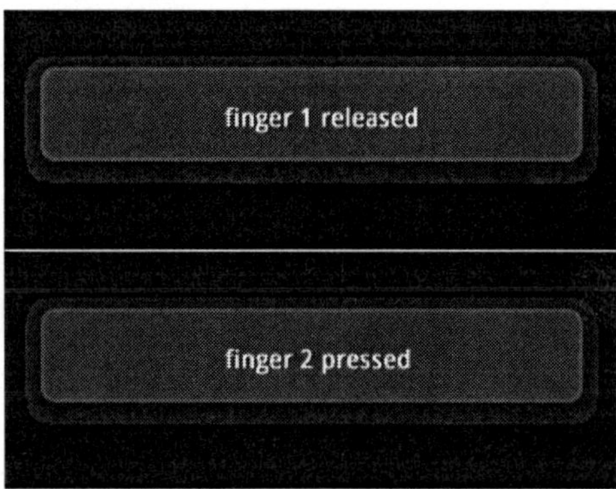

How it works...

Again, we have only used one dimension to keep the example simple, but the same principles apply equally well for both axes. The key difference here is that we now have to keep track of more than one event.

First we filtered out our action with the bit mask `MotionEvent.ACTION_MASK`, so that we could handle it with a switch statement as we did before. The MotionEvent values `ACTION_POINTER_UP` and `ACTION_POINTER_DOWN` are returned instead of `ACTION_UP` and `ACTION_DOWN` when a secondary pointer is detected. Then we obtained the **index** of our individual **pointer** by ANDing (>>) another bit mask, `MotionEvent.ACTION_POINTER_INDEX_MASK` with our action code and shifting it up or down with `MotionEvent.ACTION_POINTER_INDEX_SHIFT`, which keeps track of the number of pointers.

Once we can identify a pointer by its index, we can locate it: `getX()`, `getY()`, and their variants can all take an `int` parameter that represents a pointer's index. For example `getX(1)` will return the X coordinate of the second pointer placed on that view. The MotionEvent class also has a `getPointerCount()` method which returns the current number of pointer events.

It might seem that having a pointer's index is all we need but it is simple to confuse this system with three or more points over time. Fortunately Android provides a way for us to give each pointer an **ID** that will remain consistent over many individual events. This is far simpler than obtaining the index as MotionEvent provides the `getPointerId(int index)` method which we used here. To see the difference between referring to a multi-touch event by its **index** and its **ID**, replace id with index in the **Toast** statements in the code.

Recognizing gestures

The techniques outlined here allow us to detect, locate, and discriminate between any number of touch events. Using **MotionEvent** methods such as `getX()` and `getY()` to determine an event's position and `getEventTime()`, `getDownTime()` and others to provide information about when these events took place, we can build all sorts of complex shape recognition routines.

Constructing high level gestures this way could soon become cumbersome. Android provides the **GestureDetector** class along with one or two subclasses that allow us to detect gestures such as scrolling, flinging, and long-pressing.

Getting ready

This recipe shows how to recognize a **fling gesture**. This is when a user quickly moves and then releases a finger in a specific direction. As we only demonstrate how to capture the event and interpret its data here, you can apply these techniques to any application you wish.

Start up a new Android project in Eclipse.

How to do it...

1. First declare the following gesture detector in our main Java activity class:

```
private GestureDetector mGestureDetector;
```

2. Create a new inner class that extends a gesture listener subclass as shown here and give it an `onFling()` callback:

```
class MyGestureListener extends GestureDetector.OnGestureListener
{
  @Override
  public boolean onFling(MotionEvent e1,
    MotionEvent e2, float vX, float vY) {
    Toast.makeText(getBaseContext(),
      "velocity " + vX + " x " + vY, Toast.LENGTH_SHORT);
    return true;
  }
}
```

3. Next assign our gesture detector with the class we just created:

```
mGestureDetector = new GestureDetector(this, new
MyGestureListener());
```

4. Now add an `onTouchEvent()` method and fill it out with the single line of code seen below:

```
@Override
public boolean onTouchEvent(MotionEvent event) {
    return mGestureDetector.onTouchEvent(event);
}
```

5. Test your application on a handset or emulator to view the results.

How it works...

The way gesture detection works is relatively straightforward. The **GestureDetector** object is not used directly, but rather one of its subclasses is used to report, as was seen here with **OnGestureListener**.

We still overrode `onTouchEvent()` but passed the event directly to the **GestureDetector**. This means that we can still hook **MotionEvents** in the way did earlier in the chapter from within the `onTouchEvent()` method but our routine can now capture single motions and gestures together.

The `onFling()` callback provides us with four items of data describing the gesture. The first two are **MotionEvents**: The `ACTION_DOWN` that started the fling and the `ACTION_MOVE` that followed it. The two float values returned represent the velocity (in pixels per second) of the fling along the X and Y axes respectively.

The **OnGestureListener** class provides six gesture callbacks in total, their return values and parameters are laid out in the following table:

Method	Returns	Parameters	Notes
onDown()	boolean	MotionEvent	A single tap down event
onFling()	boolean	MotionEvent	Initial down event
		MotionEvent	Consequent move event
		float	X velocity in px/sec
		float	Y velocity in px/sec
onLongPress()	void	MotionEvent	The down event that triggered a long press
onScroll()	boolean	MotionEvent	Initial down event
		MotionEvent	Movement that caused the scroll
		float	X distance traveled in px
		float	Y distance traveled in px
onShowPress()	void	MotionEvent	Like a long press but called before
onSingleTapUp()	boolean	MotionEvent	A single tap up event

There's more...

As mentioned before, **OnGestureListener** is not the only subclass of **GestureDetector**. There is also a listener for **double-taps** and a convenience listener that combines the functionality of both.

Detecting double-taps

The **GestureDetector.OnDoubleTapListener** class has three public methods for detecting double-taps:

- onDoubleTap(MotionEvent) is called when a double-tap has occurred
- onDoubleTapEvent(MotionEvent) is called after a single MotionEvent within a double-tap
- onSingleTapConfirmed(MotionEvent) is called after the first tap

These hooks all return `true` when an event is successfully completed and `false` otherwise.

Detecting all gesture events

Simply for convenience, Android has included a further subclass of GestureDetector, **SimpleOnGestureListener**. This listener implements both the OnGestureListener and the OnDoubleTapListener and is a useful class for extending and creating custom listeners.

Handling multi-touch gestures

Gesture recognition on mobile devices is not restricted to single pointer inputs such as the double-taps and flings we met earlier in this chapter, and functions such as pinch-zoom would be difficult to perform on a touch-screen with fewer than two fingers.

Again we will make use of a gesture detector and its listeners. In this case we will be using the **ScaleGestureDetector** and its **OnScaleGestureListener**, which provide measurements useful for pinch-zooming but are flexible enough to apply to any number of situations.

Getting ready

The structure behind detecting multi-touch gestures is the same as for the single pointed gestures we covered earlier in the chapter. Load up any project you wish and we will create the listener as an inner class that you can apply as you wish.

How to do it...

1. Select the activity or class that you wish to add a scale detector to, and declare the following class-wide field:

```
private ScaleGestureDetector mDetector;
```

2. Now include the following inner class in this activity:

```
private class MyScaleDetector
    extends ScaleGestureDetector.OnScaleGestureListener {

@Override
public boolean onScaleBegin(ScaleGestureDetector detector) {
// called when the gesture starts

return true;
}

@Override
public boolean onScale(ScaleGestureDetector detector) {
// called for every MotionEvent within the gesture

  if (detector.getScaleFactor() >= 1) {
    mIsZoomingOut = true;
  } else {
    mIsPinchingIn = true;
  }

  return true;
}

@Override
public boolean onScaleEnd(ScaleGestureDetector detector) {
// called when the gesture is consumed

return true;
}

}
```

3. You will, no doubt want to include you own text within the `onScale()` method. When done, compile and run your code in the usual way.

How it works...

The way that motion detectors and listeners work should be familiar by now. The difference with multi-touch gesture detection lies in the nature of the data that is captured. As before, the detector supplies a series of getters that we can use to interrogate events that make up our gestures.

The distance (in pixels) between the two pointers can be captured with
`ScaleGestureDetector.getCurrentSpan()` and the time (ms) that it occurred is
available through `getEventTime()`. To make the detector truly useful, methods are provided
to record data from the previous scaling event as well. In particular, `getPreviousSpan()`
which gives us the last distance between pointers and `getTimeDelta()` which returns the
time between events.

These values need to be compared to yield useful results and Android saves us some
time here with the `getScaleFactor()` method which we employed and which is a ratio
equivalent to `getCurrentSpan()` divided by `getPreviousSpan()`. It is common, with fast
finger movements for this number to grow too large or too small to be meaningful and it is
normal to include some preventative measures such as:

```
mScaleFactor = Math.max(0.1f, Math.min(mScaleFactor, 10.f));
```

The **ScaleGestureDetector** has three callbacks that are fired at least once during each gesture:

- `onScaleBegin()`—This is called once, at the beginning of each gesture
- `onScale()`—This is called for every `MotionEvent` that is part of the gesture
- `onScaleEnd()`—Called when the gesture has been completed

We only looked at one or two of the public methods available to us through the
OnScaleGestureListener, although there are several more all of which are useful, so below is
a table outlining each of them:

Method	Purpose and unit
`getCurrentSpan(float)`	The current distance between the pointers in pixels
`getEventTime(long)`	The time in milliseconds when the event occurred
`getFocusX(float)`	The X coordinate (px) of the current focal point, this is the center point between all pointers
`getFocusY(float)`	The Y coordinate (px) of the current focal point
`getPreviousSpan(float)`	The distance between the pointers during the previous scale event
`getScaleFactor(float)`	A ratio equal to (current span/previous span)
`getTimeDelta(long)`	The time, in milliseconds, between the previous event and the current one
`isInProgress(boolean)`	A test to inquire if a gesture is in progress, so that execution can be delayed if necessary

Controlling on screen keyboards

There is one form of user activity that we have thus far neglected, but which is in many applications, the most used input method of all. That is the **soft keyboard** that appears when a user taps on an **EditText** widget:

More often than not it is sufficient only to work with the resultant text that a user has input rather than consider the keyboard itself. However the limited screen size on many Android handsets means that it can be important to control how these keyboards appear in our applications.

There are also a number of things that we can do to help the system select the most appropriate keyboard layout based on our desired **input type**. Here we will learn how to set soft keyboard appearances to two of three configurations according to our activity's needs and have the system select keyboard layout based on our input type.

Getting ready

We will need a way of calling up the soft keyboard, so start a new project in Eclipse and add three EditText widgets to the main layout.

How to do it...

1. We will return to our EditText in a moment. First open up the project's `AndroidManifest.xml` file.

2. Inside the `<activity>` tag include the following attribute:

```
<activity
    ...
    android:windowSoftInputMode="stateVisible|adjustResize">
```

3. Now return to our `main.xml` layout file and add to each EditText box the attributes shown here:

```
<EditText
    . . .
    android:id="@+id/edit_text1"
    android:inputType="text"
    android:layout_width="match_parent"
    android:layout_height="match_parent"
    android:layout_weight="1" />

<EditText
    . . .
    android:id="@+id/edit_text2"
    android:inputType="number"
    android:layout_width="match_parent"
    android:layout_height="match_parent"
    android:layout_weight="1" />

<EditText
    . . .
    android:id="@+id/edit_text3"
    android:inputType="phone"
    android:layout_width="match_parent"
    android:layout_height="match_parent"
    android:layout_weight="1" />
```

4. Run this application on a handset and test each of the edit boxes.

5. Having seen how each view behaves, change the `inputType` lines in the first and third `EditText`s to the following:

```
android:inputType="textCapSentences|textAutoCorrect"

android:inputType="textEmailAddress|textAutoComplete"
```

6. Run the project again, experimenting with each text view and observe the difference in behavior.

7. Return finally to the manifest and change the line that we entered earlier to:

```
android:windowSoftInputMode="stateVisible|adjustPan">
```

How it works...

There is quite a lot going on here. Firstly we handled the way that Android manages screen space when a soft keyboard is required. There are three possible modes for this behavior, one is applied automatically and we will deal with it at the end of this recipe.

The other two are controlled with the `windowSoftInputMode` attribute in the manifest. We applied two attributes here, separated by a pipe character (|). The first, `stateVisible`, simply ensures that the keyboard displays correctly when requested, it is the other two that control our keyboard display mode. As you probably saw during the exercise, when the input mode is set to `adjustPan`, the keyboard scrolls our activity to make room. On the other hand the setting `adjustResize` will cause our activity to resize to fit the remaining space:

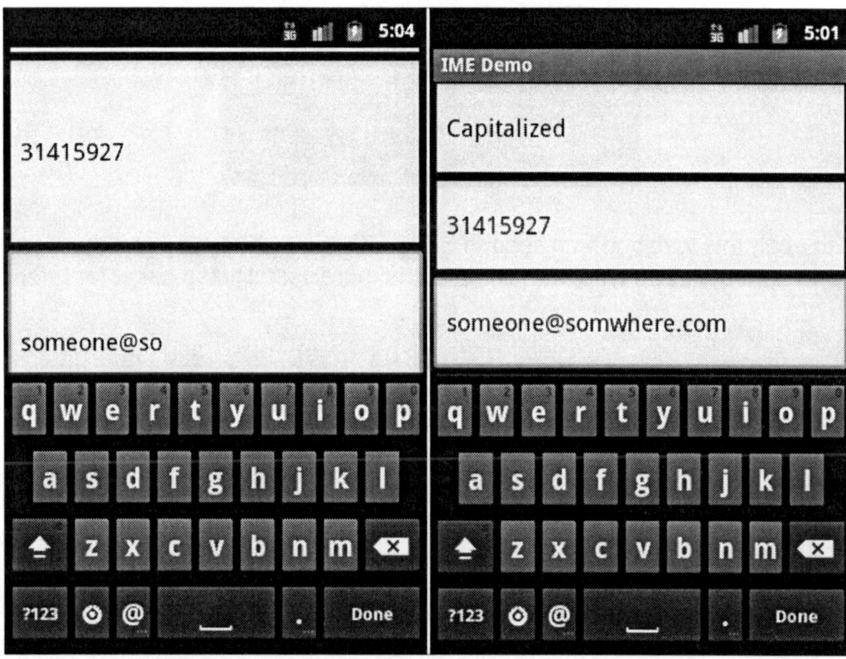

Having made sure that our application is making the best possible use of screen space, we can concentrate on the input itself, in particular the input type. There are five basic input types: `text`, `number`, `phone`, `date`, and `datetime`, and at their simplest they control the keyboard layout that is chosen by the system, for example, an `inputType` of `number` causes the numeric keyboard to display:

These basic types can be enhanced by any number of variations, separated by a pipe (**|**), and we used one or two of them here, for example the `textEmailAddress` caused the resultant keyboard to have a "@" character clearly displayed:

All we did to apply this variation was append `text` with `EmailAddress` and there are many other variations on the `text` type, with some of the more useful listed below for reference:

- `textCapCharacters`
- `textCapWords`
- `textCapSentences`
- `textAutoCorrect`
- `textAutoComplete`
- `textMultiLine`
- `textNoSuggestions`
- `textEmailAddress`
- `textPassword`
- `textVisiblePassword`

The `number` input type is the only other type that can take variations and these are limited to `numberDecimal` and `numberSigned`.

There's more...

We mentioned earlier that there was a third soft keyboard layout mode. This is the **exclude** mode and it is applied when the system considers that there is insufficient space to display *any* part of an activity, as is often the case when a screen is in landscape orientation. When this occurs, Android provides default buttons for the user to return to our activity or continue to the next field depending on how our activity is laid out.

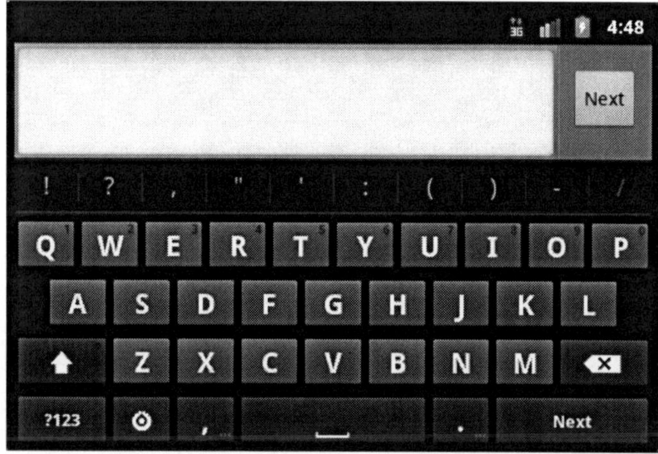

We have seen now how to take advantage of many of the features found on today's mobile devices such as touchscreens and motion sensors, and how to use the data they provide to develop applications that can be accessed in intuitive and imaginative ways. Now it is time for the information to flow the other way and to explore the different ways we can provide information to the user.

7

Notifying the User

In this chapter, we will cover the following topics:

- Displaying an alert dialog
- Displaying a progress dialog
- Customizing a dialog
- Making a Toast
- Notifying the user with the status bar
- Using the Notification.Builder class

Introduction

The efficient management of screen space is of utmost importance when it comes to programming mobile devices, and there are many occasions when an application will need to notify the user of some event or another. We could of course create text views or other widgets of our own, but as one would expect, Android provides several techniques specifically designed for this purpose.

Perhaps the most useful way to inform users is the **dialog box** and Android comes equipped with some flexible dialog objects that suit almost any purpose. It is also quite possible and not at all that difficult to create custom dialog boxes that match more precisely the appearance or function of our applications.

Android also provides a handy little pop-up that requires no dismissing called a **Toast**. We have encountered these in earlier chapters but here we will explore them in more detail, explaining how we can gain finer control over their positioning and even how to customize them.

As with most smartphones, Android handsets will display a small *notification* in the **status bar**, (most often to be found at the top of the screen) that contains iconic information usually regarding the general state of the device. We can take advantage of the notification bar and this is especially useful when our application is running in the background.

The notification bar also gives us access to to a **sliding drawer** tool, which drops down from the status bar as seen in the following screenshot:

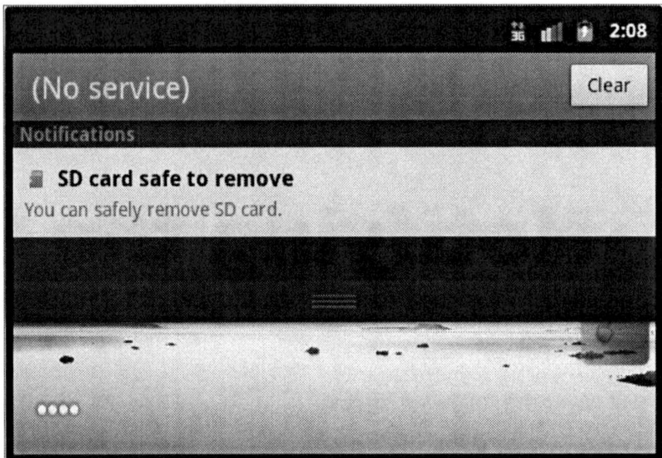

The sliding drawer mechanism permits us to notify a user with the bar and then provide further information with the sliding drawer but without taking the user away from the activity they are engaged in. From Android 3.0 (API level 11) onwards the **Notification.Builder** class has been available and this has considerably simplified this form of notification.

Displaying an alert dialog

AlertDialog is the most common form of built-in **dialog box** on the Android platform, and probably the most useful as well. It can be used to present the user with a variety of just activity-specific information in the form of a temporary window that partially obscures the screen, and more often than not allows the user to respond to that information by providing one or more clickable buttons or selectable items:

Here we will see how to generate such windows and how to provide them with components that will notify the user and also allow them to take an action.

Getting ready

Android makes the production of an **AlertDialog** box remarkably simple. To follow the instructions in this task simply start up a new Android project in Eclipse.

There is no need to add or identify any new widgets but you may want to remove the default text view the wizard includes in new projects.

How to do it...

1. We need some way to refer to our dialog box, so open the Java activity file and declare and assign the following static variable:

```
static final int DIALOG_ID = 0;
```

2. We will have our dialog appear as soon as our activity starts up so add the `showDialog()` call shown below, at the end of the `onCreate()` method:

```
@Override
    public void onCreate(Bundle state) {
        ...
        showDialog(DIALOG_ID);
    }
```

3. Now we need to handle the creation of the dialog, which is done generally with the `onCreateDialog()` method. Enter the following routine to create a simple dialog creator:

```
@Override
protected Dialog onCreateDialog(int id) {
AlertDialog.Builder builder = new AlertDialog.Builder(this);

builder.setTitle("An alert dialog")
        .setMessage("This dialog does nothing")
        .setPositiveButton("OK",
          new DialogInterface.OnClickListener() {
        public void onClick(DialogInterface dialog, int id) {

            // when the user clicks the OK button
            // do something

            dialog.dismiss();
        }
    });

    return builder.create();
}
```

4. That's all there is to creating an alert dialog. Run the code on your handset or an emulator to view the results.

How it works...

It will be obvious that the use of the final int `DIALOG_ID` is not strictly required for this code to run successfully and it is included simply to demonstrate how we might handle situations where we are employing more than one dialog box and need to distinguish between them: we could just as easily have conjured up our alert dialog using `showDialog(0)`, or even `showDialog()`.

We called up our dialog from within the `onCreate()` hook but this was for ease of demonstration and often we would have to be more specific about when we called this routine. Nevertheless the `showDialog()` method is the key to how dialogs are employed. The other side of this process is managed by another Activity member, the `onCreateDialog()` method and a specific **AlertDialog** descendant, the **Builder**. Dialog builders do what their name suggests and allow us to put together the components of each alert by stringing these parts together as we did here, stringing together a **title**, a **message** and a single **button**.

The Builder method's `setTitle()` and `setMessage()` were passed character sequences in this demonstration but the use of resource ID integers is also permitted and, for longer passages of text, provides a far tidier approach, for example `setMessage(R.id.my_message_string)`.

We included a button on our dialog box and caught it with a `DialogInterface.OnClickListener` which behaves as other listeners do. The use of a "positive" button requires some explanation as there are also `setNegativeButton()` and `setNeutralButton()` methods that allow us up to three buttons per alert dialog. These names however are somewhat arbitrary and there is no reason, other than a certain semantic clarity, to have them behave as their names suggest.

There's more...

The dialog box we created here was rather simple and there are a number of other things we could have done to enhance it, such as include an icon, supply a list of selectable items as our dialog content, or respond specifically to dialog dismissals and cancellations.

Adding an icon to an alert dialog

Including an icon within our alert dialog is simply a matter of adding another setter to the builder chain. To see this in action add the following line to our builder:

```
setIcon(R.drawable.icon)
```

Here we have used the default application icon but would more usually design one of our own that was specific to our purpose.

Employing lists in dialogs

Alert dialogs are often used to present the user with a selectable list of items and this is achieved with another method, `setItems()` which takes a **list** and a **listener**. To create such a dialog with the example here insert the following code into our `onCreateDialog()` callback.

```
builder.setItems(items, new DialogInterface.OnClickListener() {
    public void onClick(DialogInterface dialog, int item) {
    }
});
```

Here **items** can be either a resource int ID or a character sequence such as the following:

```
final CharSequence[] items =
    { "Bath", "Birmingham", "Bradford", "Brighton" };
```

There are often situations where we might like our user to be able to select more than one item and Android allows the use of multiple choice selections with the `setMultiChoiceItems()` method, which then includes **check boxes** beside each item. Furthermore, the system will retain information regarding which items were selected as long as the calling activity is active.

There is also a `setSingleChoiceItems()` method which produces radio buttons by each item and is also managed by the system.

Listening for dialog cancellations and dismissals

It is easy to imagine situations where we would need listeners to tell us more than just which button or item had been selected and Android provides methods that listen for the actual **cancellation** or **dismissal** of a dialog. This can be done with the `onDialogCancelled()` and `onDialogDismissed()` callback methods.

See also

To see how to customize an alert dialog see the recipe *Customizing a dialog* later in this chapter.

For more on lists and list views, refer to the recipe *Using ListViews and ListAdapters* in *Chapter 2, Layouts*.

Displaying a progress dialog

No matter how hard we try or how fast a particular hardware might be, there will inevitably be times when the user is required to wait for certain events to complete, such as retrieving a large file, and it will come as no surprise to learn that Android provides **progress dialogs** and **progress bars** to keep the user informed of when and how long they will be required to wait.

Getting ready

Once again we will be calling up our dialog the moment our application begins to run just as we did with the alert dialog in the previous task and, in fact, the **ProgressDialog** descends directly from the **AlertDialog** and in its simplest form is even easier to render.

Start up a new project in Eclipse and open up the Java activity source.

How to do it...

1. A non-specific progress alert can be produced with a single line. Add the `ProgressDialog.show()` command to the `onCreate()` method as follows:

```java
@Override
public void onCreate(Bundle state) {
   super.onCreate(state);
   setContentView(R.layout.main);

   ProgressDialog.show(this, "title (normally omitted)",
      "doing something - please wait...", true);
}
```

2. Run the project on your handset or an emulator to see what this code does and then return to this task:

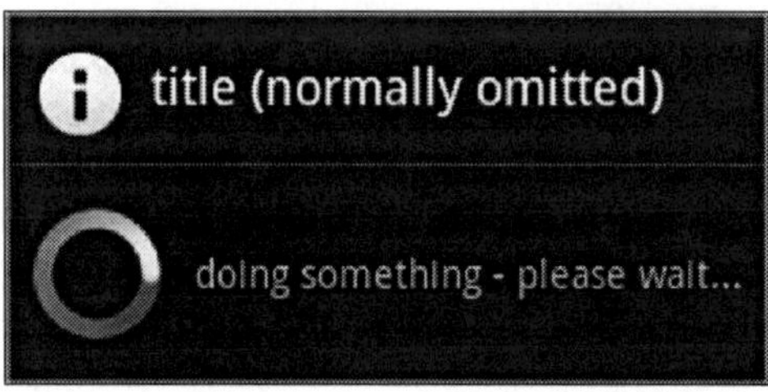

3. For a granular progress bar replace the final line of the previous code snippet with the following:

```
ProgressDialog dialog = new ProgressDialog(this);

dialog.setProgressStyle(ProgressDialog.STYLE_HORIZONTAL);
dialog.setMessage("doing something...");
dialog.setCancelable(true);

dialog.show();
```

4. Again, run the project to view the output:

5. Finally add the following lines beneath the `dialog.show()` call:

```
dialog.setProgress(41);
dialog.incrementProgressBy(1);
```

6. The progress bar will now appear like the one seen here:

How it works...

There are really two kinds of progress dialog boxes that we have created here, a **spinner** for when we do not know how long a task will take and a **horizontal bar** for when we do and wish to indicate this to the user. We made this switch in the second half of this exercise with the `setProgressStyle(ProgressDialog.STYLE_HORIZONTAL)` instruction and also demonstrated a slightly neater way to set the box's other attributes such as the message. The `setCancelable(true)` command allows the user to escape the process with the *BACK* key and is generally preferable to blocking this action with `setCancelable(false)`.

The `ProgressDialog.show()` method takes three arguments, the context (usually the owning activity), the character sequence to be displayed, and a Boolean value controlling whether the dialog can be canceled.

When setting the actual value of a progress bar, most of the code would be tied up with whatever action was being carried out but the two methods, `setProgress()` and `incrementProgressBy()`, are all we need to reflect this behavior on the dialog.

There's more...

It is often very useful to be able to hide a dialog without dismissing or canceling it, and dialogs can be hidden from view like this with the `Dialog.hide()` command.

Another useful tool is the ability to send the user a message upon cancellation and this can be achieved with the `setCancelMessage("a message")` call.

Customizing a dialog

The Android dialogs that we have used so far all have a similar appearance to them which may not match the specific look of our activities. Fortunately we can create customized dialogs in XML and maintain a consistent feel to our applications.

Getting ready

Once a custom dialog has been defined it can be summoned in exactly the same way as any other dialog, so either start up a new project or load any of those we have used in this chapter thus far.

How to do it...

1. We define our customized dialog box with an XML layout. Begin by creating a new Android XML file in the `res/layout` folder, alongside `main.xml` called `my_custom_dialog.xml` or some such name.

2. We only need one view to demonstrate how to customize a dialog box. Add the **TextView** below to a vertical **LinearLayout**:

```xml
<LinearLayout
    xmlns:android="http://schemas.android.com/apk/res/android"
    android:layout_width="match_parent"
    android:layout_height="match_parent"
    android:orientation="vertical"
    android:padding="6dip">
    <TextView
        android:layout_width="match_parent"
        android:layout_height="match_parent"
        android:background="#0F0"
        android:textColor="#000"
        android:textSize="20sp"
        android:typeface="serif"
        android:text="This dialog has some custom settings."
        android:padding="6dip" />
</LinearLayout>
```

3. Now open up the Java source code for the activity and complete the `onCreate()` method like so:

```java
@Override
public void onCreate(Bundle state) {
    super.onCreate(state);
    setContentView(R.layout.main);

    Dialog dialog = new Dialog(this);

    dialog.setContentView(R.layout.my_dialog);
    dialog.setTitle("My custom dialog");

    dialog.show();
}
```

4. Run this code on an emulator or handset to observe our applied XML:

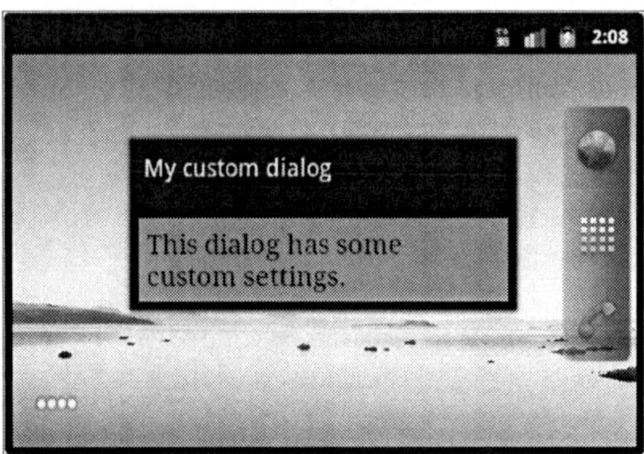

How it works...

Constructing a custom dialog is remarkably simple. All the skills acquired when we learned how to design **activity layouts** can be applied to our dialog design. And any view or widget that can be included in a normal layout can be added to our custom dialogs. Furthermore, once we have constructed our dialog we can treat it exactly as if it were a system-built one. All we had to do to set this up was reference the XML from Java with `Dialog.setContentView(int resource ID)` in a very familiar fashion.

We also used `Dialog.setTitle()` and `Dialog.show()` but any of the Dialog members encountered in this chapter can be applied.

> It is worth noting that if the method `setTitle()` is not called then an empty space will appear at the top of the box. If you want to create a custom dialog with no title at all you will need to customize an **AlertDialog** rather than the **Dialog** object.

See also

To learn how to customize other types of widget see the recipe *Creating a custom component* in *Chapter 3, Widgets*.

Making a Toast

Small rectangular pop-up notifications known as **Toasts** are by far the simplest way to inform a user of an application event, such as the completion of a download. Toasts are a fantastic way to notify a user of an event that he or she need not respond to, as Toasts dismiss themselves, do not interrupt any processes, or shift application or processor focus.

We have encountered Toasts already in this book simply because they are so easy to implement, but now it is time to take a closer look.

Getting ready

Toasts are great mainly because they can be implemented in a single line of code. Here however, we will deconstruct the process somewhat, to show the inner workings in greater detail. Start up a new Android project in Eclipse and make your way to the main Java activity code.

How to do it...

1. Within the `onCreate()` method and immediately following the `setContentView(R.layout.main)` call, add these declarations and assignments:

   ```
   Context context = this;
   CharSequence chrSeq = "this is a toast";
   int time = Toast.LENGTH_LONG;
   ```

2. Following this, add this line to call up our **Toast**:

   ```
   Toast toast = Toast.makeText(context, chrSeq, time).show();
   ```

3. Compile and run this code on an emulator or handset. The Toast will appear near the bottom of the screen for a second.

4. Now, replace the line we just added with the three shown here:

   ```
   Toast toast = Toast.makeText(context, chrSeq, time);
   toast.setGravity(Gravity.TOP | Gravity.RIGHT, 0, 30);
   toast.show();
   ```

5. Finally, compile and run the code again. This time we will see the Toast appear near to the upper right-hand side of the screen.

How it works...

There should be nothing unfamiliar in the three parameters taken by the `Toast.makeText()` method that we used here. The **context** is simply the calling component, which here is our single activity. We used **this** but in less trivial applications we would probably find ourselves using `getApplicationContext()` instead. The use of a character sequence is obvious but the `makeText()` method is overloaded so that a **resource ID** would be equally permitted. The `time` (int) argument refers, quite naturally, to the toast's duration on the screen. `LENGTH_LONG` and `LENGTH_SHORT` are provided for us and represent durations of 1000 and 500 milliseconds respectively, but it is very easy to set these to user defined values if it suits the need of our application better.

Nothing of what we did in this task was any different from the way we have made toasts before, using a single line of code, until we reached the `Toast.setGravity()` method which allows us to not only chain together relative screen constants such as `Gravity.TOP` and `Gravity.RIGHT` with the pipe character (**|**) but also to take finer control by including horizontal and vertical offsets (in pixels) with the second and third (int) parameters.

There's more...

Just like many other Android widgets and dialogs, it is also possible to create custom Toasts to suit the needs of our applications more thoroughly.

Customizing Toasts

Customizing a Toast pop-up is managed in a similar fashion to the way we customized alert dialogs earlier in the chapter by defining our new view group in XML. For example, create the following file inside the `res/layout` folder and call it `my_toast.xml`:

```xml
<LinearLayout
    xmlns:android="http://schemas.android.com/apk/res/android"
        android:id="@+id/toast_layout"
        android:orientation="horizontal"
        android:layout_width="match_parent"
        android:layout_height="match_parent" >

    <TextView android:id="@+id/text_view"
        android:layout_width="wrap_content"
        android:layout_height="match_parent" />

    <ImageView android:id="@+id/image_view"
        android:layout_width="wrap_content"
        android:layout_height="match_parent" />

</LinearLayout>
```

There is slightly more to the way we call up a custom toast than there is with a dialog, and we need to make use of the **LayoutInflater** object.

```
LayoutInflater inflater = getLayoutInflater();
View view =
  inflater.inflate(R.layout.my_toast,
    (ViewGroup) findViewById(R.id.toast_layout));
```

The rest of the code required is what we might imagine and should be familiar with, probably along the lines of the following snippet:

```
ImageView image = (ImageView) view.findViewById(R.id.image_view);
image.setImageResource(R.drawable.icon);
TextView text = (TextView) view.findViewById(R.id.text_view);
text.setText("this is a custom toast view");

Toast toast = new Toast(this);
toast.setGravity(Gravity.TOP, 0, 40);
toast.setView(view);
toast.setDuration(Toast.LENGTH_LONG);
toast.show();
```

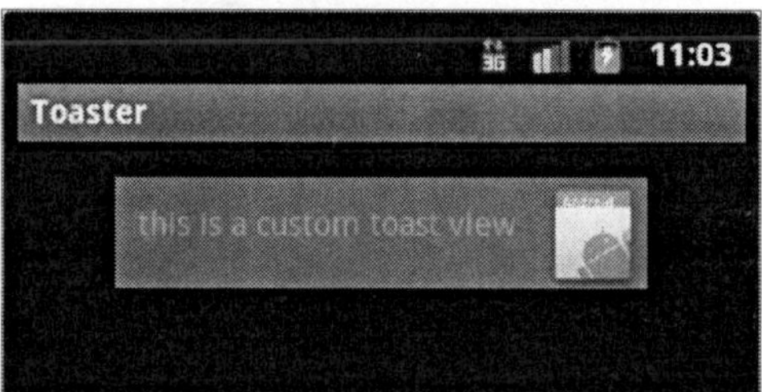

See also

For information on how to apply gravity to other screen components, such as layouts, see the recipe *Applying gravity and weight* in *Chapter 2, Layouts*.

Notifying the user with the status bar

Perhaps the least intrusive way of notifying a user is with the **status bar**. This **notification area** allows us to display an icon, along with a scrolling 'ticker' style message which, if responded to with a long click, opens a 'sliding drawer' window that provides more message space and the opportunity for the user to generate some resultant action, usually the firing of an **Intent** and the starting of an **Activity**.

Both **Activities** and **Services** are able to produce status bar notifications. More often than not, we would use this from within a Service, that is, when our application is running in the background. Here for the sake of brevity we will call our notification from the main activity as the principles remain the same and this approach allows us to concentrate on how status bars work without having to worry about setting up extra components.

Getting ready

We will be doing all the work here from within the main Java activity but we will also need an icon. Create a 24 bit, transparent, PNG image that is 24 pixels wide and 38 pixels high. Place any graphic you like inside but ensure the top seven, and bottom seven rows are left transparent.

Now start up a new Android project in Eclipse and place the icon we just created in the `res/drawable-hdpi` folder and call it `status_bar_icon.png`.

How to do it...

1. Open the project's main Java source and, following the `setContentView()` call in the `onCreate()` method, and create and assign the variables as follows:

```
final int NOTIFICATION_ID = 0;
int icon = R.drawable.status_bar_icon;
CharSequence tickerText = "this is the ticker text";
Notification note =
   new Notification(icon,
      tickerText, System.currentTimeMillis());
```

2. To connect to the system's built-in notification manager insert the following line, after the code we just entered:

```
NotificationManager manager =
   (NotificationManager)
      getSystemService(Context.NOTIFICATION_SERVICE);
```

3. We need to set up the details of our notification now so continue the code with:

```
Context context = getApplicationContext();
Intent intent = new Intent(context, SomeActivity.class);
PendingIntent contentIntent =
   PendingIntent.getActivity(this, 0, intent, 0);
```

4. The class `SomeActivity` does not yet exist, so we need to create it. A quick and simple way to do this is to take advantage of Eclipse's *quick fix* function by hovering over the text `SomeActivity.class`, which the IDE will have identified as an error. Then simply select **Create class 'SomeActivity'** from the list of fixes and then click the **Finish** button on the subsequent dialog:

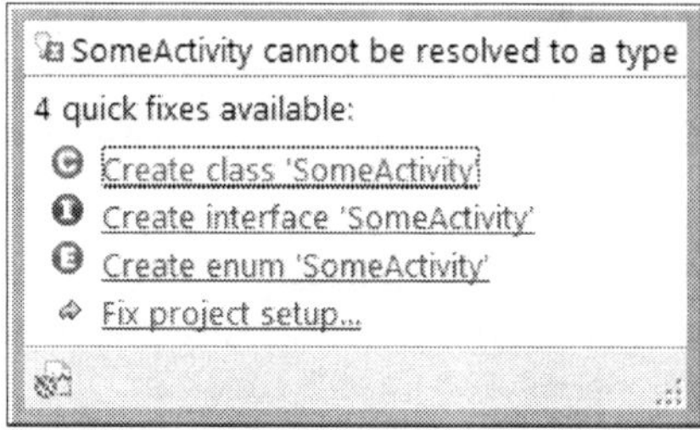

5. Finally we want the **NotificationManager** to trigger our notification. Enter the last two lines of code shown here:

```
note.setLatestEventInfo(context,
   "a notification", "this is the content text", contentIntent);
manager.notify(NOTIFICATION_ID, note);
```

6. Run the project on a handset or emulator. The notification will appear along with the ticker message:

7. A long press on the icon will enable the sliding drawer containing our other elements to be dragged downwards:

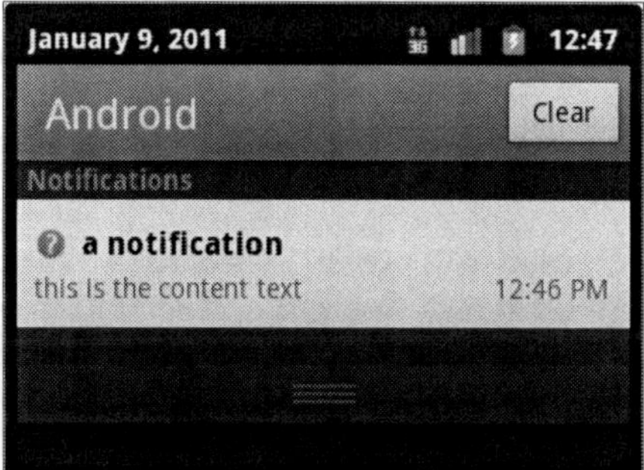

How it works...

First we created a new **Notification** with three arguments: a resource pointer to our icon, our ticker text, and the time when we wish the notification to take place with `System.currentTimeMillis()` simply meaning 'now'. The declaration of the int `NOTIFICATION_ID` does not come up again until later but that is how we would refer to notifications when we have more than one.

This brings us onto the **NotificationManager**, which is the key class here and manages all system notifications. Notification managers are simple to set up; we can call on `Context.getSystemService()` as we have before but using the string constant `NOTIFICATION_SERVICE`.

We created an Intent that started an Activity that did nothing here but would, in most applications, represent the point of the notification and we also used **PendingIntent** which is really just a way of combining Contexts and Intents together.

There's more...

For times when the user is not actually using the handset, we can set it to beep or vibrate when the notification is called.

Adding a sound to a notification

To include the user's default notification sound with our notification use:

```
note.defaults |= Notification.DEFAULT_SOUND;
```

If you want to provide your own sound file then replace this line with:

```
note.sound =
  Uri.parse(
    Environment.getExternalStorageDirectory() + "/my_note.mp3"
  );
```

Adding a flashing light to a notification

If the user's device has any LED lights, then it is equally simple to cause these to flash by including the following line:

```
note.defaults |= Notification.DEFAULT_LIGHTS;
```

Custom light settings can be created with `note.ledARGB = long` (ARGB color value), `note.ledOnMS = long` (light on in ms), and `note.ledOffMS = long` (light off in ms), followed by `note.flags |= Notification.FLAG_SHOW_LIGHTS`.

Adding a vibration to a notification

Vibrations are just as easy to include in a notification and `notification.defaults |= Notification.DEFAULT_VIBRATE;` will do this.

See also

To learn more on designing compliant icons see the recipe *Designing Android compliant menu icons* in *Chapter 4, Menus*.

For programming status bar notification in applications targeting Android 3.0 (API level 11) and above, see the next recipe *Using the Notification.Builder* class.

Using the Notifcation.Builder class

For applications targeting API level 11 (Android 3.0) and above, developers can take advantage of the **Notification.Builder** class, which makes the production of notifications far simpler than with earlier versions and also provides some extra functionality such as changing the size of the associated icon.

Here we will reproduce the status bar notification from the previous recipe for the Android 3.0 Honeycomb status bar.

Getting ready

Start up a new Android project in Eclipse, making sure that it is built against **API level 11** or greater.

How to do it...

1. In the `onCreate()` method, underneath the `setContentView()` statement add the following declarations:

    ```java
    final int NOTIFICATION_ID = 0;
    NotificationManager manager =
        (NotificationManager) getSystemService(NOTIFICATION_SERVICE);
    ```

2. Beneath this set up a `Notification.Builder`, as follows:

    ```java
    Notification.Builder builder = new Notification.Builder(this);
    builder.setSmallIcon(R.drawable.icon);
    builder.setContentText("This is the content text");
    ```

3. Underneath that, add this line to call the notification:

    ```java
    manager.notify(NOTIFICATION_ID, builder.getNotification());
    ```

4. Now run the code on a handset or emulator running Android 3.0 or higher to view the notification:

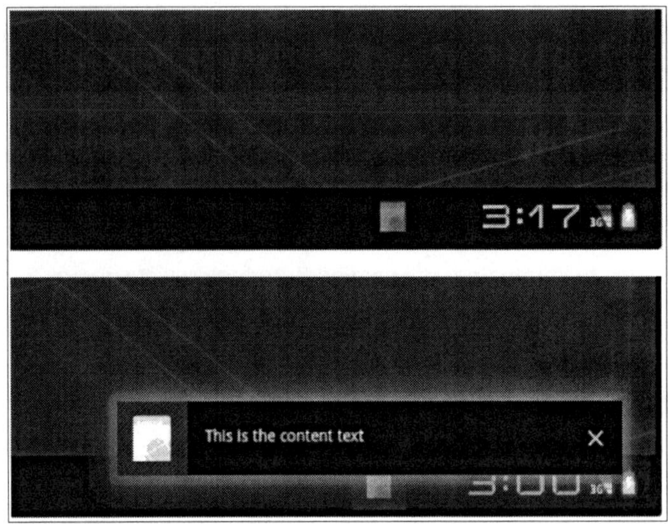

Note that `Notification.Builder` is not available to applications using the Android compatibility package.

How it works...

Using a Notification.Builder is similar to using the Notification class that is used in Android versions prior to 3.0 in that it is initialized with the use of a NotificationManager and then called from the Notification.Manager's `notify()` method. However, in this example we passed the output of the builder's `getNotification()` method rather than the Notification itself.

Here only the icon and the content text were set but but the notification builder has plenty of other useful methods, for example there is also a `setLargeIcon()` method that is great for thumbnail images.

Other handy Builder methods include `setTicker(character sequence)` for defining the text that appears when the notification icon first appears and `setWhen(long)`, which controls the moment the alert took place.

The `Notification.Builder` class also makes associating and defining flashing lights, sounds, and vibrations simpler with `setLights (int ARGB, int onMs, int offMs)`, `setSound (Uri)`, and `setVibrate (long[])`.

Having covered user input and output in this and the previous chapter it is time to include a little glamour in our applications by looking at Android graphics and animation.

8
Graphics and Animation

In this chapter, we will cover the following topics:

- Adding graphics to the ImageView class
- Rotating an image with a matrix
- Using ShapeDrawable and Paint
- Drawing with a Canvas
- Using tween animations
- Animating with Honeycomb APIs
- Creating stop frame animations
- Working with OpenGL

Introduction

Android offers a variety of tools that allow us to produce graphic images and animations. From simple **color and shape control** and **transitional animations** to full blown **3D rendering**, this wide range of functionality means that we can produce graphics that best suit the needs of our applications and the demands of our target devices.

Android has a powerful **2D graphics** library and unless an application requires fast, responsive animations, it is well worth first considering the **android.graphics.drawable** and the **android.view.animation** packages.

Generally speaking, when dealing with the `android.graphics.drawable` package we use the abstract class **Drawable**, or rather we use extensions of it such as **BitmapDrawable**, **AnimationDrawable**, or **ShapeDrawable**.

The simplest way to produce 2D graphics is to *draw* them directly onto a view (generally an **ImageView**). This way, the system's view hierarchy takes care of displaying our graphics.

For greater control, Android provides the **BitmapFactory** class, which can generate **Bitmaps** dynamically from a variety of sources, and the **Matrix** object for applying transformations.

In situations when we want more control over an image we can make use of the **Canvas** class, which allows us to call our **Drawable** subclasses' `draw()` method directly.

Another powerful yet simple set of tools that we can use are provided by the `android.view.animation` package which, amongst other things, allows us to produce inbetweening (**tweening**) animations. We can also create **stop frame animations** using individual bitmaps as frames.

A whole new animation package was introduced with the release of Android 3.0 (API level 11) that enables the animation of objects and properties other than views, and which is far simpler and quite a bit more powerful than its view-based counterpart.

The production of high level 3D graphics animations is even possible with Android although this is done through the **OpenGL** graphics library.

Adding graphics to the ImageView class

It is quite possible to draw a graphic onto any view, by setting its background property, but the **ImageView** subclass is designed for this purpose and here we will see two different ways of setting an ImageView's content with a graphic.

Getting ready

We are going to use **ImageViews** to display two images here but we will use the built-in icon PNG file for one of them. For the other, select any PNG image that you wish and, once you have started up a new Android project in Eclipse, save it in any of the `res/drawable` folders as `my_drawable_image.png`.

How to do it...

1. Eclipse should have automatically generated a TextView in `main.xml`, and if so provide it with the following `android:id`:

    ```
    android:id="@+id/text_view"
    ```

2. Beneath this TextView add the following two **ImageViews**:

    ```
    <ImageView
        android:src="@drawable/icon"
        android:tint="#5f00"
    ```

```
    android:layout_width="wrap_content"
    android:layout_height="wrap_content" />
<ImageView
    android:id="@+id/my_resource_image"
    android:layout_width="wrap_content"
    android:layout_height="wrap_content" />
```

3. View this using the **Graphical Layout** tab. The TextView and the icon should be visible:

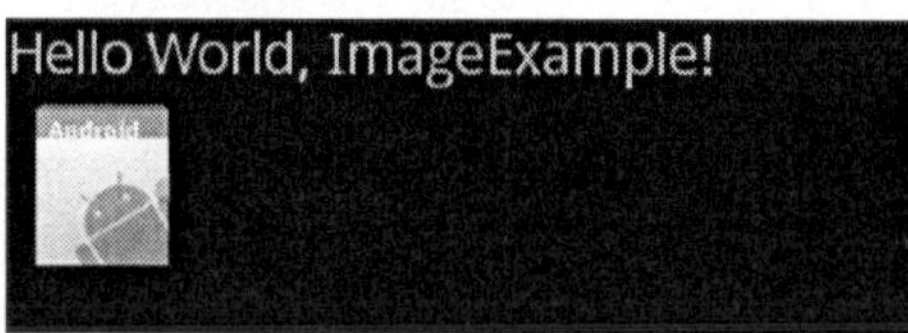

4. From the main Java activity, associate the TextView from the previous steps by adding this line after the `setContentView(R.layout.main);` line in the `onCreate()` method:

```
TextView textView = (TextView) findViewById(R.id.text_view);
```

5. Do the same with the image view and set the image resource as seen here:

```
ImageView imageView =
    (ImageView) findViewById(R.id.my_resource_image);
imageView.setImageResource(R.drawable.my_drawable_image);
```

6. Finally, set the text box to display the default **scale type**, like so:

```
textView.setText(imageView.getScaleType().toString());
```

7. Now run the project on a handset or an emulator to view both the images:

How it works...

As this has been quite an easy exercise we have actually been able to combine two tasks: how to set an **ImageView's** content from XML and how to do this with Java, and by now this should not be an unfamiliar distinction.

The use of `android:src` to set the graphical content of the top image view is a very straightforward way to do this, provided we do not wish to change the image at any point. If we had wanted to do this, we could have used the `setImageResource()` method, which is the Java equivalent of `android:src`, to dynamically change the image any number of times.

As this was such a simple task we added a line to display the enum `ImageView.ScaleType`, which is a very handy way to control how an image will be laid out within a view. This can be done with `ImageView.setScaleType(ImageView.ScaleType)`, where `ScaleType` is a string constant with the following possible values:

Value	Explanation
CENTER	Centers the image but does not scale it.
CENTER_CROP	Scales the image without changing the aspect ratio, cropping it if it's larger than the view.
CENTER_INSIDE	Scales the image to fit inside the view without changing the aspect ratio. If the image is smaller than the view, no scaling takes place.
FIT_CENTER	Centers the image and scales it to fit along at least one axis.
FIT_END	Scales and aligns the image to the bottom right of the view.
FIT_START	Scales and aligns the image to the top left of the view.
FIT_XY	Scales the image to fit exactly within the view with respect to the original aspect ratio.
FIT_MATRIX	Scales the image according to its matrix.

Our use of `ImageView.setImageResource()` is often not the best way to produce graphics in a view as it uses the UI thread and can cause an application to stutter. Very often it is preferable to define our image as a **Bitmap** or a **Drawable** and we will cover how to do this in the next few recipes. Nevertheless, for static graphics the `setImageResource()` method is quite adequate.

Although Android can manage BMP, PNG, JPG and GIF file formats, the system far prefers PNG images to the other three and, when size is an issue, JPG is preferable to BMP or GIF.

There's more...

The ability to control scaling type is not the only useful formatting tool available to the images within our **ImageViews**. We can also set constraints on their size and control how aspect ratio is managed.

Setting an image's maximum dimensions

Often we do not want an image to take up more than a certain amount of screen space. This can be easily achieved with the **ImageView** methods `setMaxHeight(int)` and `setMaxWidth(int)`. Both these methods expect their single argument to be in pixels.

 We can achieve precisely the same effect from within XML if we want with `android:maxWidth` and `android:maxHeight`.

Controlling an image's aspect ratio

To force an image to be displayed with its original aspect ratio, use `setAdjustViewBounds(true)` or `android:adjustViewBounds="true"` from XML.

Naturally, using `false` will switch this option off.

See also

To see how to use ImageViews in custom widgets see the recipe *Creating a custom component* in *Chapter 3, Widgets*.

For an example of applying an ImageView to a Google map refer to the recipe *Overlaying a map* in *Chapter 11, GPS, Locations, and Maps*

Rotating an image with a matrix

The methods applied in the previous recipe, although simple to apply, are restricted. Ideally we would like to take control of a bitmap directly so that we can impose more sophisticated transformations.

In this recipe we will create a bitmap with a **BitmapFactory** and rotate it with a **Matrix**. Both these objects belong to the **android.graphics** package.

Getting ready

This recipe is quite similar to the preceding one. If you wish, you can edit it to match what you find here or simply start a new project in eclipse. Either way we will need an image file stored in any of the `res/drawable` folders called `my_image.png`.

How to do it...

1. We do not need the TextView included by the wizard, so remove this and provide the layout in `main.xml` with the single ImageView as follows:

```xml
<?xml version="1.0" encoding="utf-8"?>
<LinearLayout
    xmlns:android="http://schemas.android.com/apk/res/android"
    android:orientation="vertical"
    android:layout_width="match_parent"
    android:layout_height="match_parent">

    <ImageView
        android:id="@+id/my_image"
        android:layout_width="wrap_content"
        android:layout_height="wrap_content" />

</LinearLayout>
```

2. Inside the Java activity source complete the `onCreate()` method so that it matches the code here:

```java
@Override
public void onCreate(Bundle state) {
    super.onCreate(state);
    setContentView(R.layout.main);

    ImageView imageView =
        (ImageView) findViewById(R.id.my_image);

    Bitmap bmp =
        BitmapFactory.decodeResource(getResources(),
            R.drawable.my_image);
    Matrix matrix = new Matrix();

    matrix.setRotate(60);
    bmp =
        Bitmap.createBitmap(bmp, 0, 0, bmp.getWidth(),
            bmp.getHeight(), matrix, false);
    imageView.setImageBitmap(bmp);
}
```

3. That's all there is to it. Run the project on a handset or in an emulator to view the rotated bitmap.

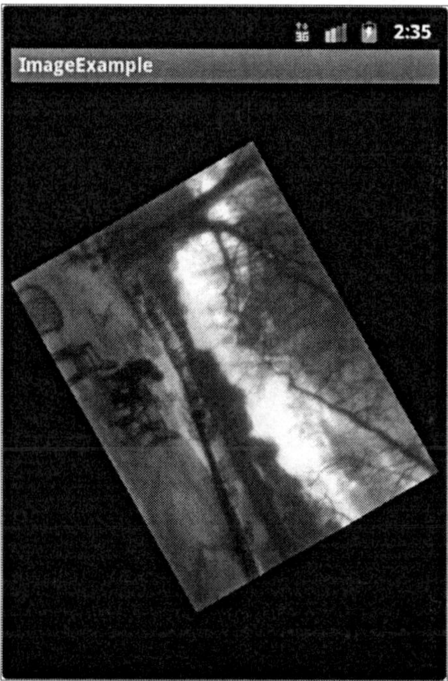

How it works...

Despite being a relatively short exercise there is actually quite a lot going on here. However, everything other than the **BitmapFactory** and the **Matrix** should be familiar to you by now.

We first used the **BitmapFactory** to create the bitmap `bmp`, using its `decodeResource(Resources, int)` method where `getResources()` returns the **Resources** object of the application package and the `int` refers to our image's ID that we declared in the XML. Once established this way, we used `Bitmap.createBitmap()` to rotate the image according to our **Matrix**. The `createBitmap()` method takes seven arguments:

- Bitmap—the bitmap in question
- int—x offset (in pixels)
- int—y offset (in pixels)
- int—image width (in pixels)
- int—image height (in pixels)
- Matrix—transformation matrix
- Boolean—true if the source image is to be filtered

The **Matrix** object is far more sophisticated than the simple `setRotate()` method that we used here suggests. It is in fact a three by three transformation vector whose values can be set directly with `Matrix.setValues(float[])` or read with `getValues(float[])`.

There's more...

It is not always necessary to resort to adjusting the elements of our matrix individually if we want to perform simple transformations such as **scaling** and **skewing,** as the Matrix object provides similar methods to `setRotate()`. Try using any of the following lines instead of `matrix.setRotate()` in the previous code:

```
matrix.setSkew(0.5f, 0.1f);

matrix.setScale(1.1f, 0.9f);

matrix.setTranslate(30, 50);
```

To apply more than one transformation replace the `set` prefix of the command with `post`, for example:

```
matrix.setRotate(60);
matrix.postSkew(0.5f, 0.1f);
```

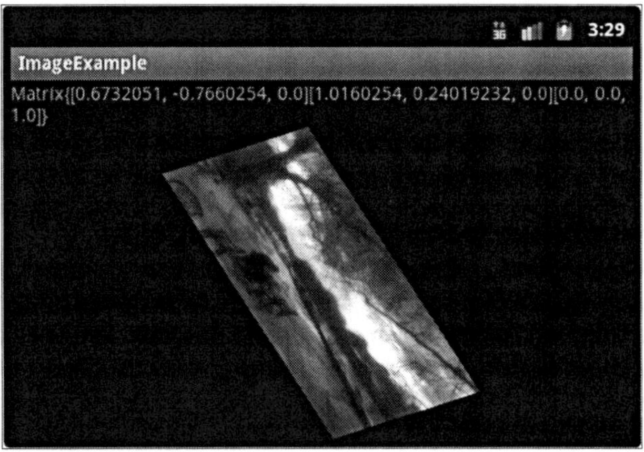

The readout of the Matrix's values in the screenshot here was achieved with `Matrix.toString()`.

See also

For more information on including images see the recipe *Adding graphics to the ImageView* class earlier in this chapter.

To rotate components using a different technique refer to the *Using tween animations* recipe later in this chapter.

For animation methods in Android 3.0 and higher there is a recipe later in this chapter called *Animations for Honeycomb APIs*.

Using ShapeDrawable and Paint

Another useful extension of the **Drawable** class is the **ShapeDrawable**, which allows us to define basic geometrical shapes such as arcs, ovals, and rounded rectangles. **ShapeDrawables** are often used alongside the **Paint** class which provides a way of applying drawing styles. A common way to achieve this is by extending the View class and overriding its `onDraw()` callback.

Getting ready

Everything that is done in this task is generated by the system and there is no need to import any graphic file. Simply start a new Android project in Eclipse and open the Java editor on the Activity file.

How to do it...

1. Within our main Activity, create a new inner class that extends View as follows:

    ```java
    public class MyShape extends View {
        private final ShapeDrawable mShape;

    }
    ```

2. Give the new class the constructor shown here:

    ```java
    public MyShape(Context context) {
        super(context);

        Paint paint = new Paint();
        paint.setARGB(255, 255, 255, 0);
        paint.setStyle(Paint.Style.STROKE);
        paint.setStrokeWidth(4.0f);

        mShape = new ShapeDrawable(new ArcShape(0, 180));
        mShape.getPaint().set(paint);
        mShape.setBounds(0, 0, 300, 200);
    }
    ```

3. Override its `onDraw()` method as follows:

    ```java
    @Override
    protected void onDraw(Canvas canvas) {
    ```

```
        mShape.draw(canvas);
    }
```

4. Now change the activity's `onCreate()` method so that it inflates our new view rather than `main.xml`:

```
@Override
public void onCreate(Bundle state) {
    super.onCreate(state);
    setContentView(new MyShape(this));
}
```

5. Run the project on a handset or emulator to view the ShapeDrawable:

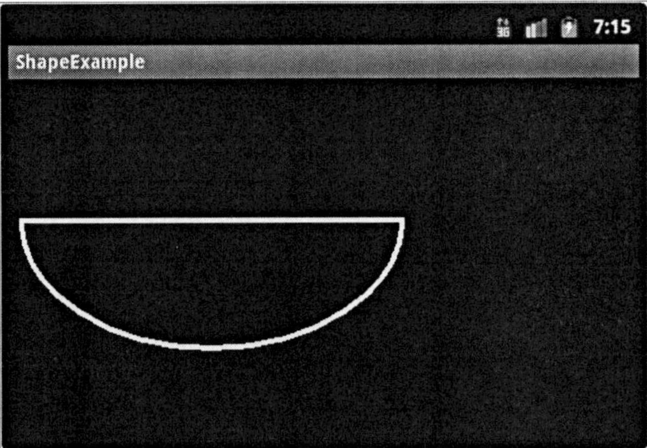

How it works...

When we set up our new class we created a **Paint** object to control the look of our drawable. We only set color, style, and stroke-width here, but Paint has many more public methods that simplify the styling of our shapes. The `setARGB()` method is straightforward enough and is a handy way to control color through `alpha`, `red`, `green`, and `blue` arguments.

> We used `setARGB()` here to control color because it provides a lot of flexibility but if we'd been feeling lazy we could have just used `paint.setColor(Color.YELLOW)`.

We set the style to STROKE but we could have used FILL or FILL_AND_STROKE if we'd preferred.

There are three shapes available to the ShapeDrawable class: **ArcShape**, **RoundRectShape**, and **OvalShape**. The arc that we drew here is defined by two floats representing the start angle and the angle of sweep (both in degrees). The rounded rectangle takes arrays of floats to define the inner and outer radii of each corner and can also take another inner rectangle to create a ring shape. The oval shape draws an ellipse and its proportions are dependent on the size and proportions of the view containing it.

Applying our paint object to our drawable was a simple matter and the `setBounds()` method requires four integer values representing the left, top, right, and bottom edges of the bounding rectangle. It is also possible to define these rectangles as **Rect** objects and we could have defined one with something like `myRect = new Rect(0,0,300,200)` and then `mShape.setBounds(myRect)`.

See also

We briefly introduced a new object here with **Canvas** which is a class for handling all our *drawing* calls. We will cover Canvases more thoroughly in the next recipe but it was provided automatically here by our custom View's `onDraw()` method and passed to our Drawable's `draw()` method.

Drawing with a Canvas

We briefly introduced the **Canvas** class in the previous recipe, using it to draw a shape. Objects that have an `onDraw()` callback, like Views, provide one for us, but the real power of the Canvas is that it gives us control over all our `draw()` calls so that we can change our graphics in real time.

Here we will use a Canvas, along with a Paint object to produce a graphic that will follow the user's finger as it moves across a touch screen.

Getting ready

This task is similar to the previous one. If you like, load it up and edit it according to what you find here. Otherwise start up a new project from scratch in Eclipse.

If you have not yet come across touch listeners, you might want to take a quick look at the recipes in *Chapter 6, Detecting User Activity* first as they are explained in more detail there.

How to do it...

1. As before we are going to set a custom view of our own as the activity content view, so as to make it immediately visible when the application runs. Edit the `onCreate()` method in the Java source code to match what you see here:

```java
@Override
public void onCreate(Bundle state) {
   super.onCreate(state);
   setContentView(new MyShape(this));

}
```

2. Now we need to define our new class. Make it extend **View** as before but also provide the **OnTouchListener** interface and the fields seen here:

```java
public class MyShape extends View implements OnTouchListener {
   float y;
   float x;
   Paint paint = new Paint();

}
```

3. Add this constructor to the `MyShape` class:

```java
public MyShape(Context context) {
   super(context);

   paint.setColor(Color.YELLOW);
   paint.setStyle(Paint.Style.STROKE);
   paint.setStrokeWidth(4.0f);
   paint.setAntiAlias(true)

   this.setOnTouchListener(this);
}
```

4. Next give our view something to do when its `onDraw()` method is called:

```java
@Override
public void onDraw(Canvas canvas) {
   canvas.drawCircle(x, y, 20, paint);
}
```

Finally add a response to any motion event with an `onTouch()` callback:

```java
public boolean onTouch(View view, MotionEvent event) {
   x = event.getX();
   y = event.getY();
   invalidate();
   return true;
}
```

5. Run the code on a handset or emulator and run your finger across the touchscreen to observe our canvas in action:

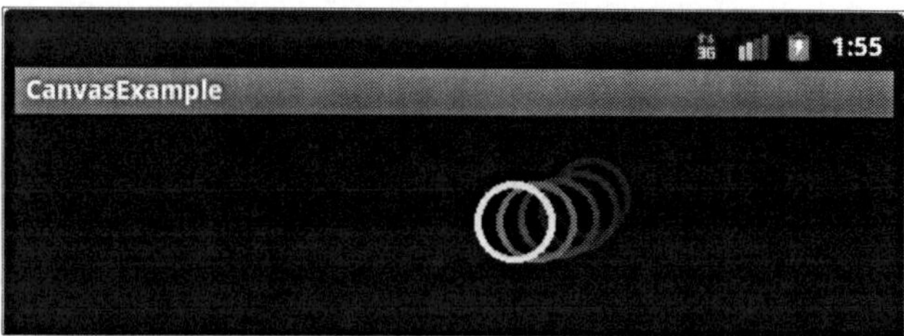

How it works...

The structure of this program is very similar to the previous recipe, using an extended View, a **Paint** definition, and an overridden `onDraw()` callback. The most significant difference here is that instead of calling `Drawable.draw(Canvas)` to produce an image, we called the **Canvas** directly to draw a circle with a radius of 20 pixels, using our defined Paint at the point of the last touchscreen event.

The Canvas class has many such useful methods, and if we declare a bitmap as an activity wide field like this:

```
Bitmap bmp =
    BitmapFactory.decodeResource(getResources(), R.drawable.icon);
```

And then replace the `drawCircle()` call in `onDraw()` with the following line, the circle is replaced with a bitmap:

```
canvas.drawBitmap(bmp, null, paint);
```

If its text we want to display, we could try something like:

```
canvas.drawText("text", x, y, paint);
```

Although it may be worth including `paint.setTextSize(72.0f)` and `paint.setStrokeJoin(Paint.Join.ROUND)` in the Paint definition to improve appearance:

See also

For a more thorough look at touch events, refer to the *Recognizing touch events* and *Detecting multi-touch elements* recipes in *Chapter 6, Detecting User Activity*.

Using tween animations

Android's built-in **tweening** (or more correctly **inbetweening)** functions are often overlooked as being unable to produce more than simple translations but the `android.view.animation` package allows us to **fade**, **stretch**, and **rotate** the contents of a view and to combine these effects with each other and also a neat **speed interpolator**. Furthermore, tweening is often easier on system resources than the direct manipulation of bitmaps and drawables.

Getting ready

When possible, tween animations are best defined in XML. Start up a new Android project in Eclipse and create a new folder named `anim` inside the `res` folder.

How to do it...

1. In the `res/anim` folder create a **New Android XML** file called `my_tween_anim.xml`:

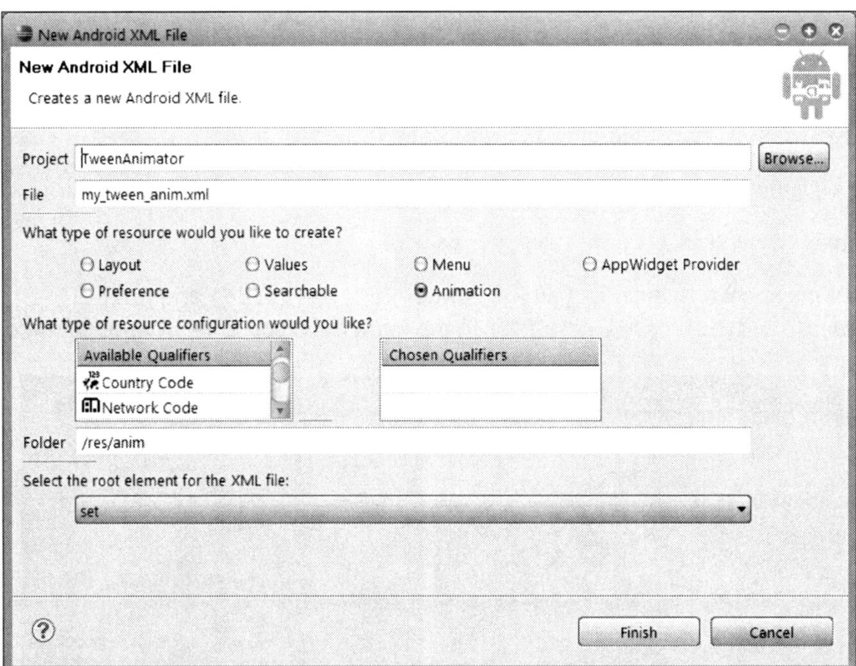

2. If you used the **New** wizard to create the file and selected **set** as the **root element**, the file should look something like this:

```xml
<?xml version="1.0" encoding="utf-8"?>
<set
    xmlns:android="http://schemas.android.com/apk/res/android">
</set>
```

3. We want our graphic to move in from the right, so add the following element inside the set tag:

```xml
<translate
    android:interpolator="@android:anim/accelerate_interpolator"
    android:fromXDelta="100%p"
    android:toXDelta="0"
    android:duration="1000" />
```

4. Next, to create a fade-in effect, add the following **alpha** element beneath the **translate** element:

```xml
<alpha
    android:fromAlpha="0.0"
    android:toAlpha="1.0"
    android:duration="2500" />
```

5. Beneath this add a new set element:

```xml
<set
    android:interpolator="@android:anim/decelerate_interpolator">
</set>
```

6. Now, within this second set element add the **rotate** tag as follows:

```xml
<rotate
    android:fromDegrees="0"
    android:toDegrees="-90"
    android:pivotX="50%"
    android:pivotY="0%"
    android:startOffset="1000"
    android:duration="3000" />
```

7. Now, open up the main Java activity code and and edit the onCreate() method to match the one found here:

```java
public void onCreate(Bundle state) {
    super.onCreate(state);
    setContentView(R.layout.main);

    final LinearLayout layout =
        (LinearLayout) findViewById(R.id.my_layout);
```

```
final Animation myAnim =
    AnimationUtils.loadAnimation(this, R.anim.my_anim);

layout.startAnimation(myAnim);
}
```

8. We referred to a LinearLayout here but have not set one up. However, the project wizard provided us with one in `main.xml`. Open the file and provide it with the appropriate ID. I also changed the text in the TextView:

   ```
   android:id="@+id/my_layout"
   ```

9. Now run the project on your emulator or device to view the animation. As this animation is called whenever our activity is created, simply turn the phone, or hit *Ctrl + F12* to repeat it:

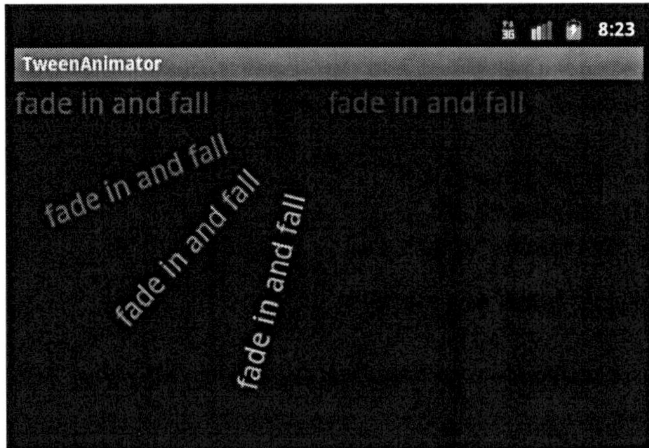

How it works...

The concepts behind what we have just done, such as rotate and translate, should be reasonably apparent. However, some of the notations used may require some explanation.

There are four kinds of basic transformation that we can apply. These are **scaling, translation, rotation** and **transparency**. We can control the time (in milliseconds) that transformations take to complete with the `duration` attribute and we can delay their start with `startOffset`.

The **<translate>** element controls the movement of a graphic from the point described by `fromXDelta` and `fromYDelta` to the point `toXDelta, toYDelta`. Depending on the notation used, there are three different metrics we can apply:

1. To translate a view to an absolute number of pixels, apply a value that is made up of digits only, for example `toXDelta="100"`.

2. Suffixing the value with a percent sign allows us to apply a movement that is relative to the animated view, so `toXDelta="100%"` would refer to the width of the view.

3. To apply a transformation that is relative to the whole screen, append the value with a 'p', as in `toXDelta="100%p"`.

Setting transparency with **<alpha>** is far simpler with the value 0.0 producing a wholly see-through image, and 1.0 a wholly opaque one.

The **<rotate>** element allows us to not only rotate our view contents (in degrees) from one angle to another but also to select a **pivot point**. As with the scale animation we can place this point absolutely, or relatively with '%' and 'p'.

We did not use the **<scale>** element in our example but its make up is straightforward and self explanatory. Attributes include `fromXScale` and `fromYScale` with 1.0 meaning no difference. It is also possible to control the point at which this scaling is centered using `pivotX` and `pivotY`.

Interpolators allow us to control the speed and movement of our animations and can be applied to whole `set` element as well as individual transformations, which is why we nested one `set` within another here.

There are several other neat interpolators that allow us to apply fancy transformation effects with a minimum effort. Given next is a list of `@android:anim/` values and it is well worth inserting them into the exercise code to see how they work:

- `accelerate_decelerate_interpolator`
- `accelerate_interpolator`
- `anticipate_interpolator`
- `anticipate_overshoot_interpolator`
- `bounce_interpolator`
- `cycle_interpolator`
- `decelerate_interpolator`
- `linear_interpolator`
- `overshoot_interpolator`

There was nothing complex about the Java in this task. The **AnimationUtils** class provides a few other animation based functions such as load interpolators and return the current animation's time.

See also

For animation techniques for platforms higher than 3.0 (API 11) see the next recipe.

Animating with Honeycomb APIs

Android 3.0 (API level 11) brought with it a whole new animation package, **android.animation**. It is easier to use and more powerful than the **android.view.animation** package. It can be used to animate object values and properties as well as views.

This exercise makes use of the **ObjectAnimator** to set up and trigger a transition animation and the `AnimatorListenerAdapter` interface to detect the completion of the animation.

Getting ready

Start a new Android project in Eclipse and open the `main.xml` file.

How to do it...

1. Either using the **Graphical Layout** menu or by editing the XML directly, edit the following three properties:

```
android:id="@+id/text_view"
android:textSize="26sp"
android:layout_marginTop="150dip"
```

2. Everything in this example can go straight into the `onCreate()` method. Underneath the `setContentView()` statement add these fields:

```
final TextView textView =
    (TextView) findViewById(R.id.text_view);

ObjectAnimator twirl =

    ObjectAnimator.ofFloat(textView, "rotation", 0f, 360f);
```

3. Now, beneath this, set up the animator like so:

```
twirl.setDuration(2000);
twirl.setStartDelay(100);
twirl.setRepeatCount(2);
twirl.setRepeatMode(ObjectAnimator.REVERSE);
twirl.start();
```

4. Next, give our animator a listener:

```
twirl.addListener(new AnimatorListenerAdapter() {

  @Override
  public void onAnimationEnd(Animator twirl) {
    textView.setText("Finished");
  }

});
```

5. Compile and run the example on a handset or emulator to view the animation:

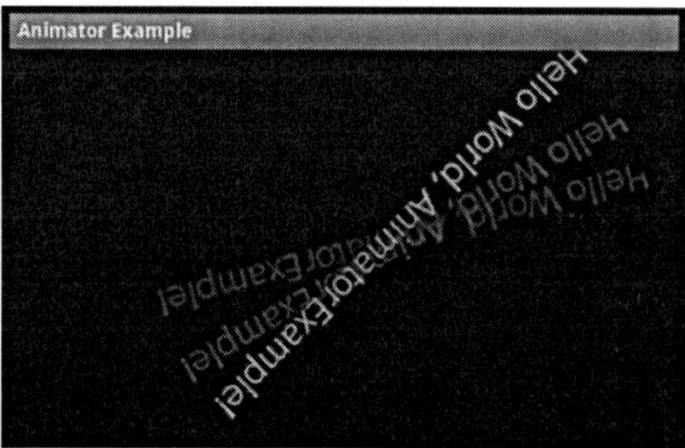

How it works...

The **ObjectAnimator** class is the object that does a bulk of the work here. It is descended from the **ValueAnimator** which itself is descended from **android.animation.Animator**. Animator itself is not used directly (although custom animators can be extended from it) instead either `ObjectAnimators` or `ValueAnimators` are used, the difference between them being that the ValueAnimator calculates the values of the properties being animated and controls the timing, whilst the ObjectAnimator does both this and the actual animating.

The ObjectAnimator here was constructed to calculate floats, `ObjectAnimator.ofFloat()` but we could have calculated integers with `.ofInt()` or ARGB color values with `.ofObject()`.

It is also possible to animate arbitrary object properties with the **TypeEvaluator** interface.

The arguments we passed to `ObjectAnimator.ofFloat()` are the the object to be animated, the property to be changed, and the desired start and end points of the transition—here expressed in degrees.

These properties can also be set with `setTarget(object)`, `setPropertyName(String)`, `setValueFrom(valueType)`, and `setValueTo(valueType)`.

The `rotation` property used in this example was added to View in Android 3.0 (API level 11), and there are several others. We could have used `rotationX` or `rotationY` to animate in all three dimensions and we can change these values at any time, as we would any property with a setter, for example with `setRotationX(float)`. Honeycomb also introduced `scale` and `pivot` properties, along with X and Y variants for 3D transitions.

Translation can be handled with `translationX` and `translationY` properties based on an object's position within its container view group or absolutely with `X` and `Y` properties. Transparency can also be managed with the `alpha` property with 1.0 equal to fully opaque and 0.0 fully transparent. All arguments are in pixels or degrees and all have appropriate setter and getter methods.

A useful feature of the ObjectAnimator constructors is that if the start point is omitted from the arguments, then it will start the transition using the current value.

Setting the properties of our ObjectAnimator was pretty straightforward and easy to follow, and as you would imagine this can be achieved from within a static XML file. The example here would look like the following:

```xml
<objectAnimator
    xmlns:android="http://schemas.android.com/apk/res/android"
    android:propertyName="rotation"
      android:valueFrom="0"
    android:valueTo="360"
    android:valueType="floatType"
      android:duration="2000"
    android:startDelay="100"
    android:repeatCount="7"
    android:repeatMode="reverse"/>
```

Note that one property that cannot be set from within XML is the target.

Animators have listeners to detect various events in a transition's lifecycle. Here we used a special kind of listener, an **AnimatorListenerAdapter**, which is a convenient interface so we do not have to override callbacks that are not needed. The other callbacks we could have used are `onAnimationStart()`, `onAnimationRepeat()`, and `onAnimationCancel()`.

Another handy listener is the `AnimatorUpdateListener` which calls `onAnimationUpdate()` on every frame change. Use `getAnimatedValue(String propertyName)`.

There's more...

Another great feature of the android.animation API is the **AnimationSet** class which allows us to group several animations and play them back in a desired order, either before, alongside, or after each other. Previously defined animators can be combined into an **AnimationSet** as follows:

```
AnimatorSet mySet =
   new AnimatorSet().play(anim1).before(anim2).with(anim3);
mySet.play(anim4).after(anim3);
mySet.start();
```

To implement animation sets in XML use the `<set>` tag.

See also

To animate a view on platforms earlier than Android 3.0 see the previous recipe *Using tween animations*.

Creating stop frame animations

Traditional animations can be constructed using a series of images, and Android provides the **AnimationDrawable** that can accomplish the same. Any number of slightly differing bitmaps can be defined as a list in XML and played in sequence to produce a stop frame animation.

Getting ready

Before we start we will require a number of images to act as the frames of our animation. As few as three or four is enough for demonstration purposes—we used the following:

As always with Android, the PNG format is preferred over other formats, although BMP, JPG and GIF are permitted. Depending on the screen density of your target device, store these bitmaps in the appropriate `res/drawable` folder. We called them `image01.png`, `image02.png`, and so on.

 When developing fully blown applications, it is more than likely that you will have to prepare three versions of these files.

How to do it...

1. Create a new XML file called `my_frames.xml` in the `res/drawable` folder (or folders) you are using. This is easier to do if you use **New XML** rather than **New Android XML File**, as the resource type we are using is not provided by the wizard.

2. Fill out `my_frames.xml` so as to match the code here:

```xml
<animation-list
    xmlns:android="http://schemas.android.com/apk/res/android"
    android:oneshot="false">

    <item android:drawable="@drawable/image01"
        android:duration="200" />
    <item android:drawable="@drawable/image02"
        android:duration="200" />
    <item android:drawable="@drawable/image03"
        android:duration="200" />
    <item android:drawable="@drawable/image04"
        android:duration="200" />

</animation-list>
```

3. We need a view to contain our animation so add the following `ImageView` to the `main.xml` layout definition:

```xml
<ImageView
    android:id="@+id/my_anim"
    android:layout_width="wrap_content"
    android:layout_height="wrap_content" />
```

4. In the Java activity code, declare this Activity wide field:

```java
AnimationDrawable myAnimation;
```

5. Now, edit the `onCreate()` callback, associate our view with its XML counterpart, and set its background resource:

```java
@Override
public void onCreate(Bundle state) {
    super.onCreate(state);
    setContentView(R.layout.main);

    ImageView view = (ImageView) findViewById(R.id.my_anim);
    view.setBackgroundResource(R.drawable.my_frames);
    myAnimation = (AnimationDrawable) view.getBackground();

}
```

6. Add a touch listener to trigger our animation:

```java
@Override
public boolean onTouchEvent(MotionEvent event) {
    if (event.getAction() == MotionEvent.ACTION_UP) {
      myAnimation.start();
      return true;
    }

    return super.onTouchEvent(event);

}
```

7. Now run the application on your handset or an emulator and tap the screen to start the stop frame animation:

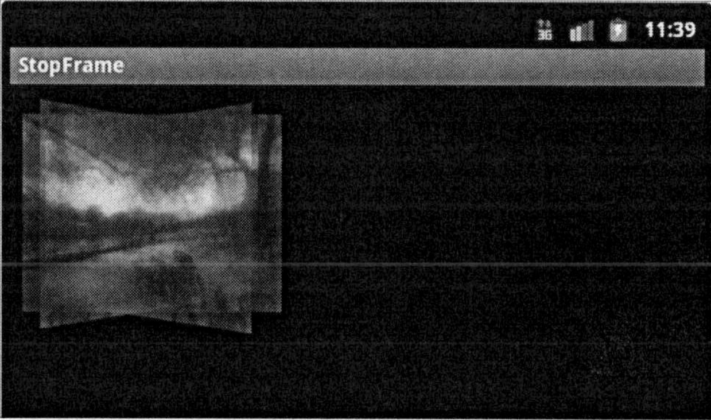

How it works...

The XML definition of our animation that we added at the beginning of the exercise is a straightforward list of drawable resources and durations (in milliseconds), and the system plays them in the order they appear. The attribute `oneshot` allows us to play the animation just once or in a repeating loop.

Once we have connected our ImageView with the element in our layout XML, it is a simple matter of setting its background resources to our XML animation definition and then assigning this background to our **AnimationDrawable**.

There's more...

We included a touch event in this exercise to trigger the animation. However, we would not have been able to call it directly from `onCreate()` as one might expect. This is due to the fact that the `AnimationDrawable` would not have finished configuring by the time the method concludes. It is nevertheless possible to have an animation run automatically when an activity starts.

Using window focus to trigger an animation

The Activity callback `onWindowFocusChanged()` *will* trigger once the `AnimationDrawable` is ready. Simply override the method and call `Animation.start()` from within it to have an animation play on start up:

```
@Override
public void onWindowFocusChanged() {
   myAnimation.start();
}
```

Working with OpenGL

Many modern smartphone applications require fast, color, 3D animations of complex, textured surfaces. To achieve this, Android provides support for an OpenGL API, specifically the OpenGL ES 1.0 API. It is beyond the scope of this book to go into the workings of graphics libraries and it is assumed that the reader has some familiarity with the subject. OpenGL is developed by the Khronos Group and their site at `www.khronos.org/opengles` contains a wealth of information for the beginner and expert alike.

In this recipe we explain how to set up an OpenGL **Renderer** from an activity and what such a renderer may look like.

Getting ready

This recipe assumes that the reader already has an OpenGL object that they wish to render. This needs to be in the form of a Java class. If you are unsure about OpenGL, there are plenty of places on the web where sample objects can be downloaded, such as `www.opengl.org`.

Start a new Android project in Eclipse and import the OpenGL object class into the same folder as the Java activity file, `/src`. Here we have called it `Cube`. It will need a method called `draw()` that takes a GL10 interface as an argument.

How to do it...

1. We need to set a **GLSurfaceView**, with a renderer, as our main content so edit the projects Java activity code to match the lines here:

    ```
    @Override
    protected void onCreate(Bundle state) {
       super.onCreate(state);

       mGLView = new GLSurfaceView(this);

       mGLView.setRenderer(new MyRenderer());

       setContentView(mGLView);
    }
    ```

2. To stop and start the animation along with the activity, include the `onResume()` and `onPause()` methods:

```java
@Override
protected void onResume() {
  super.onResume();
  mGLView.onResume();
}

@Override
protected void onPause() {
  super.onPause();
  mGLView.onPause();
}
```

3. Now, complete the MyRenderer, implementing a **GLSurfaceView.Renderer**, below:

```java
class MyRenderer implements GLSurfaceView.Renderer {
  private final Cube mCube;
  private float mRotate;

  public MyRenderer() {
    mCube = new Cube();
  }

  public void onDrawFrame(GL10 gl) {
    gl.glClear(GL10.GL_COLOR_BUFFER_BIT |
      GL10.GL_DEPTH_BUFFER_BIT);

    gl.glMatrixMode(GL10.GL_MODELVIEW);
    gl.glLoadIdentity();
    gl.glTranslatef(0, 0, -2.5f);
    gl.glRotatef(mRotate, 1.5f, 1.5f, 0);

    gl.glEnableClientState(GL10.GL_VERTEX_ARRAY);
    gl.glEnableClientState(GL10.GL_COLOR_ARRAY);

    mCube.draw(gl);

    mRotate += 2.0f;
  }
  public void onSurfaceChanged(GL10 gl,
    int width, int height) {
      float ratio = (float) width / height;
      gl.glViewport(0, 0, width, height);
      gl.glMatrixMode(GL10.GL_PROJECTION);
      gl.glLoadIdentity();
      gl.glFrustumf(-ratio, ratio, -1, 1, 1, 10);
  }
  public void onSurfaceCreated(GL10 gl, EGLConfig config) {
    gl.glEnable(GL10.GL_CULL_FACE);
  }
}
```

4. Provided that you have an OpenGL object saved as `Cube.java` in the same folder, this should run on a handset or emulator:

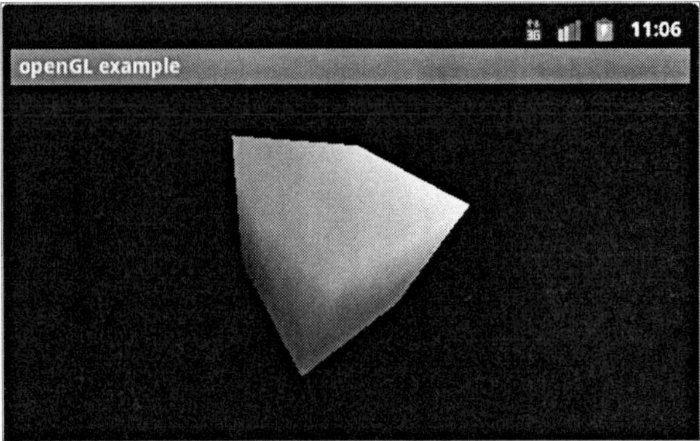

How it works...

Although most of the work done here requires some knowledge of OpenGL, from an Android point of view it is the `android.opengl.GLSurfaceView` that is of interest. This descendant of `android.view.SurfaceView` is what provides us with the Renderer in our `onCreate()` method. It is important that we call `onPause()` and `onResume()` on our **GLSurfaceView** when the holding activity loses and gains focus to prevent memory leakage, and 3D rendering can leak a *lot* of memory.

As for the implementation of the renderer, there is no room here to go into detail. To anyone with OpenGL experience it should appear straightforward, and for those who are not it will hopefully provide a clue or two as to how it works.

There's more...

On more recent devices it is now possible to use a certain amount of native code for programming 3D graphics and also to apply hardware graphic acceleration when available.

The Renderscript system

Staring with Honeycomb (API 11) it has been possible, for those readers that are comfortable developing in native code, to maximize graphic performance with the **Renderscript** API code written in C and saved as Renderscript files (`.rs`), included in the application's `.apk` file. Some examples are shipped with the SDK and can be found in the `android-sdk/samples/android-11/Renderscript` folder.

Hardware acceleration

From Android 3.0 onwards it has been possible to provide hardware acceleration on devices that have the appropriate hardware. Simply include `android:hardwareAccelerated=` `"true"` in the manifest's `<application>` element.

Now that we have covered various aspects of image control it seems only right that we should venture into the world of Android sound and video.

9
Multimedia

In this chapter, we will cover the following topics:

- Playing an audio file from within an application
- Playing back video from external memory
- Playing multiple sounds with a SoundPool
- Recording audio
- Recording video
- Capturing photos with the camera

Introduction

As the computing power of mobile devices has increased, so has their ability to play and record a variety of media such as audio and video. Android provides some useful tools for managing multimedia.

Very few successful applications are completely silent or have only static graphics, and in order that Android developers take full advantage of the advanced multimedia capabilities of today's smartphones, the system provides the **android.media** package, which contains many useful classes.

The **MediaPlayer** class allows the playback of both audio and video from raw resources, files, and network streams, and the **MediaRecorder** class makes it possible to record both sound and images.

Android also offers ways to manipulate sounds and create interactive effects through the use of the **SoundPool** class, which allows us to not only bend the pitch of our sounds but also to play more than one at a time.

One of the most pleasing aspects of the Android system is the way that it allows us to take near-complete control over hardware such as cameras and although this process requires a little setting up we can nevertheless incorporate these cameras into our applications and have them take photographs.

Playing an audio file from within an application

One of the first things that we may want to do with regards to multimedia is play back an audio file. Android provides the **android.media.MediaPlayer** class for us and this makes playback and most media related functions remarkably simple.

In this recipe we will create a simple media player that will play a single audio file.

Getting ready

Before we start this project we will need an audio file for playback. Android can decode audio with any of the following file extensions:

- `.3GP`
- `.MP4`
- `.M4A`
- `.MP3`
- `.OGG`
- `.WAV`

There are also quite a few MIDI file formats that are acceptable but have not been included here as their use is less common and their availability often depends on whether a device is running the standard Android platform or a specific vendor extension.

Before you start this exercise create or find a short sound sample in one of the given formats. We used a five second Ogg Vorbis file and called it `my_sound_file.ogg`.

How to do it...

1. Start up a new Android project in Eclipse and create a new folder: `res/raw`.
2. Place the sound file that you just prepared in this folder. In this example we refer to it as `my_sound_file`.

3. Using either the **Graphical Layout** or the **main.xml** panel edit the file `res/layout/main.xml` to contain three buttons, as seen in the following screenshot:

4. Call these buttons `play_button`, `pause_button` and `stop_button`.

5. In the Java activity code declare a **MediaPlayer** in the `onCreate()` method:

```java
@Override
public void onCreate(Bundle state) {
    super.onCreate(state);
    setContentView(R.layout.main);

    final MediaPlayer mPlayer;
```

6. Associate the buttons we added in step 3 with Java variables by adding the following lines to `onCreate()`:

```java
Button playButton =
    (Button) findViewById(R.id.play_button);
Button pauseButton =
    (Button) findViewById(R.id.pause_button);
Button stopButton =
    (Button) findViewById(R.id.stop_button);
```

7. We need a click listener for our **play** button. This also can be defined from within `onCreate()`:

```java
playButton.setOnClickListener(new OnClickListener() {
    public void onClick(View v) {
        mPlayer = MediaPlayer.create(this, R.raw.my_sound_file);
        mPlayer.setLooping(true);
        mPlayer.start();
    }
});
```

8. Next add a listener for the **pause** button as follows:

```java
pauseButton.setOnClickListener(new OnClickListener() {
    public void onClick(View v) {
        mPlayer.pause();
    }
});
```

9. Finally, include a listener for the **stop** button:

```java
stopButton.setOnClickListener(new OnClickListener() {
  public void onClick(View v) {
    mPlayer.stop();
    mPlayer.reset();
  }
});
```

10. Now run this code on an emulator or your handset and test each of the buttons.

How it works...

The **MediaPlayer** class provides some useful functions and the use of `start()`, `pause()`, `stop()`, and `setLooping()` should be clear. However, if you are thinking that calling `MediaPlayer.create(context, ID)` every time the start button is pressed is overkill, you would be correct. This is because once `stop()` has been called on the **MediaPlayer**, the media needs to be **reset** and **prepared** (with `reset()` and `prepare()`) before `start()` can be called again. Fortunately `MediaPlayer.create()` also calls `prepare()` so that the first time we play an audio file we do not have to worry about this.

The lifecycle of the MediaPlayer is not always straightforward and the order in which it takes on various states is best explained diagrammatically:

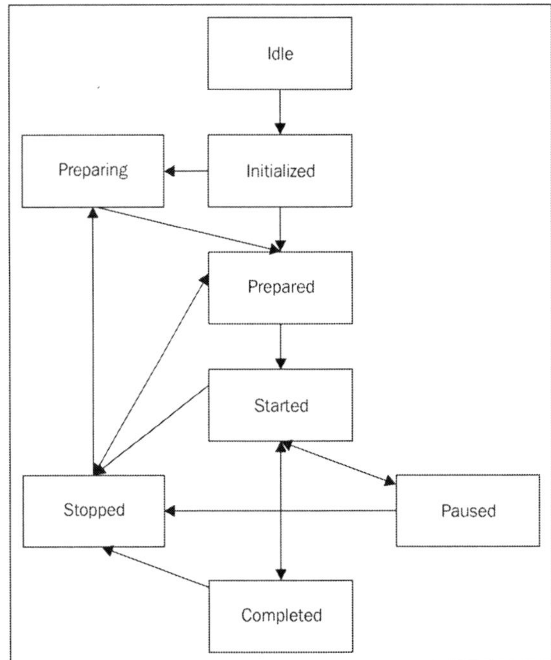

Otherwise, MediaPlayer has lots of useful methods such as `isPlaying()`, which will return a Boolean telling us whether our file is being played or not, or `getDuration()` and `getCurrentPosition()`, which inform us of how long the sample is and how far through it we are. There are also some useful hooks that we can employ using MediaPlayer and the most commonly used are `onCompletionListener()` and `onErrorListener()`.

There's more...

We are not restricted to playing back raw resources. We can also playback local files or even stream audio.

Playing back a file or a stream

Use the `MediaPlayer.setDataSource(String)` method to play an audio file or stream. In the case of streaming audio this will need to be a URL representing a media file that is capable of being played progressively, and you will need to prepare the media player each time it runs:

```
MediaPlayer player = new MediaPlayer();
player.setDataSource("string value of your file path or URL");
player.prepare();
player.start();
```

It is essential to surround `setDataSource()` with a `try/catch` clause in case the source does not exist when dealing with removable or online media.

See also

For playing more than one sound file at a time see the recipe *Playing multiple sounds with a SoundPool* later in this chapter.

Playing back video from external memory

The **MediaPlayer** class that we met in the previous recipe works for video in the same manner that it does for audio and so as not to make this task a near copy of the last, here we will look at how to play back video files stored on an SD card using the **VideoView** object.

Getting ready

This recipe requires a video file for our application to playback. Android can decode **H.263**, **H.264** and **MPEG-4** files; generally speaking this means files with `.3gp` and `.mp4` file extensions. For platforms since 3.0 (API level 11) it is also possible to manage **H.264 AVC** files.

Find a short video clip in one of these compatible formats and save it on the SD card of your handset. Alternatively you can create an emulator with an SD card enabled and **push** your video file onto it. This can be done easily through Eclipse's **DDMS perspective** from the **File Explorer** tab:

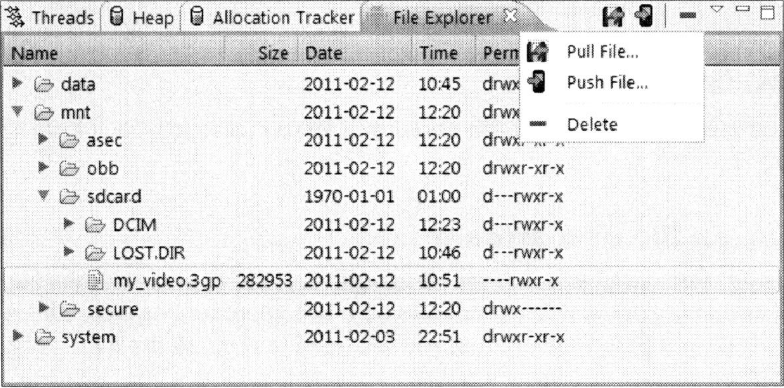

In this example we called our video file `my_video.3gp`.

How to do it...

1. Start a new project in Eclipse and navigate to the `main.xml` file. Replace the prepared `TextView` with the following `VideoView`:

```xml
<VideoView
    android:layout_height="fill_parent"
    android:layout_width="fill_parent"
    android:id="@+id/video_view" />
```

2. Associate this view with a Java variable in the usual manner from within the `onCreate()` method:

```java
@Override
public void onCreate(Bundle state) {
    super.onCreate(state);
    setContentView(R.layout.main);

    VideoView view =
        (VideoView) findViewById(R.id.video_view);
```

3. Directly underneath this, set a path to our video with this line:

```java
view.setVideoPath(Environment.getExternalStorageDirectory()
    + "/myvideo.3gp");
```

4. Now add a command to play the video:

```java
view.start();
```

5. Run this code on your handset or emulator. The video will play as soon as the application starts:

How it works...

We have not encountered the **VideoView** object before but nevertheless it is very similar to the View subclasses that we saw earlier in the book. However, it also implements the **MediaController.MediaPlayerControl** class and this gives us access to some of the useful methods that we used with the MediaPlayer earlier in the chapter such as `isPlaying()`, `getDuration()`, and `getCurrentPosition()`, and like other views it has an `onTouchEvent(MotionEvent)` callback which can prove very useful.

 For Android platforms 3.0 onwards it has been possible to run HTTP live streaming sessions by passing an M3U playlist URL to the media framework.

There's more...

When it comes to adding common media controls such as **play**, **pause** and **seek**, Android provides a very handy little widget in the form of the **MediaPlayerControl** interface that can be accessed through the `android.widget.MediaController` class, and which automatically synchronizes with the active media and floats above it.

Adding a MediaPlayerControl to a view

A **MediaPlayerControl** can be created with something along the lines of:

```
myPlayerControl = new MediaController.MediaPlayerControl()
```

This will necessitate the implementing of several methods that give us further control over the widget's appearance and behavior.

Once defined, we can apply the widget to our media using:

```
myMediaController.setMediaPlayer(myPlayerControls)
```

We can also select which view it hovers over with:

```
myMediaController.setAnchorView(some_view)
```

The media player control will take care of when it appears by itself. To force it to be displayed use `MediaController.show(int)`, where `int` is the number of milliseconds to display the controls and a value of 0 will cause the widget to display as long as the related view is visible, regardless of whether media is playing or not.

Playing multiple sounds with a SoundPool

Android provides an extremely useful audio tool in the form of the **android.media.SoundPool** class. This class allows us to play more than one sound at a time and to adjust the pitch and stereo placement of these sounds programmatically. Here we will create a **SoundPool** that will play three sound files simultaneously.

Getting ready

You will need three audio files to complete this exercise. Find three short samples in one of the compatible formats, ideally noises that will not sound unpleasant when played together. Here we have used Ogg Vorbis files and named them `sound1`, `sound2`, and `sound3`.

How to do it...

1. Start up a new Android project in Eclipse and create a new folder called `raw` inside the `res` folder.
2. Place the three sound files you selected earlier inside `res/raw`.
3. As a class-wide field in the main Java activity code, declare and assign a new **SoundPool** as follows:

```
SoundPool pool =
    new SoundPool(3, AudioManager.STREAM_MUSIC, 0);
```

4. We will have our sounds play as the activity starts and use a hash map as a simple index. Amend the `onCreate()` method to match the one found here:

```java
@Override
public void onCreate(Bundle state) {
    super.onCreate(state);
    setContentView(R.layout.main);

    HashMap<Integer, Integer> map = null;
    map.put(1, pool.load(this, R.raw.sound1, 1));
    map.put(2, pool.load(this, R.raw.sound2, 1));
    map.put(3, pool.load(this, R.raw.sound3, 1));

    for (int i = 1; i < 4; i++) {
        pool.play(map.get(i), 0.8f, 0.2f, 1, 0, 1.0f);
    }
}
```

5. SoundPools need to be shut down when they are no longer needed, so add an `onPause()` method and include the following lines:

```java
@Override
public void onPause() {
    super.onPause();

    pool.release();
    pool = null;
}
```

6. This is all the code we need to play back our samples. Run the project on your handset or emulator in the usual way.

How it works...

The main object of interest in this task is the **SoundPool**. We constructed it with three `int` values. The first number tells the system about the maximum number of sounds that we wish to play at any one time, and is not limited.

The second argument is a constant member of **AudioManager** and is used to select the type of sound we want. Here we chose `STREAM_MUSIC` but there are others available and some of the most commonly used include `STREAM_ALARM` and `STREAM_RING`.

The final value represents the desired audio quality. However, as of Android 3.1, it still has not been implemented and so is left as zero.

The `SoundPool.play()` method is self explanatory in function and the purpose of each of the six required parameters is explained in the following list:

- **int** - the index of the sound.
- **float** - the left volume, between 0 and 1.
- **float** - the right volume.
- **int** - the priority. This is for situations where the number of played sounds exceeds the maximum, with higher numbers having higher priority.
- **int** - sets the number of times the sound should loop. Set to `-1` to loop indefinitely. This can be halted with `SoundPool.stop()`.
- **float** - the speed of the file's playback. Set at `2.0` to double the speed and `0.5` to halve it.

It is this last parameter to adjust the pitch of our sounds that demonstrates what is perhaps the most useful function of the SoundPool class. This can be applied to create Doppler-like effects in games or to save on memory by using a single resource to produce several notes. Another advantage of the way that SoundPools work is the way that they cut down on latency by preparing the samples during construction.

It is worth noting that although we used raw resources as our audio source it is perfectly possible and just as simple to use files from any available source.

Recording audio

Most mobile devices contain **audio recording** equipment, either as an independent **microphone** or as part of a **camcorder** setup. Provided that our target devices contain this hardware, we can use the **android.media.MediaRecorder** class to record audio samples from within our applications. In this recipe, we will create a basic audio recorder that stores captured sound on the SD card.

Getting ready

Audio recording support does not currently work with an emulator, so you will need to test this recipe with a handset.

How to do it...

1. Start up a new Android project and open up the `res/layout/main.xml` file.
2. Using either the **Graphical Layout** or the **main.xml** tab, add two buttons and give them the IDs `start_button` and `stop_button`.

3. Declare the following class-wide fields in the Java activity class:

```java
private MediaRecorder recorder = new MediaRecorder();
private Button playButton;
private Button stopButton;
```

4. Next, associate these with the views defined in `main.xml`:

```java
playButton = (Button) findViewById(R.id.start_button);
stopButton = (Button) findViewById(R.id.stop_button);
```

5. Now add a click listener for the play button:

```java
playButton.setOnClickListener(new OnClickListener() {

    @Override
    public void onClick(View v) {
    recorder.setAudioSource(MediaRecorder.AudioSource.MIC);
    recorder.setOutputFormat(MediaRecorder.OutputFormat.THREE_GPP);
    recorder.setAudioEncoder(MediaRecorder.AudioEncoder.AMR_NB);
    recorder.setOutputFile(Environment.getExternalStorageDirectory()
        + "/my_recording.3gp");

        try {
            recorder.prepare();
        } catch (IllegalStateException e) {
            e.printStackTrace();
            finish();
        } catch (IOException e) {
            e.printStackTrace();
            finish();
        }

        recorder.start();
    }
});
```

6. Finally, add a click listener for the stop button:

```java
stopButton.setOnClickListener(new OnClickListener() {

    @Override
    public void onClick(View v) {
        recorder.stop();
        recorder.release();
    }
});
```

7. Run this example on a handset. The stored audio can be found on the SD card as `my_recording.3gp`.

How it works...

The key object here is the **MediaRecorder** class and this allows us to set up everything we need to record our audio. The **AudioSource** class does little more than offer a number of constants used to identify the desired source. Here we used the device's built-in microphone, `MIC`: we could have used `CAMCORDER` or one or two others and very often we would simply use `DEFAULT`. The **OutputFormat** and **AudioEncoder** classes operate in a similar fashion.

Although `reset()` can be called at any point in a recording's process, other **MediaRecorder** methods must be executed in a certain order as the next diagram shows. Once `release()` has been called the recorder will need to be set up again:

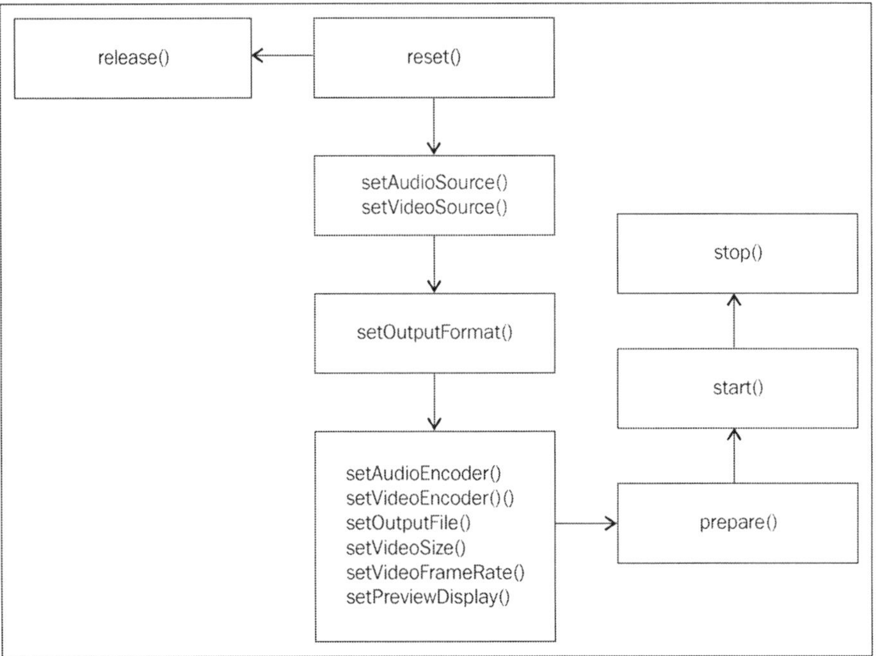

See also

Note that the previous diagram also includes details pertinent to video recording which we cover in the next recipe.

Recording video

Recording video content is remarkably similar to recording audio. In fact, both processes employ the **MediaRecorder** class. The two forms of recording are so similar that, for this exercise, we will convert the audio recorder of the previous recipe into a video recorder.

Getting ready

To prepare for this task load the project from the previous recipe. Most Android devices have video capacities built-in but if you are planning on testing this recipe on an emulator, make sure you have the hardware property **Camera support** set to **yes** when you create it.

How to do it...

1. In the `main.xml` file of the project, add a **SurfaceView**, with the ID `camera_view`, beneath the two buttons:

2. Add the following class field:

    ```
    SurfaceHolder holder;
    ```

3. Also, declare a SurfaceView and associate it with the one defined in XML:

    ```
    SurfaceView cameraView =
      (SurfaceView) findViewById(R.id.camera_view);
    ```

4. We can connect our **SurfaceHolder** and **MediaRecorder** like so:

    ```
    holder = cameraView.getHolder();
    recorder.setPreviewDisplay(holder.getSurface());
    ```

5. The start button click listener needs a video source as well as an audio one:

    ```
    recorder.setVideoSource(MediaRecorder.VideoSource.CAMERA);
    ```

6. Also, the output file type needs to be a video file type:

    ```
    recorder.setOutputFile(
      Environment.getExternalStorageDirectory()
        + "/my_recording.mp4");
    ```

7. These are the only changes that are needed to convert the previous recipe into one that records video. Run the project on your handset or emulator and touch **start** to record.

How it works...

This recipe bears such a resemblance to the previous one that little explanation is needed although there are one or two other configurations that we could have applied to our video before preparing it: once we had set the output file we could have added `recorder.setMaxDuration(int milliseconds)` to control the maximum allowed recording time, or `recorder.setMaxFileSize(long bytes)` to limit memory.

SurfaceHolder is a very useful interface for configuring and monitoring any display surface. Here we used it simply to set our preview window but it has several other useful functions and a few of the handier ones are listed next:

- `getSurfaceFrame()`—returns a `Rect` object describing the current surface
- `isCreating()`—true until creation is complete
- `setFixedSize(int, int)`—desired width and height (in pixels)
- `setKeepScreenOn(boolean)`—prevents screen timeout if true
- `setSizeFromLayout()`—adjusts the size to fit its container view

There's more...

For platforms equal to or greater than API level 11 (Honeycomb) it has been possible record **time-lapse video**. The frame rate can be controlled with:

```
android.media.MediaRecorder.setCaptureRate(double framesPerSecond)
```

The actual frame rate range can be computed with `getPreviewFpsRange(int)`.

See also

To learn how to record audio and for more details on the `MediaRecorder` class, see the previous recipe *Recording audio*.

Capturing photos with the camera

Virtually every Android device is equipped with at least one digital camera and it's nice to be able to take control of this equipment and take photographs directly from within an application. Although the **android.hardware.Camera** class makes it simple to take an actual photo, the preparation of the camera preview is relatively more complex.

In this exercise we will construct a **SurfaceView** that will take a photograph when tapped. Be warned that there is more typing involved in this task than most.

Getting ready

All you will need to prepare for this recipe is to start a new Android project in Eclipse. Make your way to the `AndroidManifest` file.

How to do it...

1. Use of the camera requires for permissions to be granted. Add the following lines to the Manifest file at the same level as the `<application>` tag:

```
<uses-permission
    android:name="android.permission.CAMERA" />

<uses-feature
    android:name="android.hardware.camera" />
```

2. We need only one view in our layout, so replace the default TextView with this **SurfaceView**:

```
<SurfaceView
    android:id="@+id/camera_view"
    android:layout_width="match_parent"
    android:layout_height="match_parent" />
```

3. Provide the following class fields to the Java activity class:

```java
private SurfaceView mView;
private SurfaceHolder mHolder;
private Camera mCamera;
private boolean mIsPreviewing;
```

4. Identify our view and connect it to the `SurfaceHolder` like so:

```java
mView = (SurfaceView) findViewById(R.id.camera_view);
mHolder = mView.getHolder();
mHolder.addCallback(this);
mHolder.setType(SurfaceHolder.SURFACE_TYPE_PUSH_BUFFERS);
```

5. Change the activity definition so that along with extending Activity, it also implements **SurfaceHolder.Callback**:

```java
public class CameraPreviewer
    extends Activity implements SurfaceHolder.Callback {
```

6. This will cause Eclipse to suggest that you add some unimplemented methods, do so.

7. Complete the `surfaceCreated()` method as shown here:

```java
@Override
public void surfaceCreated(SurfaceHolder holder) {
  mCamera = Camera.open();
}
```

8. Next, fill in the `surfaceChanged()` method:

```java
@Override
public void surfaceChanged(
    SurfaceHolder holder, int format, int w, int h) {
      if (mIsPreviewing) {
        mCamera.stopPreview();
      }

    Camera.Parameters param = mCamera.getParameters();
    param.setPreviewSize(w, h);
    mCamera.setParameters(param);

    mCamera.setPreviewDisplay(holder);
    mCamera.startPreview();

    mIsPreviewing = true;
    }
```

9. Now the `surfaceDestroyed()` method:

```java
@Override
public void surfaceDestroyed(SurfaceHolder holder) {
    mCamera.stopPreview();
    mCamera.release();

    mIsPreviewing = false;
    }
```

10. We need to create a callback for when a picture is taken. It looks like this:

```java
Camera.PictureCallback mPictureCallback =
    new Camera.PictureCallback() {
    public void onPictureTaken(byte[] image, Camera camera) {
      // manage or convert the picture here
    }
};
```

11. Finally we need a mechanism to trigger the shutter. Here we use a touch listener so that we can take photos with a tap on the preview:

```java
mView.setOnTouchListener(new OnTouchListener() {
    @Override
    public boolean onTouch(View v, MotionEvent event) {
      mCamera.takePicture(null,
        mPictureCallback, mPictureCallback);
      return true;
    }
});
```

12. With all that typing done, it is now time to test this code. This is best done on a handset as all you will get on an emulator is the sound of the shutter.

How it works...

There is a lot going on in the previous code, but hopefully most of it should make sense by now. In step 4 we hooked our SurfaceView and our SurfaceHolder together. `SurfaceView.getHolder()` gives the view access to the underlying data.

The three surface callbacks we implemented come into play as the surface reaches various stages of its life cycle. The `surfaceCreated()` and `surfaceDestroyed()` are quite easy to follow and we have created `surfaceChanged()` with only the barest essentials so as to make it easier to understand the general structure of camera enabled applications. The getting and setting of parameters enables the preview to handle screen orientation and other UI changes.

We implemented our activity with an interface (`SurfaceHolder.Callback`) that you may not have seen before. This is what gave us access to the surface callbacks as well as being able to call `addCallback()` on our `SurfaceHolder`. The `onPictureTaken()` method provides our photo as a byte array which we could convert, if we wished, with a `BitmapFactory`.

See also

For more about **SurfaceViews** see the previous recipe, *Recording video*.

For an introduction to **BitmapFactories** take a look at the recipe *Drawing with a Canvas* in *Chapter 8, Graphics and Animation*.

Now that we have covered the multimedia side of Android capabilities, we can go a step further and look at how to connect our applications to the outside world using networks and the Web.

10
Telephony, Networks, and the Web

In this chapter, we will cover the following topics:

- ▸ Initiating a phone call
- ▸ Listening for phone events
- ▸ Sending SMS messages
- ▸ Monitoring SMS messages
- ▸ Connecting to WiFi
- ▸ Connecting Bluetooth devices
- ▸ Including web content

Introduction

With so much being made of the computing power of Android devices it is easy to almost forget that they can also function as telephones. It's ironic that we do not cover this subject until the end of this book. As we deal with telephony at this point, we will also explore other network functionality.

This chapter introduces several new packages and classes, particularly the **TelephonyManager** in the **android.telephony** package. We will use these along with the system's built-in **Phone Application** to take control over the making of phone calls from within an application. We will also use the **PhoneStateListener** class to monitor the device's mobile radio.

The `android.telephony` package also provides a **SmsManager** class and this can be utilized to send text messages from our applications. The monitoring of outbound and inbound SMS messages is covered along with how to use **PendingIntent** and **BroadcastReceiver** objects to cause and detect these events.

This chapter also examines mobile **WiFi**, which is accessed through the `android.net` package that provides us with the **ConnectivityManager** for dealing with networking in general, and the **WifiManager** for managing WiFi networks specifically.

Finally, we explore the **WebView** class, which is powered by the **Webkit** engine. The **WebViewClient** class allows us to provide web content from within an application.

Initiating a phone call

Although some elements of telephony development can be quite complicated, Android provides a built-in **Phone Application** that we can call on from our own applications by making use of an **Intent** object to call an activity in one application from another.

Getting ready

This is a quick and easy exercise with very little coding and a single class. Start up a new project with Eclipse and open up the main Java activity source.

How to do it...

1. There are just three lines to add to our `onCreate()` method and they can be seen here beneath the `setContentView()` statement:

```java
@Override
public void onCreate(Bundle state) {
    super.onCreate(state);
    setContentView(R.layout.main);

    Intent intent = new Intent(Intent.ACTION_DIAL);
    intent.setData(Uri.parse("content://contacts/people/13"));
    startActivity(intent);
}
```

2. That really is all there is to it. Run the project on a handset to test this properly. If you have fewer than 13 contacts on your phone, adjust the value in the code to accommodate.

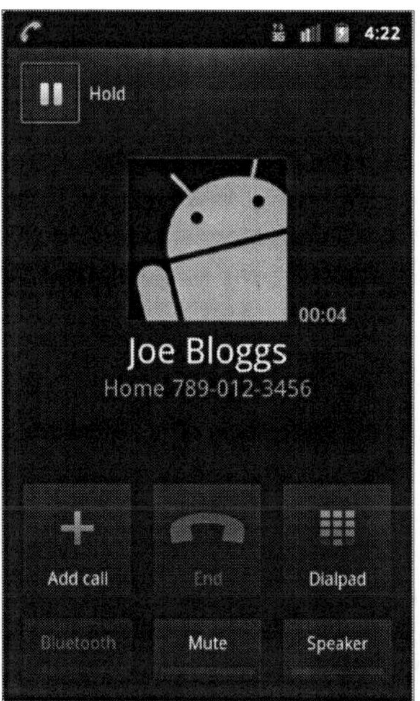

How it works...

The built-in **Phone Application** does most of the work for us here and all we did was provide our new instance of an Intent with the action `ACTION_DIAL` and the data which refers to the thirteenth person in our contact list. We also pulled the dialed number from a contacts list but we could have dialed the number specifically with `intent.setData(Uri.parse("tel:7890123456"))` instead.

If there are other installed applications on a handset that contain an `ACTION_DIAL` action, then these too may be called. The system attempts to select the most appropriate application from the data field and usually with great success.

One of the nice things, in this case, about Android's ability to call up other applications is that the Phone App does all the telephone-based error checking for us, so we do not have to think about whether the network may be down or our call interrupted. Nevertheless it is usually wise to attempt to catch 'activity-not-found' exceptions as follows:

```
try {
    Intent intent = new Intent(Intent.ACTION_DIAL);
    intent.setData(Uri.parse("content://contacts/people/13"));
    startActivity(intent);
} catch (ActivityNotFoundException notFound) {
    // error trap statements
}
```

Listening for phone events

Using the built-in Phone Application is a handy way to access telephonic functions, but it is very limited. To really get under the skin of our mobile radio we need to make use of the **android.telephony** package which contains many useful classes. Here we will use the **TelephonyManager** and the **PhoneStateListener** classes to create a simple application that records the phone's state during incoming and outgoing calls while the application is running.

Getting ready

This application requires no external resources, so simply start up a new Android project in Eclipse and open the Manifest file.

How to do it...

1. To allow our application to use the phone device, include the following permission inside the `<activity>` node:

```
<uses-permission
   android:name="READ_PHONE_STATE" />
```

2. Open the `res/layout/main.xml` file, remove the `android:text` element, and provide this resource ID:

```
android:id="@+id/text_view"
```

3. We will place all our Java code within the `onCreate()` method of our Java activity. First declare and assign a `TextView` and a `TelephonyManager`:

```
final TextView textView =
   (TextView) findViewById(R.id.text_view);

final TelephonyManager phoneManager =
   (TelephonyManager)
     getSystemService(Context.TELEPHONY_SERVICE);
```

4. Next, call the Phone Application with these two lines:

```
Intent intent = new Intent(Intent.ACTION_CALL_BUTTON);
startActivity(intent);
```

5. Now, start the phone listener with the next line:

```
phoneManager.listen(phoneListener,
   PhoneStateListener.LISTEN_CALL_STATE);
```

6. Finally, create this listener with the following inner class:

```
PhoneStateListener phoneListener = new PhoneStateListener() {
```

```
  @Override
   public void onCallStateChanged(int state, String number) {
     String phoneState = number;

     switch (state) {
     case TelephonyManager.CALL_STATE_IDLE:
       phoneState += " idle\n";
     case TelephonyManager.CALL_STATE_RINGING:
       phoneState += " ringing\n";
     case TelephonyManager.CALL_STATE_OFFHOOK:
       phoneState += " off hook\n";
     }

     textView.append(phoneState);
   }
 };
```

7. Now, we can test our project by installing it on a mobile device or emulator and making and receiving a few calls while it is running.

8. The application opens the Phone Application as soon as it starts so that we can make calls. To call an emulator with Eclipse, use the **Emulator Control** tab in the DDMS perspective:

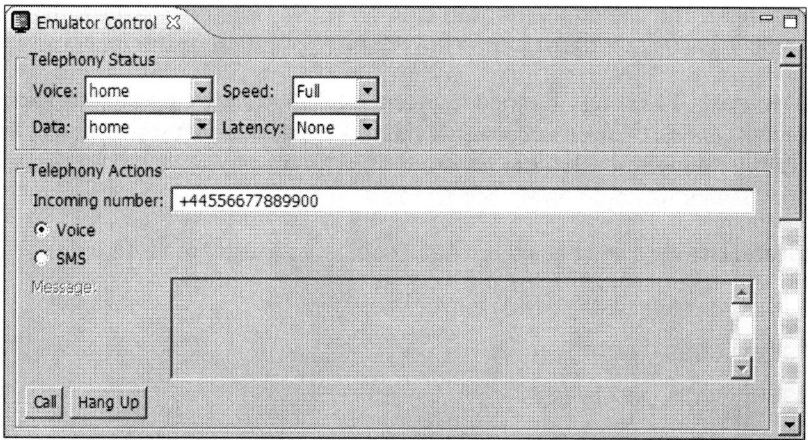

9. Once you have made a call or two, press the *back* button on the phone or emulator to view the record of events:

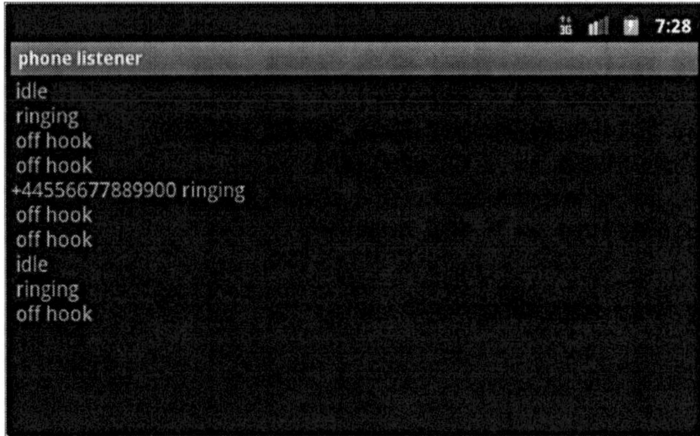

How it works...

Setting permissions and defining views has been covered earlier and we have also used Context previously. Here we used the constant `TELEPHONY_SERVICE` to retrieve a **TelephonyManager**. The use of an **Intent** to start an activity is similar to the one used in the previous example. We used it here to open the Phone Application as the program loaded.

The `phoneManager.listen()` method registers our listener with the system. Along with the listener itself (`phoneListener`), we also passed the device that we wished to listen to in the form of the **PhoneStateListener** constant `LISTEN_CALL_STATE`. If we had wanted to unregister the listener we could have used `LISTEN_NONE`.

The **PhoneStateListener** class has other useful constants which are listed here:

- `LISTEN_CALL_FORWARDING_INDICATOR`
- `LISTEN_CELL_LOCATION`
- `LISTEN_DATA_ACTIVITY`
- `LISTEN_DATA_CONNECTION_STATE`
- `LISTEN_MESSAGE_WAITING_INDICATOR`
- `LISTEN_SERVICE_STATE`
- `LISTEN_SIGNAL_STRENGTH`
- `LISTEN_SIGNAL_STRENGTHS`

> Note that these devices may well require different permissions to be set.

The listener itself is very similar to other such methods and here we used it to report the call state to our text view. Observe that the PhoneStateListener only records incoming numbers but not the numbers we dial.

Sending SMS messages

As with Android's built in Phone Application, we can call up the **SMS Messaging Application** in the same way by using an Intent. More often, when employing SMS within an application, we will want our own interface and we can achieve this with the **android.telephony. SmsManager** class.

In this exercise we will create a simple application that sends a text message to a predefined number.

Getting ready

It is not possible, and may well be illegal, to send SMS messages from an emulator to a real phone. If you intend to test this code on an emulator, then you will need to open two of them.

Either way, start up a new Android project in Eclipse and make your way to the `res/layout/main.xml` file. We will need an EditText and a button with the IDs `message_text` and `send_button`. Here we have also changed the text content:

How to do it...

1. Open the project Manifest file and include the following permission in the top level:

```
<uses-permission
  android:name="android.permission.SEND_SMS">
</uses-permission>
```

2. Now, open the main Java activity code and provide two class-wide fields:

```
EditText messageText;
Button sendButton;
```

3. Connect these with their XML counterparts with:

```
messageText = (EditText) findViewById(R.id.message_text);
sendButton = (Button) findViewById(R.id.send_button);
```

4. Now, add a click listener for the send button as follows:

```
sendButton.setOnClickListener(new OnClickListener() {

  @Override
  public void onClick(View v) {
    String message = messageText.getText().toString()
;

    SmsManager sms = SmsManager.getDefault();
    sms.sendTextMessage("5556", null, message, null, null);
  }

});
```

5. If you are testing this on a handset, replace the number 5556 with another handset's number before testing the application:

How it works...

Unlike many classes, we do not instantiate the **SmsManager** directly but instead call `getDefault()`. The SmsManager's `sendTextMessage()` method takes five parameters. The first three are Strings; the first and the third represent the destination number and the text content, while the second is the service center number and if ignored will use the device's default center. The final two parameters are both **PendingIntents** that inform the system which activity to perform, both when the message is sent and when it is received. Using PendingIntents to monitor the progress of SMS messages is covered in the next recipe.

There's more...

Text messages are generally restricted to between 70 and 160 characters in length by the mobile carriers and longer texts have to be broken down into shorter segments. Fortunately the **SmsManager** provides methods to both divide and send long messages.

The **SmsManager** does not restrict us to text alone and sending data, as byte arrays, is very similar to sending text.

Sending long text messages

The `SmsManager.divideMessage()` method has a single String argument that is the original (long) text message. It returns an ArrayList of Strings comprised of the constituent parts.

To send a multi-part SMS message use `sendMultipartTextMessage()`. This operates in the same way as the `sendTextMessage()` method, with the exception that it expects an ArrayList of Strings as the text content and ArrayLists of PendingIntents (one for each message part) for the sent and received intents.

Sending data with SMS

Byte arrays can be sent through SMS in the same way as text, and the **SmsManager** provides the `sendDataMessage()` method to facilitate this. The `sendDataMessage()` method works like `sendTextMessage()` but takes six parameters. The first two are destination number and service center as before and the last two, likewise, are PendingIntents, but the third and the fourth are a short which refers to the destination port and a byte array for the data.

See also

To learn how to detect incoming SMS messages refer to the next recipe *Monitoring SMS messages*.

For more on using the status bar see the recipe *Notifying the user with the status bar* in *Chapter 7, Notifying the User*.

Monitoring SMS messages

In the previous recipe we had no way of knowing for sure if our message had been correctly sent or not. To monitor the success or otherwise of SMS messages we need to use a **PendingIntent** to trigger some activity once the action is completed. We will also need a **BroadcastReceiver** to pick up on our message sends.

This exercise is much the same as the last but here we will provide a way of monitoring our message's progress.

Getting ready

This task picks up from where the previous one left off, so if you have not yet done so, quickly complete it now and return here, it is very short and will not take long.

How to do it...

1. Along with the button and `EditText` field declarations in the Java code add these:

```java
PendingIntent sendIntent;
PendingIntent receiveIntent;

String sent = "MESSAGE_SENT";
String received "MESSAGE_DELIVERED";

BroadcastReceiver sendBR;
BroadcastReceiver receiveBR;
```

2. Inside the `onCreate()` callback, set up a `PendingIntent` for when the message is sent and one for when it is received:

```java
sendIntent =
   PendingIntent.getBroadcast(this, 0, new Intent(sent), 0);
receiveIntent =
   PendingIntent.getBroadcast(this, 0, new Intent(received), 0);
```

3. Then, inside the `onClick()` method of the Button's `onClickListener`, change the `sendTextMessage` line to:

```java
sms.sendTextMessage("5556", null, message,
   sendIntent, receiveIntenet);
```

4. Now create some send and receive broadcast receivers:

```java
registerReceiver(new BroadcastReceiver() {
   @Override
   public void onReceive(Context context, Intent intent) {
      switch (getResultCode()) {
```

```java
      case Activity.RESULT_OK:
        messageText.append(" ... sent");
        break;
      default:
        messageText.append(" ... not sent");
        break;
      }
    }
  }, new IntentFilter(sent));

  registerReceiver(new BroadcastReceiver() {
    @Override
    public void onReceive(Context context, Intent intent) {
      switch (getResultCode()) {
      case Activity.RESULT_OK:
        messageText.append(" ... received");
        break;
      case Activity.RESULT_CANCELLED:
        messageText.append(" ... not received");
        break;
      }
    }
  }, new IntentFilter(received));
```

5. Finally add an `onStop()` callback to unregister:

```java
@Override
public void onStop() {
  super.onStop();
  unregisterReceiver(sendBR);
  unregisterReceiver(receiveBR);
}
```

6. Run the code as before with another handset or emulator running. After a moment or two, the result should look something like the next screenshot:

How it works...

To monitor the progress of our text message we needed to first broadcast two **PendingIntents** and then pick them up with two **BroadcastReceivers**. It is possible to start an activity in another application using a PendingIntent, just as it is with a standard Intent. The difference is that with a pending intent the permissions from our own application are passed to the called activity and so should be used with a certain caution.

When we register a BroadcastReceiver we override its `onReceive()` callback and use `getResultCode()` to retrieve the behavior of SMS. In the previous example we only considered `Activity.RESULT_OK`, but the SMS manager also provides results and we could have also included any of the following calls to discover the reason for the failure to send:

- `RESULT_ERROR_GENERIC_FAILURE`
- `RESULT_ERROR_NO_SERVICE`
- `RESULT_ERROR_NULL_PDU`
- `RESULT_ERROR_RADIO_OFF`

When a BroadcastReceiver is no longer needed, it can, and should, be released with `unregisterReceiver()`.

Connecting to WiFi

The **android.net** package provides two very useful classes for incorporating **WiFi** into applications, the **ConnectivityManager** and the **wifi.WifiManager**. The first of these manages and monitors the network connection and the latter is the primary class for WiFi connectivity.

In this example we will use these classes to query the network and WiFi state of a device.

Getting ready

WiFi is not available on Android Virtual Devices so to test this demonstration you will need a handset with WiFi enabled. Next, start up a new project in Eclipse.

How to do it...

1. WiFi connectivity requires the following two permissions to be declared in the Manifest:

```
<uses-permission
  android:name="android.permission.ACCESS_NETWORK_STATE" />
<uses-permission
  android:name="android.permission.ACCESS_WIFI_STATE" />
```

2. We will use three TextViews to display our information. Include these in the `res/layout/main.xml` file and give then the following resource IDs:

```
android:id="@+id/network_text"
android:id="@+id/signal_text"
android:id="@+id/connection_text"
```

3. Along with the text views, we need to declare two other class-wide fields for the two network managers:

```
ConnectivityManager conMan;
WifiManager wifiMan;

TextView networkText;
TextView signalText;
TextView connectionText;
```

4. Now, from within the `onCreate()` method, connect the Java TextViews with their XML counterparts in the usual way:

```
networkText = (TextView) findViewById(R.id.network_text);
signalText = (TextView) findViewById(R.id.signal_text);
connectionText = (TextView) findViewById(R.id.connection_text);
```

5. Still inside `onCreate()`, retrieve the two managers with these lines:

```
conMan = (ConnectivityManager)
    getSystemService(Context.CONNECTIVITY_SERVICE);
wifiMan = (WifiManager) getSystemService(Context.WIFI_SERVICE);
```

6. Directly after this calculate and display the network data:

```
String network = conMan.getNetworkInfo(
    ConnectivityManager.TYPE_WIFI).toString()
String signal = "signal strength: "
    + WifiManager.calculateSignalLevel(200, 100) + "%"
String connection = "ConnectionInfo: "
    + wifiMan.getConnectionInfo()

networkText.setText(network);
signalText.setText(signal);
connectionText.setText(connection);
```

7. Now run the project on a handset to examine its current WiFi settings:

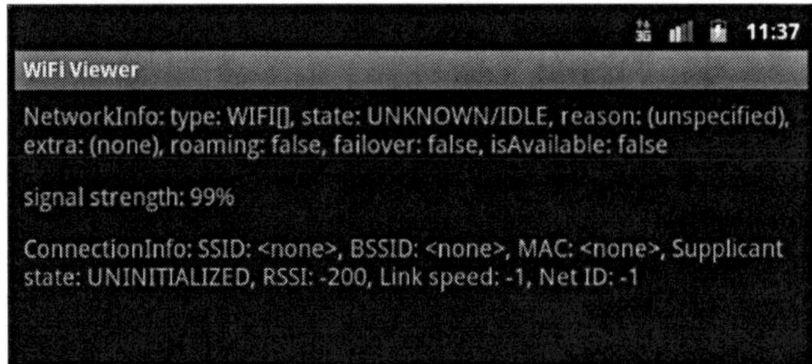

How it works...

The two classes doing all the work here are **ConnectivityManager** and **WifiManager**, and they are both retrieved with the activity's `getSystemService()` method. The ConnectivityManager provides access to and control over all network types, and swapping the constant `TYPE_WIFI` with `TYPE_MOBILE` in the code will provide mobile data and `TYPE_WIMAX`, WiMAX data.

The **WifiManager** gives us a lot of control over all available WiFi networks and here we used it to gather information about the connection and signal strength.

The two parameters in the `calculateSignalLevel()` method are both integers: the first is the power of the signal and the second the scale of the output. There is also a `compareSignalLevel()` function that takes two levels and is very useful for selecting the strongest signal from those available.

To finish using WiFi use the `WifiManager.disconnect()` method:

```
@Override
public void onStop() {
   super.onStop();
   wifiMan.disconnect();
}
```

There's more...

The **WifiManager** class also provides methods that allow us to check the state of the WiFi before we access it and to query the state at any time.

Besides querying the current network, we can create a list of all available networks.

Checking the WiFi state

To detect whether a device is WiFi enabled use the `WifiManager.isWifiEnabled()` method.

The `WifiManager.getWifiState()` method returns an integer representing the following constants:

```
0 = WIFI_STATE_DISABLING
1 = WIFI_STATE_DISABLED
2 = WIFI_STATE_ENABLING
3 = WIFI_STATE_ENABLED
4 = WIFI_STATE_UNKNOWN
```

Listing all configured WiFi networks

To view a list of available WiFi networks use the `getConfiguredNetworks()` method, although this does not return all the fields that the previous methods do:

```java
List<WifiConfiguration> configs = wifiMan.getConfiguredNetworks();
for (WifiConfiguration wc : configs) {
  networkText.setText("\n\n" + wc.toString());
}
```

Connecting Bluetooth devices

Along with WiFi and other network capabilities, Android also provides support for discovering and connecting to **Bluetooth** enabled devices. The **android.bluetooth** package contains several useful classes such as the **BluetoothAdapater**, which represents the device's own Bluetooth adapter. In this recipe the default BluetoothAdapter is used to check for already paired devices and be discovered by new devices that are in range.

Getting ready

Android emulators do not support Bluetooth so you will need a handset to test this code and you will also need another Bluetooth enabled device for the application to connect to.

When ready, start up a new Android project in Eclipse.

How to do it...

1. Bluetooth applications require at least one permission to be set, so open up the Android Manifest file and add the following permissions:

```xml
<uses-permission
  android:name="android.permission.BLUETOOTH"
  android:name="android.permission.BLUETOOTH_ADMIN" />
```

2. In the main activity Java code, in the `onCreate()` method, directly after the `setContentView()` statement, add this declaration:

```
BluetoothAdapter adapter =
   BluetoothAdapter.getDefaultAdapter();
```

3. To check for already known devices, add the following code beneath this:

```
Set<BluetoothDevice> pairedDevices =
   adapter.getBondedDevices();

if (pairedDevices.size() > 0) {

   for (BluetoothDevice device : pairedDevices) {
     Toast.makeText(this, device.getName(),
       Toast.LENGTH_LONG).show();
   }

}
```

4. Beneath this, to make our device discoverable, add this code:

```
if (adapter == null) {
   Toast.makeText(this, "Bluetooth not supported",
     Toast.LENGTH_LONG).show();
   finish();
   return;
} else {
   Intent intent = new
     Intent(BluetoothAdapter.ACTION_REQUEST_DISCOVERABLE);
     startActivity(intent);
}
```

5. Run this code on a handset with Bluetooth enabled in the presence of another Bluetooth device.

How it works...

Creating an object to represent the Bluetooth adapter of our device with `getDefaultAdapter()` is straightforward and once we have such an adapter we can easily search for all **paired** (bonded) **devices** in range; the `BluetoothAdapter.getBondedDevices()` method returns a set of all such devices.

Here we displayed the name of the discovered device in a toast but we could also have pulled the **MAC address** with `device.getAddress()`, and once we have this address we could represent any remote device by creating an instance of the **BluetoothDevice** class using `BluetoothAdapter.getRemoteDevice(String address)`.

Android devices are not discoverable by default but the BluetoothAdapter can be used to make a handset discoverable by other Bluetooth devices, and this is achieved by creating a new Intent with the adapter's built-in Action `ACTION_REQUEST_DISCOVERABLE` and starting an activity with it.

 It is worth noting that the calling of this activity will cause the system to prompt the user to switch Bluetooth on, if he or she has not already done so.

By default our device will remain discoverable for 120 seconds but this can be changed by adding `intent.putExtra(BluetoothAdapter.EXTRA_DISCOVERABLE_DURATION, int seconds)` after the Intent declaration. The int value can take any value less than 300 seconds.

Including web content

A large number of applications make use of a mobile device's ability to access the Internet and one of the most straightforward and flexible ways to do this with Android is through the purpose built **WebView** viewgroup.

Here we will create a very simple web browser with a back button.

Getting ready

This exercise can be started from scratch, start up a new Android project in Eclipse and add the following permission to the Manifest file:

```
<uses-permission
    android:name="android.permission.INTERNET" />
```

How to do it...

1. Create a simple layout in the `main.xml` file with a single Button and WebView:

```
<Button
    android:text="back"
    android:id="@+id/button"
    android:layout_width="wrap_content"
    android:layout_height="wrap_content" />
<WebView
    android:id="@+id/web_view"
    android:layout_width="match_parent"
    android:layout_height="match_parent" />
```

2. In the Java activity source declare a WebView field:

```
WebView webView;
```

3. Next, in the `onCreate()` method, set up the Button like so:

```
Button button = (Button) findViewById(R.id.button);
button.setOnClickListener(new OnClickListener() {

  @Override
  public void onClick(View view) {
    webView.goBack();
  }

});
```

4. Now, still within the `onCreate()` method, set up the WebView widget:

```
webView = (WebView) findViewById(R.id.web_view);
webView.loadUrl("http://www.packtpub.com");
webView.setWebViewClient(new MyWebViewClient());
```

5. Finally, add a WebViewClient class after the `onCreate()` method:

```
private class MyWebViewClient extends WebViewClient {

  @Override
  public boolean
    shouldOverrideUrlLoading(WebView view, String url) {
    view.loadUrl(url);
    return true;
  }

}
```

6. With this done, run the code on a handset or emulator, select a hyperlink, and then press the button to return to the previous page:

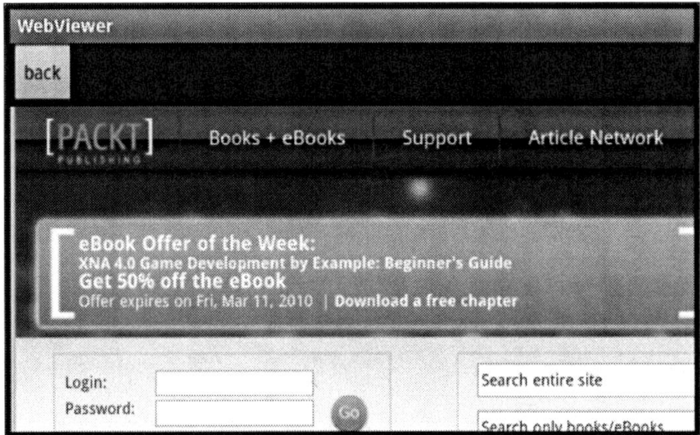

How it works...

We have introduced two new classes here: The **WebView**, which is an extension of View, and the **WebViewClient**, which belongs to the `android.webkit` package. The WebView acts like a canvas and is powered by **Webkit** which is the layout engine behind Google's Chrome and Apple's Safari browsers. It is not within the scope of this book to cover Webkit in any detail but the `android.webkit` package offers numerous ways to access and control web content from within an application and is well worth exploring.

We created just a single button to go back one page with `goBack()` but WebView has many such functions and we could have buttons calling `goForward()` and `reload()` easily.

The reason for creating a WebViewClient may not seem obvious at first but without the `shouldOverrideUrlLoading()` method the system would render all but the first page in the default browser.

Applications targeting Android 3.0 (API level 11) or higher have access to one or two extra methods that allow the developer finer control over network traffic. For example when a WebView becomes hidden from view, its `onPause()` callback will be called and this can be overridden to allow us to prevent network traffic when the user is not focused on the web view. When the WebView becomes visible again the corresponding `onResume()` callback is called.

Also introduced in API level 11 is the `saveWebArchive()` method, which unsurprisingly saves the current view on the device and the `showFindDialog()` method, which allows the user to perform a text search of the page.

There's more...

There are times when we do not want a web page to open in an application but rather open in a browser, and this is remarkably simple. There are also times when we want to render HTML directly.

Opening the browser at a specific page

To take a user directly to a site within the device's default browser, parse the URL as a String and start a new activity using a `ACTION_VIEW` intent:

```
Uri uri = Uri.parse("http://www.packtpub.com");
startActivity(new Intent(Intent.ACTION_VIEW, uri));
```

Rendering HTML in a WebView

The `WebView.loadData(String markup, String type, String format)` can be used to display HTML within a WebView like so:

```
String markup="<html><body><h1><center>Greetings!</></></></>"
webView.loadData(markup, "text/html", "UTF-8");
```

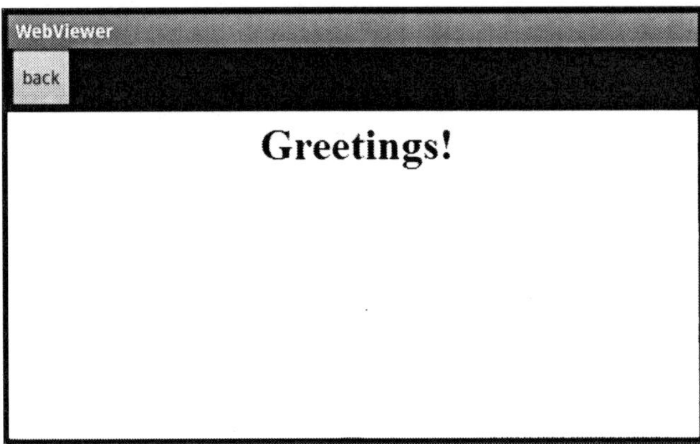

Defining and enforcing permissions in *Chapter 5, Data and Security.*

Phone calls, text messages, WiFi, and HTML make up only a part of the way in which a smartphone can communicate with the outside world but perhaps the most exciting aspect of mobile development is the ability of these devices to know where they are and next we will explore the world of GPS and maps.

11
GPS, Locations, and Maps

In this chapter, we will cover the following topics:

- Detecting a device's location
- Listening for location changes
- Setting up Google Maps
- Zooming in on a MapView
- Setting a map's location with a GeoPoint
- Marking a location on a map with an overlay

Introduction

One of the most remarkable aspects of modern smartphones is the way they can detect their location either through a **Global Positioning System (GPS)**, or cell towers and **WiFi** signal strength; and more often than not, applications use both.

For managing location based information, Android provides the **android.location** package which in turn gives us the **LocationManager** class that gives us access to location based functions such as the latitude and longitude of a device's position. Tracking a device over time is made equally convenient and the **LocationListener** class monitors changes in location as they occur.

Listening for location changes is only a part of the story, as Google provides APIs for managing Google Maps data and displaying and manipulating maps through the use of the **MapView** and **MapController** classes. These powerful tools require us to sign up with Google first, and once done enable us to zoom in and out of maps, pan to any location that we are looking for, and when we want to, include application information on a map, and even add our own layers to maps and mark locations on a Google map.

Detecting a device's location

Android locations are expressed in terms of latitude and longitude coordinates. The default format is degrees. The **Location** object can also be used to store a time-stamp and other information such as speed and distance traveled.

Although obtaining a device's last known location does not always yield the most accurate information, it is often the first reading that we may want. It is fast, simple to employ, and makes a good introduction to the **LocationManager**.

Getting ready

Start a new Android project in Eclipse and provide the following permission to the manifest file as a child of the root node:

```
<uses-permission
    android:name="android.permission.ACCESS_FINE_LOCATION" />
```

How to do it...

1. Use the TextView provided in the `main.xml` file and give it a resource ID:

   ```
   android:id="@+id/text_view"
   ```

2. Declare a TextView as a class-wide field in the Java activity code:

   ```
   TextView textView;
   ```

3. Then, find it in the usual way, from within the `onCreate()` method:

   ```
   textView = (TextView) findViewById(R.id.text_view);
   ```

4. Next, and still within `onCreate()`, declare and define our `LocationManager`:

   ```
   LocationManager manager =
       (LocationManager) getSystemService(Context.LOCATION_SERVICE);
   ```

5. Then, to retrieve the last known location using GPS and display this in the text view, add these lines:

   ```
   Location loc =
       manager.getLastKnownLocation(LocationManager.GPS_PROVIDER);
   textView.setText("latitude: " + loc.getLatitude()
       + "\nlongitude: " + loc.getLongitude());
   ```

6. Run the code on a handset or emulator to obtain its location:

How it works...

The use of a **LocationManager** to obtain the device's last known location is very straightforward. As with other system services, we obtained it with `getSystemService()` and the `getLastKnownLocation()` method returns the `Location` object itself, which can be further queried to provide latitude and longitude coordinates. We could have done more with the `Location` object, for example `Location.getAltitude()` will return altitude and `getDistance(Location)` and `getBearing(Location)` will return distance and bearing to another `Location`.

It is possible to send mock locations to an emulator using the DDMS perspective in Eclipse:

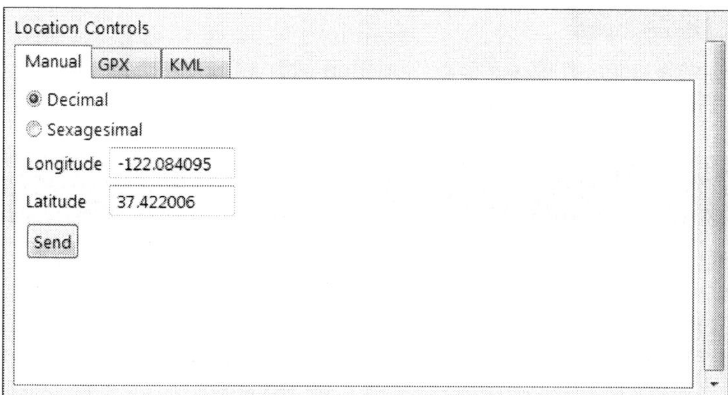

Before sending location data this way, make sure that you have set the emulator to allow mock locations under **Settings | Applications | Development**.

It is worth noting that although use of the `getLastKnownLocation()` method may not always be accurate, particularly if the device has been switched off for some time, it does have the advantage of yielding almost immediate results.

There's more...

Using GPS to obtain a location has a couple of drawbacks. Firstly, it does not work indoors; and secondly, it is very demanding on the battery. Location can be determined by comparing cell tower signal strengths, and although this method is not as accurate, it works well indoors and is much more considerate to the device's battery.

Obtaining a location with a network provider

The network provider is set up in exactly the same way as the previous GPS example, simply exchange the `Location` declaration with:

```
Location loc =
    manager.getLastKnownLocation(LocationManager.NETWORK_PROVIDER);
```

You will also need to change, or amend, the permission in the manifest file with:

```
<uses-permission
    android:name="android.permission.ACCESS_COURSE_LOCATION" />
```

See also

To see how to apply a location object in conjunction with a Google map, see the recipe *Setting a map's location with a GeoPoint* later in this chapter.

Listening for location changes

Obtaining the last known location as we did in the previous recipe is all well and good and handy for retrieving a **Location** quickly, but it can be unreliable if the handset has been switched off or if the user is on the move. Ideally we want to be able to detect location changes as they happen and to do this we employ a **LocationListener**.

In this recipe we will create a simple application that keeps track of a mobile device's movements.

Getting ready

This task can be performed most easily by starting where the previous one left off. If you have not completed that task yet, do so now—it is very short—then return here. If you have already completed the recipe then simply open it up to proceed.

How to do it...

1. First, move the declaration of our `LocationManager` so that it is a class-wide field:

```
LocationManager manager;
```

2. In the main Java activity code, before the `TextView.setText()` call, add the following three lines:

```
LocationListener listener = new MyLocationListener();
manager.requestLocationUpdates(LocationManager.GPS_PROVIDER,
    30000, 50, listener);
Location location =
    manager.getLastKnownLocation(LocationManager.GPS_PROVIDER);
```

3. Now create an inner class called `MyLocationListener` that implements `LocationListener`:

```
public class MyLocationListener implements LocationListener {

}
```

4. Eclipse will most likely insist that you add some unimplemented methods and you should do so.

5. For now, only complete one of them, the `onLocationChanged()` callback:

```
@Override
public void onLocationChanged(Location l) {
    textView.setText("/n/nlatitude: " +
        l.getLatitude() + "\nlongitude: " + l.getLongitude());
}
```

6. Leave the others as they are:

```
@Override
public void onProviderDisabled(String provider) {}

@Override
public void onProviderEnabled(String provider) {}

@Override
public void onStatusChanged(String provider,
    int status, Bundle extras) {}
```

7. If you want to test this code on an emulator, then go right ahead. However, this code will create a serious drain on the battery of a handset, and it is wise to switch our listener off when it is not needed. Here we have used the activity's `onPause()` and `onResume()` functions to control this. You may wish to include these statements in any part of your activity's life cycle that suits your application's purpose:

```
@Override
protected void onResume() {
```

```
        super.onResume();
        manager.requestLocationUpdates(LocationManager.GPS_PROVIDER,
            30000, 50, listener);
    }

    @Override
    protected void onPause() {
        super.onPause();
        manager.removeUpdates(this);
    }
```

8. If you have not already tested this application, do so now. You will need to move around if you are testing it on a real device, or send mock locations to an emulator to see the code in action:

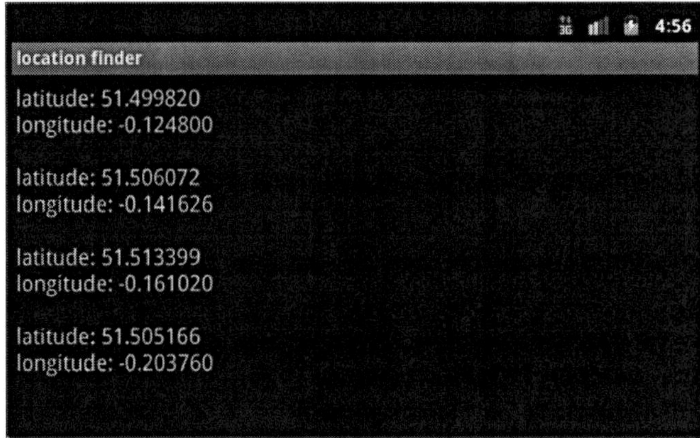

How it works...

In this recipe we used the **LocationManager** to provide location updates roughly every 30 seconds (30000 milliseconds) or whenever the location changed by more than 50 meters. We say 'roughly' because these values work only as a guide and the actual frequency of updates often varies from the values we set. Nevertheless, setting these two parameters of the `requestLocationUpdates()` method to high values can make a big difference to the amount of battery power the GPS provider consumes. Hopefully the use of the provider and the LocationListener as the other two parameters is self explanatory.

The **LocationListener** operates very much as other listeners do and the purpose of the `onProviderEnabled()` and `onProviderDisabled()` should be clear. The `onStatusChanged()` method is called whenever a provider becomes unavailable after a period of availability or vice versa. The int, status can represent 0 = `OUT_OF_SERVICE`, 1 = `TEMPORARILY_UNAVAILABLE`, or 2 = `AVAILABLE`.

See also

To see how to use locations in conjunction with Google maps see the recipes *Setting a map's location with a GeoPoint* and *Marking a location on a map with an overlay* later in this chapter.

Setting up Google Maps

When it comes to displaying **Google Maps** from within our own applications Android makes this wonderfully simple by providing the **MapView** widget, which we can treat just like we would any other View.

Unfortunately, because the data we are using belongs to Google, before we can begin working with maps we have to register for a **Google API key**. This is free and simple to do, as this recipe will demonstrate.

Getting ready

Before we start, you will need to know the whereabouts of the files that you use when signing an application. These are `debug.keystore` and `keytool.exe`. The `debug.keystore` file can usually be found somewhere like `C:\Users\<user>\.android\` on most PCs and `keytool.exe` should be in your Java program files; on my machine it was in `C:\Program Files\Java\jdk1.6.0_25\bin\`.

This exercise is designed to be run on an emulator. If you wish to run it on a handset then you will need to substitute `debug.keystore` with your own keystore file, which you will have set up when you registered as a developer with Google.

You will also need to check whether you have installed the **Google APIs** with the SDK. Although it is almost certain that you have as they install as default.

How to do it...

1. From the command prompt enter the following line, substituting the location of your keystore where different:

```
keytool.exe -list -alias androiddebugkey -keystore "C:\
Users\<user>\.android\debug.keystore" -storepass android -keypass
android
```

2. After a moment you should see the **MD5 fingerprint**, which you should copy to your clipboard:

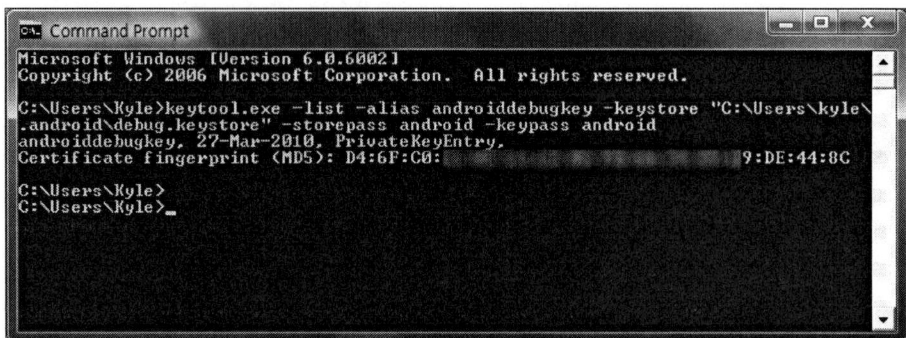

3. Next, visit `http://code.google.com/android/maps-api-signup.html` and follow the instructions there.

4. If all is successful you should receive your **API key**, which will be a long string of seemingly random alphanumeric characters. Save this somewhere secure.

5. Now start up a new Android project in Eclipse, but instead of selecting an Android API level as the **Build Target**, select **Google APIs**:

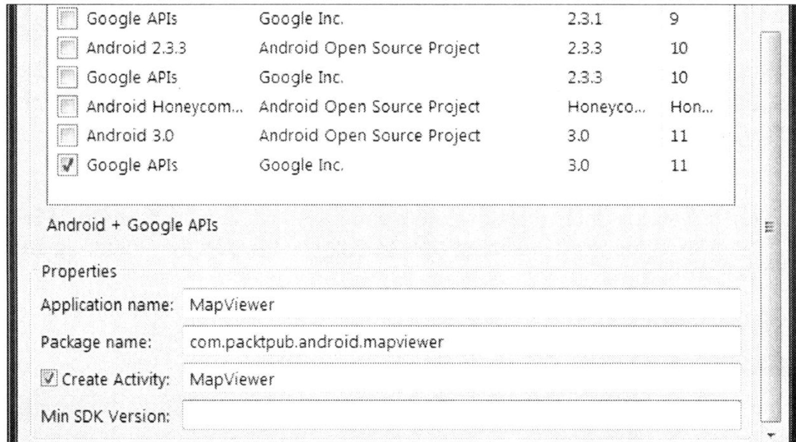

6. For Google Maps to work we need to set Internet permissions in the Manifest file as a child of the `<manifest>` element:

```
<uses-permission
    android:name="android.permission.INTERNET" />
```

7. We also need to inform the system that we are using a library. As a child of the `<application>` element include the following line:

```
<uses-library
   android:name="com.google.android.maps" />
```

8. We can create a layout from a single MapView, so edit the `main.xml` file to match the code here:

```
<?xml version="1.0" encoding="utf-8"?>
<com.google.android.maps.MapView
   xmlns:android="http://schemas.android.com/apk/res/android"
   android:layout_width="match_parent"
   android:layout_height="match_parent"
   android:clickable="true"
   android:apiKey="[your API key goes here]" />
```

9. Finally, in the Java activity code simply change the class extension from `Activity` to **MapActivity**:

```
public class MapViewer extends MapActivity {
```

10. This will cause Eclipse to ask you to implement `isRouteDisplayed()`. Ignore this for now by having it simply return false:

```
@Override
protected boolean isRouteDisplayed() {
   return false;
}
```

11. This code will now display Google Maps, although all we can do for the moment is pan around the map:

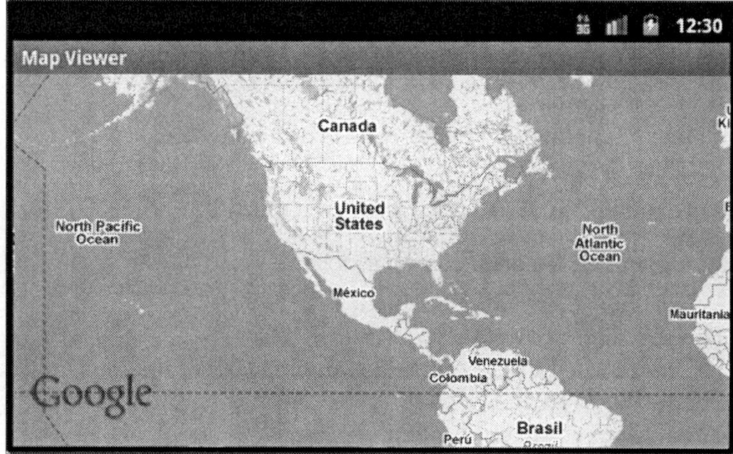

How it works...

Signing up with Google this way is a task that needs to be performed only once and is fairly straightforward. The purpose is mainly security, and **MD5** is a 128 bit Message-Digest algorithm that is widely used for checking file integrity.

Obviously a map with no zoom function is not much use and now that we have the API sign up process completed, we can concentrate on having a bit more fun with Google Maps.

Zooming in on a MapView

A map is of any use only if we can view it at particular scales and the Google Maps API allows us to achieve this by having **zoom controls** built into the **MapView** widget.

Here we will build a small application that will open Google Maps with built-in zoom controls that will allow us to view any area of the map at any allowable scale.

Getting ready

Start a new Android project in Eclipse but, as with any map based application, select a Google API as the build target.

How to do it...

1. Open the manifest file of your project and add the following library `<uses>` definition to the `<application>` element:

```
<uses-library
    android:name="com.google.android.maps" />
```

2. Now add Internet permission to the `<manifest>` element:

```
<uses-permission
    android:name="android.permission.INTERNET" />
```

3. Open the `main.xml` file and set it up as follows:

```
<?xml version="1.0" encoding="utf-8"?>
<com.google.android.maps.MapView
    xmlns:android="http://schemas.android.com/apk/res/android"
    android:id="@+id/map_view"
    android:layout_width="match_parent"
    android:layout_height="match_parent"
    android:clickable="true"
    android:apiKey="[your API key goes here]" />
```

4. In the Java activity class, declare a MapView as a class field:

```
MapView mapView;
```

5. In the `onCreate()` method of the Java activity class and after the `setContentView()` statement add the following three lines.

```
mapView = (MapView) findViewById(R.id.map_view);
mapView.setBuiltInZoomControls(true);
mapView.setSatellite(true);
```

6. Next, change the activity class itself from an Activity extension to a **MapActivity** extension, like so:

```
public class MapViewer extends MapActivity {
```

7. Finally, override the `isRouteDisplayed()` method that Eclipse will insist you implement:

```
@Override
protected boolean isRouteDisplayed() {
    return false;
}
```

8. Now run the program on an emulator or handset to test the zoom controls:

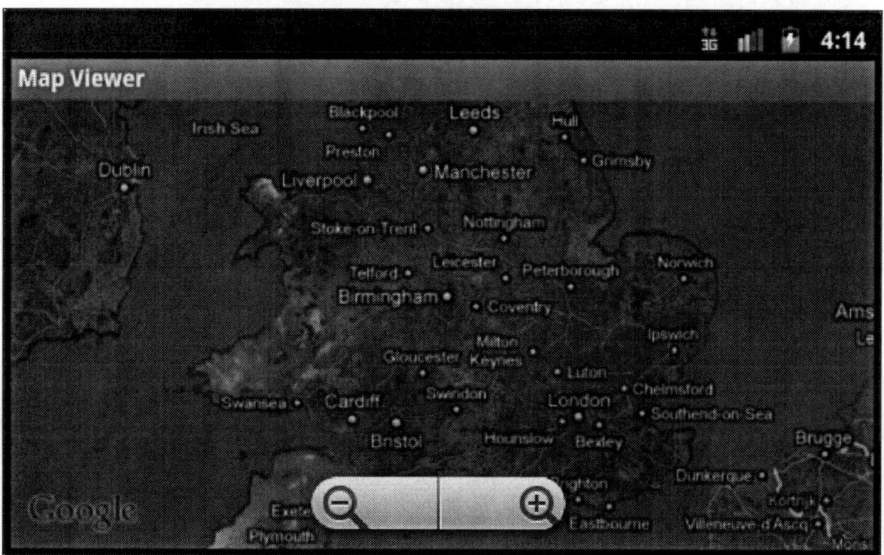

How it works...

This is another wonderful example of how simple it can be to incorporate Google Maps into our own applications. Once set up, the **MapView** widget is very easy to use and it took only a single statement to include the **built in zoom controls** and another to change to **satellite mode**.

We can gain further control still over our map with the help of a **MapController** which, amongst other things, allows us to zoom in and out programmatically. To declare a MapController for the MapView in the example above add a line like the one below after the `setSatellite()` statement:

```
MapController mapController = mapView.getController();
```

To zoom in or out one level at a time use `mapController.zoomIn()` or `mapController.zoomOut()`. To set the scale to a specific zoom level we can use `mapController.setZoom(int)` where `int` is a value between 1 and 21 with 1 being the largest scale and 21 the smallest:

There's more...

The MapController provides another handy function that allows us to zoom to a set point on the map. This is a point measured in pixels and is not the same as setting a geographical location which will be covered in the next section.

Zooming to a fixed point on a MapView

To change the zoom focus from its default center point, use `zoomInFixing(int x, int y)` with x and y being a distance in pixels from the top-left corner of the MapView.

Setting a map's location with a GeoPoint

It is pleasant enough to be able to pan around and zoom into Google Maps but most useful applications require that a map opens at a specific location, either the user's location or a location set by the developer.

Here we will use the **GeoPoint** object to control the location displayed by our map.

Getting ready

Start up a library project by setting the build target as a Google API and, if you are not planning on testing this an a real handset, set up an Android Virtual Device to match.

How to do it...

1. Start by adding the following `<uses-library>` declaration to the `<application>` element of the Android Manifest file of the project:

```
<uses-library
    android:name="com.google.android.maps" />
```

2. Also include Internet permission as a child of the `<manifest>` element itself:

```
<uses-permission
    android:name="android.permission.INTERNET" />
```

3. In the `main.xml` file create a MapView widget. Make it clickable and include your API key within it along with an ID:

```
<com.google.android.maps.MapView
    android:id="@+id/map_view"
    android:layout_width="match_parent"
    android:layout_height="match_parent"
    android:clickable="true"
    android:apiKey="[your API key goes here]" />
```

4. Now, open the main Java activity file and change the extension type from `Activity` to `MapActivity`:

```
public class MapViewer extends MapActivity {
```

5. This will mean overriding the `isRouteDisplayed()` method, but having it simply return false will effectively lead to it being ignored:

```
@Override
protected boolean isRouteDisplayed() {
   return false;
}
```

6. Within the `onCreate()` method create and associate a local MapView and set it to display in satellite mode:

```
MapView mapView = (MapView) findViewById(R.id.map_view);
mapView.setSatellite(true);
```

7. We will also need a map controller:

```
MapController mapControl = mapView.getController();
```

8. Next, define two doubles to act as our latitude and longitude. Here we have used a location in a central London park, but any legitimate coordinates will do:

```
double lat = 51.50773;
double lng = -0.16582;
```

9. Then, convert these values to a **GeoPoint**, like so:

```
GeoPoint gPoint =
new GeoPoint((int) (lat * 1E6), (int) (lng * 1E6));
```

10. Now we can call on the **MapController** to animate to our designated **GeoPoint**:

```
mapControl.animateTo(gPoint);
mapControl.setZoom(17);
mapView.invalidate();
```

11. Run the code on your handset or emulator to view the location set by the GeoPoint:

How it works...

The way we set this project up is the same as the other library projects, which is simply a matter of building against a Google API library and adding the `<uses-library>` to the `application` node of the manifest. Again we used the **MapController** class to take us to the geographic point with `animateTo`(**GeoPoint**). GeoPoints are constructed using integer units called **micro-degrees** which, as their names suggests, represent a millionth of a degree. One might just as easily have used `GeoPoint point = new GeoPoint(51507730, -165820)`.

> Note that although the `invalidate()` call is not always necessary, it does guarantee that our view will be redrawn.

Of course, it is not a difficult matter to take data provided by the GPS or network location finder to display a user's current location on the map, and this is left as an exercise for the reader.

See also

To learn how obtain the device's actual location see the recipe *Detecting a device's location* earlier in this chapter.

Marking a location on a map with an overlay

Above all else one of the best features of the **Google Maps API** is the ability to add our own content to maps by **overlaying** them with our own material.

In this final exercise we will display a map at a particular location and then overlay it with our own imagery. We will also see how to translate from geographical locations to screen positions.

Getting ready

This task is a continuation of the previous one, so make sure you have completed this first and have it open in Eclipse.

Here we have used the built in `icon.png` as our graphic but if you want to use your own, then add this first to a `res/drawable` folder, ideally as a PNG file.

How to do it...

1. Mostly what is required here is a new class, which we can add as an inner class, but first we need to convert our MapView and MapController to class wide fields:

```
MapView mapView;
MapController mapControl;
```

2. Now it is simply a matter of adding a new class to our MapActivity. It should be defined like this:

```
class MyMapOverlay extends com.google.android.maps.Overlay {

}
```

3. To take control of our overlay class we can override its `draw()` method:

```
@Override
public boolean draw(Canvas canvas, MapView mapView,
   boolean shadow, long when) {
      super.draw(canvas, mapView, shadow);

      double lat = 51.50778;
      double lng = -0.16590;
      GeoPoint oPoint =
         new GeoPoint((int) (lat * 1E6), (int) (lng * 1E6));

      Point sPoint = new Point();
      mapView.getProjection().toPixels(oPoint, sPoint);

      Bitmap bmp = BitmapFactory.decodeResource(
         getResources(), R.drawable.icon);
      canvas.drawBitmap(bmp, sPoint.x, sPoint.y, null);
      return true;

}
```

4. This is now ready to run, and as we are providing the locations ourselves, it does not matter whether this code is tested on a real handset or an AVD:

How it works...

The class of real interest here is **Overlay**, which is a library class and belongs to `com.google.android.maps`. Once established, all we had to do was override the `draw()` method to add our own layer to the map. The image is drawn onto a **Canvas** which makes the first parameter and the desired MapView the second. The boolean, `shadow`, shows only the shadow view if true and the long, `when`, controls the time that the overlay will be displayed in milliseconds after the instruction is received. If this argument is ignored in the call to the super class, then our layer will be displayed as soon as possible.

The GeoPoint of the overlay was set only meters away from the map location itself and one micro-meter is equal to around 10 centimeters, but do note that it is the top left corner of our image that the GeoPoint will locate at this point and we normally would have to adjust this to accommodate our overlay's dimensions.

Handiest of all of the MapView's methods is `getProjection().toPixels` which lets us easily convert real-world geographical coordinates to screen position in pixels and so mark any location we desire on our map.

See also

For more information on using canvases see the recipe *Drawing with a canvas* in *Chapter 8, Graphics and Animation*.

It's entirely impossible to cover everything that the Android SDK is capable of in just one book, the subject is just too vast and growing every day. However, we hope that this book will have given you what you need to turn your ideas into working applications and everyone who worked on this book wishes all its readers the very best of luck in what is without doubt the most exciting arena for imaginative people for a whole generation.

Index

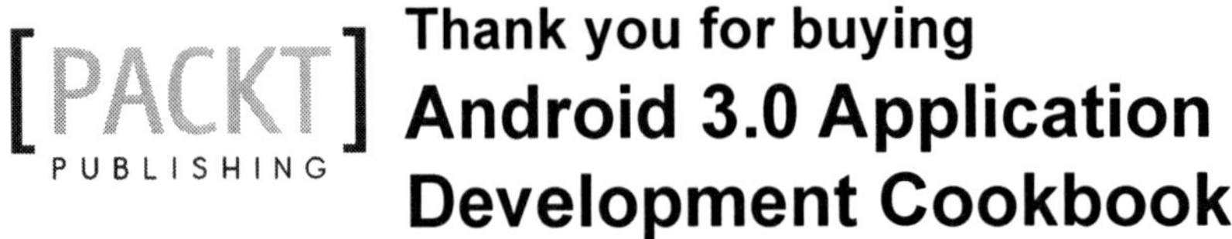

About Packt Publishing

Packt, pronounced 'packed', published its first book "*Mastering phpMyAdmin for Effective MySQL Management*" in April 2004 and subsequently continued to specialize in publishing highly focused books on specific technologies and solutions.

Our books and publications share the experiences of your fellow IT professionals in adapting and customizing today's systems, applications, and frameworks. Our solution based books give you the knowledge and power to customize the software and technologies you're using to get the job done. Packt books are more specific and less general than the IT books you have seen in the past. Our unique business model allows us to bring you more focused information, giving you more of what you need to know, and less of what you don't.

Packt is a modern, yet unique publishing company, which focuses on producing quality, cutting-edge books for communities of developers, administrators, and newbies alike. For more information, please visit our website: www.packtpub.com.

Writing for Packt

We welcome all inquiries from people who are interested in authoring. Book proposals should be sent to author@packtpub.com. If your book idea is still at an early stage and you would like to discuss it first before writing a formal book proposal, contact us; one of our commissioning editors will get in touch with you.

We're not just looking for published authors; if you have strong technical skills but no writing experience, our experienced editors can help you develop a writing career, or simply get some additional reward for your expertise.

MeeGo 1.0 Mobile Application Development Cookbook

ISBN: 978-1-84969-032-4   Paperback: 300pages

Simple and effective recipes for professional MeeGo mobile applications supporting calls, SMS, UI, display, GPS, multimedia, and much more

1. A step-by-step guide to creating feature-rich, powerful Qt mobile applications in Python rapidly

2. Quick recipes for building professional Smartphone applications for UI, display, GPS, multimedia, and games

3. Plenty of code examples to help you develop your own applications

4. No Qt experience required

Mobile Web Development

ISBN: 978-1-847193-43-8   Paperback: 236 pages

Building mobile websites, SMS and MMS messaging, mobile payments, and automated voice call systems with XHTML MP, WCSS, and mobile AJAX

1. Build mobile-friendly sites and applications

2. Adapt presentation to different devices

3. Build mobile front ends to server-side applications

4. Use SMS and MMS and take mobile payments

Please check **www.PacktPub.com** for information on our titles

Lightning Source UK Ltd.
Milton Keynes UK
UKOW040210240212

187848UK00001B/65/P